COMPUTER   TELECOMMUNICAT

T0124091

MANAGING
THE DATA-BASE
ENVIRONMENT

TELEPROCESSING
NETWORK
ORGANIZATION

DISTRIBUTED FILE
AND DATA-
BASE DESIGN

← →

STRATEGIC
DATA-PLANNING
METHODOLOGIES

SYSTEMS ANALYSIS
FOR DATA
TRANSMISSION

← →

DESIGN AND STRATEGY
FOR DISTRIBUTED
DATA PROCESSING

COMPUTER
DATA-BASE
ORGANIZATION

(second edition)

INTRODUCTION
TO COMPUTER
NETWORKS

← →

COMPUTER NETWORKS
AND DISTRIBUTED
PROCESSING

PRINCIPLES
OF DATA-BASE
MANAGEMENT

INTRODUCTION
TO
TELEPROCESSING

PRINCIPLES OF
DISTRIBUTED
PROCESSING

AN END-USER'S
GUIDE TO
DATA BASE

**APPLICATION
DEVELOPMENT
WITHOUT
PROGRAMMERS**

A *James Martin* **BOOK**

APPLICATION

DEVELOPMENT WITHOUT PROGRAMMERS

JAMES MARTIN

with research by Richard Murch

PRENTICE-HALL, INC., Englewood Cliffs, New Jersey 07632

Library of Congress Cataloging in Publication Data

Martin, James
  Application development without programmers.

  Includes bibliographical references and
index.
   1. Electronic digital computers—Programming.
2. Electronic data processing. I. Title.
QA76.6.M3613   001.64   81–15736
ISBN 0-13-038943-9   AACR2

Application Development Without Programmers
James Martin

© 1982 by James Martin

Editorial/production supervision by *Linda Paskiet*
Jacket design by *Mark A. Binn*
Manufacturing buyer: *Gordon Osbourne*

Printed in the United States of America

10 9 8 7 6 5 4 3

ISBN 0-13-038943-9

PRENTICE-HALL INTERNATIONAL, INC., *London*
PRENTICE-HALL OF AUSTRALIA PTY. LIMITED, *Sydney*
PRENTICE-HALL OF CANADA, LTD., *Toronto*
PRENTICE-HALL OF INDIA PRIVATE LIMITED, *New Delhi*
PRENTICE-HALL OF JAPAN, INC., *Tokyo*
PRENTICE-HALL OF SOUTHEAST ASIA PTE. LTD., *Singapore*
WHITEHALL BOOKS LIMITED, *Wellington, New Zealand*

TO CORINTHIA

CONTENTS

Figure 2.1 is referred to throughout the book. For convenience it is reproduced here.

	Suitable for End Users	Suitable for DP Professionals
Simple-Query Facilities		
Complex-Query Languages		
Report Generators		
Graphics Languages		
Application Generators		
Very High-Level Programming Languages		
Parameterized Application Packages		

Figure 2.1 Categorization of facilities for application creation without conventional programming. The reader might fill in the matrix with facilities with which he is familiar. (See Fig. 2.2 and Box 2.1 for examples.)

Table of boxes

PREFACE

This book is dedicated to the view that a higher level of automation is needed in developing data processing applications. This higher automation must come by breaking away from procedural languages wherever possible.

Applications development did not change much for 20 years, but now a new wave is crashing in. A rich diversity of nonprocedural techniques and languages are emerging. As these languages improve, they promise to change the entire fabric of DP development.

This means a major change for many of the personnel involved in DP, from the DP manager to the junior programmer. DP personnel have always welcomed new hardware and software, but it is not as easy to accept fundamental changes in the nature of one's job. Many DP professionals and, not surprisingly, programmers will instinctively resist some of the methods described in this book. If they wish to articulate their defense, they might turn to Box 3.2, which lists how DP personnel rationalize the preservation of the status quo.

Unfortunately, the winds of change are sometimes irreversible. The continuing drop in cost of computers has now passed the point at which computers have become cheaper than people. The number of programmers available *per computer* is shrinking so fast that most computers in the future will have to work at least in part without programmers. In this book a wide spectrum of methods is described. Each has its place, and the ability to apply the right approach to each task becomes an essential new DP skill.

Application development without programmers is not a free lunch. To maximize productivity with the aids described in this book requires good data-base design and administration, networking, planning of distributed systems, and evolution of office-of-the-future techniques. These, and the changes they bring, are the subject of my five-day seminars held throughout the world.

I would like to thank the Savant Research Institute and Mr. and Mrs. Collins for assisting with this material and publishing my associated reports.

Thanks are due to Ms. E. Schaefer and Dr. Carma McClure for their valuable comments, also Mr. W. Clarke of National C.S.S. for help on the NOMAD chapter.

I would also like to thank Mr. Richard Murch for intrepid research assistance. We would like to hear about experiences related to the software we discuss, either from vendors or users. Mr. Murch's address for this purpose is Bryn Morpha, Bailey's Bay, Bermuda. Readers might also note that Mr. Murch is researching a further work to be called *Fourth-Generation Languages*. Any vendors or users who are interested should write to Mr. Murch at the address indicated.

James Martin

APPLICATION
DEVELOPMENT
WITHOUT
PROGRAMMERS

A *James Martin* BOOK

1 THE PROGRAMMING DILEMMA

INTRODUCTION   Before World War I the telephone industry was one
of the rising stars of Wall Street. It was growing furiously rather like the computer industry is today. However, those few persons who thought about its future were concerned. All telephone calls had to
be switched manually. If there were only a small number of users, this process
was easy. However, with a large population of users, many separate switching
processes had to be performed in different locations in order to complete
one call. The number of persons needed for switching had a much higher
growth rate than the number of persons making calls. A dream of Wall Street
was that eventually most offices and many homes would have telephones.
However, the pessimists calculated that this could never happen because
almost the entire work force of the United States would be needed to switch
the calls.

The salvation of the telephone industry was, of course, automatic
telephone switching equipment. It was invented by a mortician (undertaker)
called Strowger in a small midwestern town when the other mortician in the
town married the lady who operated the town telephone exchange. Strowger's business was tending to go to the competition, so with Yankee ingenuity (which incorporates more political skill than is often credited) he
persuaded the town authorities to install the world's first Strowger switch
exchange. The telephone industry and Strowger both flourished.

Today computers are dropping in cost. Mass-production techniques are
in sight which could turn out computers like newsprint. We will eventually
have an IBM–370–like computer on a single chip. No white-collar worker
should be without one.

In the next 10 years computers will increase in speed by a factor of at
least 10, perhaps much more. As they plunge in cost, many will be sold. It is
estimated that the number of computers used for scientific and commercial

applications will continue to grow at 25% per year at least. It is growing faster than that now.

However, as with telephone switching there is a problem inherent in such growth. The application programs take a long time to write.

If we assume no increase in programming productivity, the figures above indicate that in 10 years' time the industry will need 93.1 times as many programmers as now. There are approximately 300,000 programmers in the United States today. That suggests about 28 million programmers in 10 years' time. Before long the entire American work force would be needed to program its computers. Ridiculous!

Another way of looking at the same figures is that the number of applications in today's data processing centers is growing at 45% per year. This figure comes from an IBM survey. The growth seems likely to continue. Many potential applications that users need are never mentioned by users today because the *documented* application backlog is so great. Ten years' growth of 45% per year multiplies the number of applications by 41.1. At the same time the number of data processing centers will grow, perhaps by a factor of ten in the next ten years because of the rapidly dropping cost of computers.

Any set of estimates of computing power 10 years hence indicates that the *productivity of application development needs to increase by two orders of magnitude* during the next 10 years.

The productivity of writing programs in languages such as COBOL, FORTRAN, or PL/1 is indeed improving, but only slowly. Authorities on better programming advocate structured techniques. In installations where it has been used well, structured programming has improved programmer productivity. Typical installations quote a 10% or so improvement. It is rare to find a case where structured programming (without any other change) has in reality increased programmer productivity by more than 25% [1]. Some installations state that there is no measurable improvement. It appears that structured programming might reduce the figure of 28 million programmers to about 20 million or so if we are optimistic about it!

Worse, the program coding is only part of the task. In a typical installation writing and testing new application program code takes only 14% of the human DP resources. The rest is spent on system analysis, writing program specifications, documenting the programs, and maintenance. (This figure is also from an IBM survey of its major customers. Other surveys have produced differing figures. The percentage of programming and testing is higher in complex *software* development than in conventional DP *application* development.)

Clearly, if the computer industry is to find markets for the acres of silicon chips that it will produce, fundamentally new methods of application development are needed. Indeed, if this is not done, it is doubtful whether some of the large computer vendors will survive the plunge in costs of their hardware. Like Strowger, we must automate what is today done by hand.

**PEOPLE COSTS
VERSUS COMPUTER
COSTS**

Figure 1.1 shows how the costs of computer time and people time are changing. In 1979, the curves of Fig. 1.1 crossed, making computer time (of the power shown) cheaper than people time. The vertical scale of Fig. 1.1 is logarithmic, so the rate of change is great. Before long the cost of a person for an hour will be ten times greater than the cost of a computer for an hour.

In the United States the average overall cost of a single debugged instruction of programming is about $10. This is more expensive than the cost of a cheap microcomputer. A U.S. Department of Defense study showed development costs for Air Force avionics applications averaging $75 per instruction [2]. One can buy a computer for less than the cost of one program instruction! The microcomputer instruction often runs on thousands of microcomputers, but the instruction for typical corporate application development runs on only one computer.

The number of computers being delivered is increasing very rapidly. This is not reflected in the curves of Fig. 1.1. By the time the curves in Fig.

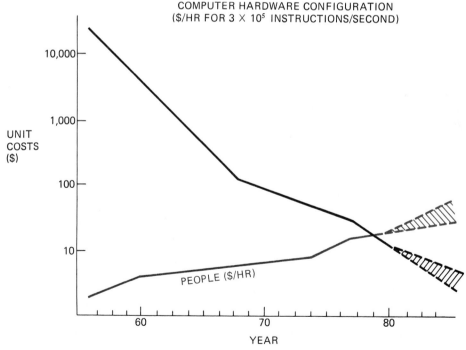

Figure 1.1 Comparison of the cost of computers with the cost of people (U.S. dollars per hour). In 1979, computer time (at 3×10^5 instructions/second) became cheaper than people time. (Note that the vertical scale is logarithmic.)

3

1.1 crossed over, the United States was delivering more computers per year than it was producing science and engineering graduates per year.

Corporate DP (data processing) departments *must* learn to acquire the applications they need without programmers wherever this is possible. This is becoming possible for most, but not all, commercial DP applications.

**APPLICATION
BACKLOG**

In most well-managed corporations the demand for new applications is rising faster than DP can supply them. The imbalance between demand and supply is steadily becoming worse.

Because of this, the backlog of applications which are needed is growing. Most corporations now have a backlog of three or four years. One New York bank informed us that its backlog was seven years. This situation is likely to become worse as machines drop in cost, unless better methods of creating applications are found.

The term *end user* is employed for the ultimate user of computer applications: the accountants, production schedulers, purchasing officers, planning executives, and so on. The long backlog and inability of DP to respond to end users' needs quickly is very frustrating for them. In some cases the end users have felt that they cannot wait for DP and have obtained their own departmental minicomputer.

**INVISIBLE
BACKLOG**

Even though today's application backlogs are so long, they reveal only part of the story. When the documented backlog is several years (as it is in most installations), the end users do not even consider making requests for many of the applications they need. There is thus an *invisible backlog.*

The invisible backlog cannot easily be measured. Its size is indicated in those installations where end users have acquired a capability to develop applications quickly, as described later in the book. Such examples indicate that the *invisible* backlog is often larger than the *documented* backlog.

**ALTERNATIVES TO
PROGRAMMERS**

If we are to avoid programmers in the development of applications, there are three possible sources of applications.

1. End users could be given powerful tools with which they can create their own applications.

2. Systems analysts or consultants working with the end users can use tools with which they can create the applications rather than writing programming specifications.

3. Preprogrammed application packages can be purchased from outside sources.

THE CHANGING DP ENVIRONMENT   Large corporations will not get rid of programmers quickly. Figure 1.2 shows the changing environment in a giant petroleum company. In 1978, 97% of applications were created by DP programmers. By 1983 it is intended that only 70% will be built by DP and much of this 70% will be *generated* by sys-

	1978	1980	1983
Applications Using Data Base	10%	20%	60%
Source of Applications	97% Built by DP 3% Purchased by DP	91% Built by DP 7% Purchased by DP 2% Purchased by end users	70% Built by DP 17% Purchased by DP 10% Built by end users 3% Purchased by end users
Application Classes	80% Operational 10% Management control 10% Planning and analysis	65% Operational 20% Management control 15% Planning and analysis	45% Operational 30% Management control 25% Planning and analysis
Batch vs. Nonbatch	75% Batch 20% On-line transaction 5% Interactive	68% Batch 25% On-line transaction 7% Interactive	40% Batch 35% On-line transaction 25% Interactive

1984–1989 Strategic Objectives

● End users can access and manipulate information (numeric, text, and graphics) required to solve their problems 50% of time without DP help.

● 30% of applications can be generated or supplied directly from business requirements (without programming).

● 70% of applications can be supplied with no more than 30% procedural code.

Figure 1.2 The changing DP environment in a giant petroleum company.

tems analysts rather than *programmed* in COBOL or PL/1. Seventeen percent
will be *purchased* by DP and 3% by end users (a major growth in the use of
application software packages). Ten percent will be built by end users with
high-level tools or languages.

The strategic objective of this giant corporation is that by the 1984–
1989 time frame, the end users should be able to access and manipulate the
information required to solve their problems *without DP help 50% of the
time*. This refers to numeric, text, and graphics information.

**SMALL
CORPORATIONS**
Small corporations, fairly new to computing, often
acquire a higher proportion of their applications
without programmers than large corporations.
Small corporations of 100 people or so can afford a minicomputer but not a
programming staff. They are not burdened with many applications of the
past, written in COBOL or PL/1, which now need heavy maintenance.

The small corporation can often adapt itself more easily to the use of
application packages and applications created with the new development
tools. Some minicomputer vendors have realized that their key to sales
success is application development without programmers and have created
software for accomplishing this in small corporations.

Many small corporations have no dedicated programming staff. They
have systems analysts who can create the screens for interactive applications
and generate the programs for billing, sending orders, and producing reports.
The general-purpose systems analyst may also program occasionally in a
language such as BASIC, APL, or NOMAD.

Figure 1.3 shows the DP environment in a small, aggressive, rapidly
growing corporation with sales of $20 million and 250 employees. The DP
department is relatively new. It uses some time-sharing employing the language NOMAD, and has a minicomputer. The main difference between this
and the environment of Fig. 1.2 is that only 8% of the applications are
created by a programmer. The organization has one programmer who programs in COBOL. Many applications are purchased packages. Many are generated by the systems analysts. Some end users are beginning to create their
own applications with NOMAD. The NOMAD system uses a relational data
base. The data-base management system TOTAL is also used.

This is contrasted in Fig. 1.4 with a typical installation in a medium-
sized company with a long-established DP department. The top DP executive
regards the operation as tightly controlled and well managed. All programmers use the same language—COBOL. A growing proportion use structured
programming. The DP department deliberately avoids pioneering because
"pioneers often get killed." Much of the programming work is on maintenance and modification of old programs. The programming backlog is such
that only applications perceived as high priority are tackled. The rest are
tabled, forgotten, or the end users never request them.

Applications Using Data Base	40%
Source of Applications	45% Purchased by DP 8% Created by programmers 41% Created by systems analysts 6% Created by end users
Application Classes	70% Operational 30% Management control and planning
Batch vs. Nonbatch	55% Batch 45% Interactive
DP Staff	1 DP manager 1 Systems expert 1 Programmer 2 Systems analysts who create applications

Figure 1.3 The DP environment in a rapidly growing small corporation (sales of $20 million) and recently implemented DP.

Applications Using Data Base	5%
Source of Applications	100% Programmed in COBOL
Application Classes	90% Operational 10% Management control and planning
Batch vs. Nonbatch	90% Batch 10% Interactive
DP Staff	30 Programmers (of which 16 are designated "maintenance programmers") 28 Systems analysts 6 DP managers

Figure 1.4 The DP environment in a medium-sized corporation (sales of $660 million) with a 20-year-old DP department.

END-USER PARTICIPATION   To achieve the degree of end-user participation in computing required by the strategy in Fig. 1.2 is a major change. It requires "user-friendly, nonthreatening" software and application dialogues. It requires a massive number of users to be trained. It requires a change in the role of the systems analyst who will increasingly assume a consultant role, guiding and teaching the users, showing them the possibilities, acting as salepersons of new methods, solving the users' problems, and generally handholding. It will require an understanding by senior management that they must motivate the users to participate, putting statements in their management-by-objectives forms (or councils and appraisals), which instruct and encourage users at all levels to apply the new DP tools.

An opinion commonly held by DP professionals and by computer manufacturers' development staff is that end users are not mentally equipped to participate in the DP creation process. In practice, whether they participate and how well they participate depends, to a large extent, on their motivation. Some learning and practice is needed. Many users feel that they are too busy or have something more important to do. Many are frightened of terminals and do not use them because they might appear foolish in front of their colleagues. Some have a slightly arrogant attitude and will not learn, in the same way that a manager will not learn to type. Users often need to be encouraged or instructed from above to get over the hurdle which prevents them making better use to today's computers. DP needs to arrange user courses which are of the right level and not too technical.

There are now many examples of end users participating in the DP process with results much better than those that would have come from DP professionals, because the end users know the subtleties of what they want to accomplish. To make this happen on a large scale needs software and tools quite different from those which the traditional programmer uses. Those facilities now exist and will rapidly improve.

The imbalance between the demand for new applications and DP's ability to supply them can only be solved in most corporations by increasing the end users' role in creating applications.

DP PRODUCTIVITY

Although the users should have this role, many applications cannot and should not be created by user departments.

For DP-developed applications a *productivity* of application development is needed many times higher than today. This will not be achieved with structured programming or today's structured analysis.

Research into the impact of structured programming shows that there are very few installations where the move to structured programming by itself gives an overall programming productivity increase of greater than 25% [1]. Usually, it is less. In installations where it is used well, Jackson methodology [3] appears to give a better improvement than other forms of structured programming which are in common use. Structured analysis as commonly practiced usually takes longer than conventional systems analysis (albeit for good reason). It is clear that much better techniques are both possible and essential as computers continue to plunge in cost.

It is the imbalance of demand and supply of DP applications that is causing corporations to create strategies such as that in Fig. 1.2. Even with a high pressure for end-user development and purchased packages, DP on the right-hand side of Fig. 1.2 are still creating 70% of the applications. This is a much larger *number* of applications than 5 years previously because the rate of development is increasing.

To achieve the improvement necessary in DP development productivity, the following are needed:

- The use of high-level *nonprocedural* languages with which applications can be generated quickly. In other words, application development without conventional programming. A diverse variety of such languages are now in use.

- The use of appropriately designed data-base systems with high-level data-base facilities for creating applications. The data bases need better logical design than most that were implemented during the 1970s. Extensive use is then needed of data-base query languages, report generators, and application generators (described later).

- The use of high-level programming languages such as APL or NOMAD, where appropriate.

- Top-down planning of data and procedures to avoid creating redundant programs which exist in profusion in some organizations.

- Conversion of old systems to data-base operation with high-level generators where this can lessen the *maintenance* work load.

- Avoidance of development methods that lead to excessive maintenance.

- Avoidance of hardware and software configurations that lead to excessive maintenance.

- Avoidance of slow time-consuming systems analysis methods and a change to fast, data-base-oriented methods which create the applications wherever possible without programmers.

- Use of self-documenting techniques to avoid the time-consuming burden of documentation.

- Avoidance, where possible, of the writing of program specifications. Instead, the analyst *creates* the application while interacting with the end users, or prototypes it and adjusts it to what the end users need.

We have deliberately not mentioned structured programming in the list above. This is not because we have anything against structuring programs; structured programs are clearly better than nonstructured ones. However, structured programming has been sold as a productivity aid when it increases productivity much less than is necessary. The way to change productivity is to *avoid* programming with languages of the level of COBOL or PL/1 where possible. DP organizations ought to be seeking every opportunity to avoid writing such programs.

THE CHANGING ROLE OF THE SYSTEMS ANALYST

The traditional techniques of systems analysis are very time consuming. The vital search for DP productivity needs to speed up systems analysis as much as it needs to speed up or eliminate programming.

The high-level facilities for application creation are often tools for the systems analyst, not tools for the end user. They eliminate the need for flow-charts, and often for data-flow diagrams. They are often self-documenting and often avoid the need to write program specifications.

The existence of well-thought-out data bases is a key to improving the systems analysis process. The analyst can specify events or triggers that affect the data base and the actions these cause. He or she can generate reports or screens from the data base and can generate data-entry dialogues for updating the data base. High-level data-base languages permit entire applications to be specified with an interactive or form-filling technique.

The task of designing the data shifts in part from the systems analyst to the data administrator. The same data are then designed *once* instead of many times as with non-data-base approaches. The data administrator has tools that automate the data-base design, enforce good design principles, and facilitate end-user participation in it [4].

The systems analyst builds on top of the data base, using higher-level data-base languages or application generators. We describe such tools later in the report. With them the systems analyst should not create specifications for a programmer except where the use of a low-level language such as COBOL or PL/1 is unavoidable. The systems analysts should create the application themselves wherever possible and interact directly with end users in adjusting it to their needs.

As well as creating applications directly, the systems analysts should advise and encourage the end users in employing new systems. They should assist them, where applicable, in creating their own applications. The role of the systems analyst, then, swings toward being a consultant to end users.

The systems analysts should be motivated in their management-by-objective or appraisal forms to speed up greatly the creation of applications and the acceptance of these by end users. They should become expert on the facilities for creating applications without programmers.

WHAT IS GOING TO HAPPEN TO ALL THE PROGRAMMERS?

The theme of this book must cause programmers to wonder about their job future.

In the short term we do not think they have much need to worry. The dilemma we describe in the opening page is a desperate *shortage* of programmers.

Will this shortage not end quickly as the new methods are adopted? Probably not. There will always be lots of backward corporations and backward DP managers who will run homes for old COBOL programmers. And not all applications are susceptible to the new application creation software. (You would not program the moonshot in RPG or ADF.) So some application development with conventional programming will still be needed even when the new software improves.

Large military systems, refinery control, weather forecasting, space vehicle control, air traffic systems, and the like will need their usual hoards of programmers. Also, fundamentally new types of computer uses will need programming.

One of the most interesting forms of programming is working with a staff of senior management to answer the many "what if" questions that arise. This generally needs to be done *fast* with languages more powerful than COBOL or PL/1. APL is often used. There is a rapidly growing demand for fast-moving APL programmers with the ability to understand the management computations that are needed. But this would require most programmers to learn a new language and fit into a different type of environment.

Creation of software such as operating systems, data-base management systems, and application development software itself will be a major industry demanding highly skilled programmers, but not COBOL programmers. The software industrial will be one of the fastest growing in the years ahead.

What advice should be given to the COBOL programmers who are comfortably coding away and who like their job? If they want to be promoted and have job security, they should take a keen interest in any means of improving application development productivity. They should learn to use the new facilities for application creation. These are fun to use and will make programmers more powerful in creating results. Programmers should consider promotion to being systems analysts who use the new tools and who create applications rather than creating programming specifications. Many good programmers will find more lucrative employment in the software industry.

SOFTWARE FIRMS   As computers drop in cost software firms acquire a larger marketplace and spend more on creating both application packages and general-purpose software. It is estimated that the number of programmers employed by software houses in the United States in five years time will be 125,000 [5]. This does not include the programmers employed by computer vendors.

Figure 1.5 shows the growth in the programmer population of the United States and the rise in numbers of programmers in the software industry. It suggests that the total number of programmers available to DP departments will not grow in the 1980s. Some projections show this number rapidly declining [5] in spite of the rising maintenance needs, the growing end-user awareness of computing, and the myriad of new applications made economic by the falling costs.

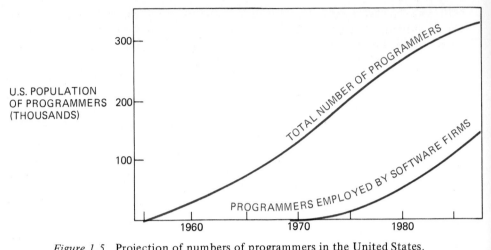

Figure 1.5 Projection of numbers of programmers in the United States. In spite of the vast growth in numbers of computers, the programming talent available to DP departments will probably not grow because of absorption of the best programmers by software firms.

To make matters even worse, the software firms are hiring the best programmers. They are in a highly competitive industry. They need high-quality efficient code. And they need it fast. Software will be a $10 billion industry soon and skilled programmers are its production resource. If the best programmers are expensive, the software company will raise the prices of its software (perhaps by one-fourth of the increase in cost of programmers because these are only part of the firm's costs). DP managers, then, will be faced with rapidly growing end-user demands, a severe programmer shortage, and good programmers looking for employment in the software industry.

TWO TYPES OF PROGRAMMER PERSONALITY

Programmers can be divided into two types of personality. One type has good human skills and the potential to work well with end users. They are broad enough to be able to learn how a business works and understand the rich diversity of user concerns. The other type is often brilliant at manipulating code and logic but does not want to be involved in people problems. We might refer to these two types as the *consultant* and the *bit-twiddler*. Both will be in high demand in the future if they are good.

The *consultant* type will be desperately needed and under pressure to obtain results for end users quickly. To do so, they must learn to be skilled with the powerful application generators, report generators, and query languages. They must develop the human skills needed to encourage, handhold, and communicate with the end users. They must acquire diplomacy and salesmanship.

The *bit-twiddler* often does not want to work with accountants, fore-men, and budget planners. The accountants, on the other hand, sometimes show unreasonable skepticism for this breed of programmer, especially if they have waist-length hair, chew bubble gum, and sit with bare feet on their desks. The future of the bit-twiddler may be as a systems programmer or in software houses. Most software houses have great difficulty finding as-sembler language programmers or programmers who can optimize table and logic design. A few complex corporate applications will also remain in which such skills are needed.

Many programmers vehemently resist the application generators and other new methods. They look for any argument in favor of the techniques they know. It costs much human effort to become a skilled COBOL or PL/1 programmer, and it is unpleasant to think of having to start again or to use that much effort to learn something new. They are not sure that they could become equally skilled in something new. They do not want to be the new kid on the block again.

Arguments against the new application creation facilities can be mus-tered easily. Such facilities take more machine time. They do not have the flexibility of conventional programming. Compromises may be needed to fit the application to the technique. Programmers often persuade their managers that COBOL or PL/1 are the best approach after all, when in fact the new techniques would be greatly preferable.

In the long run, however, low-productivity application programming is doomed because computers will continue to plunge in cost.

REFERENCES

1. T.C. Jones, "The Limits to Programming Productivity," Guide and Share Application Development Symposium, *Proceedings,* Share, New York, 1979.

2. W.L. Trainer, "Software—From Satan to Saviour," in *Proceedings,* NAE-CON Conf., May 1973.

3. Michael Jackson, *Principles of Program Design,* Academic Press, London, 1977.

4. James Martin, *Managing the Data Base Environment,* Prentice-Hall, Inc., Englewood Cliffs, NJ, 1982.

5. G.T. Orwick, "The Plight of Programming," *Computerworld EXTRA,* September 1980. (G.T. Orwick is director of product planning at MSA, Inc., the second largest U.S. software firm.)

2 SOFTWARE FOR APPLICATION DEVELOPMENT WITHOUT CONVENTIONAL PROGRAMMING

INTRODUCTION Nobody wrote books on application development without programmers until the 1980s. What made the difference was the advent of more powerful software for application creation. Some such software existed in the 1970s, but it was not yet good enough (and machines cheap enough) to constitute a revolution in DP management.

SEVEN TYPES OF SOFTWARE The software with which users or systems analysts can create applications falls into seven categories:

1. Simple-Query Facilities

These have existed since the earliest disc storage devices. They enable stored records to be printed or displayed in a suitable format.

2. Complex-Query Languages

These are data-base user languages which permit the formulation of queries that may relate to multiple records. The queries sometimes invoke complex data-base searching or the *joining* of multiple records. For example, "LIST ALL U.S. SHIPS WITHIN 500 MILES OF THE STRAITS OF HORMUZ CARRYING CREWMEMBERS WITH EXPERIENCE IN DESERT COMBAT." Because of the searching and joining, only certain data-base systems are appropriate for on-line use of such languages.

Many data-base user languages now exist. They differ greatly in their syntax and structure. Some are marketed by the vendors of their host database management systems; others are marketed by independent software houses.

Many query languages permit the users to enter and *update* data as well as query it. With some, users can create their own files.

3. Report Generators

These are facilities for extracting data from a file or data base and formatting it into reports. Good report generators allow substantial arithmetic or logic to be performed on the data before they are displayed or printed.

Some report generators are independent of data-base or query facilities. Others are an extension of data-base query languages. Ideally, an end user should be able to start by learning to make simple data-base queries and should steadily extend her or his skill to data manipulation and report formatting. The report generator should be an extension of the query language; many are not.

4. Graphics Languages

Graphics terminals are dropping in cost and give a particularly attractive way for certain types of end users to display and manipulate data. Software for interactive graphics is steadily improving. It can enable users to ask for data and specify how they want it charted. They can search files or data bases and chart information according to different criteria. Like report generators, some graphics packages allow considerable arithmetical and logical manipulation of the data.

5. Application Generators

These contain modules that permit an entire application to be generated. The input can be specified, its validation, what action it causes to happen, details of that action, what arithmetic and logic is performed, and what output is created. Most application generators operate with data bases. They can greatly speed up application development.

Some applications can be only partially generated. They require certain operations which the application generator cannot create. It is still useful to employ the generator provided that it has an *escape* mechanism which permits the inclusion of routines written in a program language.

Some application generators are designed to create heavy-duty applications in which efficient coding and data accesses are needed because of the high transaction volumes.

6. Very High-Level Programming Languages

Some programming languages are designed for end users. Some are designed so that they use a much smaller number of instructions than a language such as COBOL, FORTRAN, or PL/1 and permit much faster application development.

Languages employed by sophisticated end users include BASIC and

APL (Chapter 13). More powerful (in that it uses fewer instructions) is NOMAD (Chapter 14), which is designed to operate with a relational data base.

With high-level languages such as NOMAD, the user does not have to specify every detail of procedures that are used. He can say LIST, TITLE, INSERT, AVERAGE, SORT, SUM, and so on. He need not describe in code the format of a report. The interpreter selects a reasonable format and the user can adjust it if he wishes.

Cost studies have indicated that the cost per line of code is typically $10 in the United States (although it varies from $5 to over $300) [1]. This cost is usually lower with very-high-level languages. A COBOL program often has 20 to 40 times as many lines of code as the same application written in a very high level language.

7. Parameterized Application Packages

Packages can be purchased for running certain applications. These pre-programmed packages are increasing in number, diversity, and quality. They often require a considerable amount of tailoring to fit the organization that installs them and are designed with parameters that can be chosen to modify their operation. This parameterization is the key to success in many cases. As the marketplace for packages grows, they tend to be built with a richer set of parameters so that they have wider applicability.

Some application packages are marketed directly to end users so that they can avoid involvement with their DP department. Some are designed to operate on end-user minicomputers.

Some are marketed with "turnkey" installation so that the users need no installation skills.

SUITABLE FOR END USERS?   There are many types of software in the foregoing categories. Most vendors of such software claim that it is "designed for end users." In many cases this claim is questionable because the software requires more skill and training than most users will acquire. In many cases the software should be used by systems analysts who work with the end users.

Some of the software described above is excellent for end users. Some of the best data-base query and update facilities can be employed by users who have never touched a terminal before, for example, viewdata sets [2], IBM's QUERY-BY-EXAMPLE (Chapter 9), and Cullinane's ON-LINE ENGLISH (Chapter 9).

We might classify something as "suitable for end users" if typical end users can learn how to use it and obtain valuable results in a 2-day training course and then not forget how to use it if they leave it for several weeks. (They *would* forget codes and mnemonics.) End users could not adapt fully to IBM's application generator ADF (discussed later), for example, in a 2-day course. With this criterion we can categorize the software *for application development without conventional programming* with the matrix in Fig. 2.1.

The reader might like to fill in Fig. 2.1 with software with which he or she is familiar. There is scope for argument about which compartment in Fig. 2.1 certain facilities fit into. Many fit into more than one. For example, a good data-base language might be *both* a complex query language *and* a report generator. A language might be categorized as suitable for end users *and* suitable for DP professionals, because the users can learn (in two days) to use *some* of its facilities, but not all. This is the case with the programming language APL, for example. A child can learn to use a small subset of APL in two days, but it takes a skilled professional months to master all of APL's capabilities.

A desirable property of a language is that *to start to use it should be easy,* but that the user can continue to learn more about it and improve his* skills for a long time. Languages with this property should be taught in subsets. If a language has a beginners' subset which can be well learned in *one* day, many users will cross the threshold from being mystified outsiders to being initiated members of the club.

	Suitable for End Users	Suitable for DP Professionals
Simple-Query Facilities		
Complex-Query Languages		
Report Generators		
Graphics Languages		
Application Generators		
Very High-Level Programming Languages		
Parameterized Application Packages		

Figure 2.1 Categorization of facilities for application creation without conventional programming. The reader might fill in the matrix with facilities with which he or she is familiar. (See Fig. 2.2 and Box 2.1 for examples).

---

*The author has given much thought to the problem of avoiding words with a sexist connotation. It is possible to avoid words such as "man," "manpower," "mankind," but to avoid the use of "he," "his," and "him" makes sentences clumsy. In this book whenever these words appear, please assume that the meaning is "he or she," "his or her," and "him or her."

We sometimes use the term *end user* as though it referred to one breed of creature. In reality computer end users vary across the entire spectrum of humanity both in skills and in motivation. Some budget planners and production schedulers work wonders with APL. But most users are frightened of terminals and do not yet dream that they could instruct computers to go to work for them. A sensitive seduction process is needed to encourage them to join the club—and many are too set in their ways to be seduced.

In the long run it is certain that much computing will be user-driven. In the early days of the motor car its users employed a chauffeur. Technology improved and a chauffeur became unnecessary. Technology will increasingly improve the user interface to computers so that for many applications users will not need a computer-chauffeur.

INTEGRATED LANGUAGES   Although some languages fall into one of the seven categories in Fig. 2.1, it is desirable to have languages which are in multiple categories. Some report generators, for example, are entirely separate from query languages and some data-base query languages do not have a report-generation capability. It would be preferable for a user to learn a query language with which he could steadily extend his skills and become able to create reports with useful formats. He should also be able to create business graphics. Similarly, the language should be extendable so that it is a full application generator. Some of the languages in Fig. 2.1 can be called by conventional programming languages. This is true with IBM's SQL (pronounced "Sequel"), for example. COBOL, PL/1 or assembler language programs can call routines written in SQL.

ESCAPE FEATURE   Application generators are not capable of generating *all* applications. Sometimes they lack the capability to generate particular logic or algorithms which are needed. Too often a generator is rejected for this reason. An important feature of a generator is the capability to associate with it modules of logic written in programming languages. This is sometimes called an *escape* feature. Where possible it is desirable that the user of the generator can also use the language to which the escape is made.

In some cases a programmer is required to handle the *escape* language, but if the programmer is part of the DP department doing conventional coding, then the problems with programming backlog affect the use of the generator.

Ideally, then, the products in Fig. 2.1 should be integrated as much as possible. The query language should support the creation of reports and graphics, and be the basis of an application generator. A high-level programming language should be available both for use in its own right and for *escape* from the application generator. Most products in existence today do not yet have this degree of integration. Computer manufacturers and software houses have often created separate languages for data-base query, report generation, graphics, application generation, and high-level programming.

Some of the products in Fig. 2.1 have the capability to call preprogrammed subroutines. These can be custom built for a particular installation. Like the use of an escape feature, they extend the versatility of the products.

EXISTING PRODUCTS   Figure 2.2 lists some existing products of the types discussed in this book.

There is *much* software of these types on the market. Box 2.1 gives a longer list of some of the products that are available.

	Suitable for End Users*		Suitable for DP Professionals	
		Vendor		Vendor
Data-Base Query Languages	QUERY-BY-EXAMPLE SQL ON-LINE ENGLISH QWICK QWERY EASYTRIEVE ASI/INQUIRY DATATRIEVE	IBM IBM Cullinane Caci Pansophic ASI DEC	SQL QWICK QWERY EASYTRIEVE GIS MARK IV DATATRIEVE	IBM CACI Pansophic IBM Informatics DEC
Information Retrieval Systems	STAIRS CAFS	IBM ICL		
Report Generators	NOMAD QWICK QWERY	NCSS CACI	NOMAD QWICK QWERY GIS IBM SYSTEM 34 UTILITIES RPG II RPG III ADRS MARK IV/REPORTER	NCSS CACI IBM IBM Various IBM IBM Informatics
Application Generators	MAPPER RAMIS II FOCUS	Univac Mathematica, Inc. Information Builders	ADF RAMIS II DMS ADMINS 11 USER 11 ADS	IBM Mathematica, Inc. IBM ADMINS Northcounty Comp., Inc. Cullinane
Very High-Level Programming Languages	APL (simple functions) NOMAD (simple functions)	Various NCSS	APL APL-PLUS ADRS NOMAD MANTIS	Various STSC IBM NCSS CINCOM

*What is "suitable for end users" and what is not is always open to debate. Box 8.2 gives a test to determine this suitability.

Figure 2.2   Examples of the types of software discussed in this chapter and elsewhere in the book. Some of the above products fall into multiple categories. There are *many* other examples; see Box 2.1.

BOX 2.1 Some products of the type discussed in this chapter. This list is not intended to be complete or comprehensive. The software is changing rapidly.

Product	Query Language	Report Generator	Graphics Generator	Application Generator	High-Level Programming	Vendor	Machine Type	On-Line?	Suitable for End Users?	Data Base?
ADAM				✓		San Francisco Intelligent Machine Corp.	Own Machine			
ADMINS/11		✓		✓		ADMINS Corp.	PDP/11	✓	✓	Its own files
ADPAC		✓	✓			Adpac Computer Languages Corp.	IBM			
ADRS (APL-based)	✓	✓			✓	IBM	370	✓	✓	DL/I
APG	✓	✓				I.D.S.B.	DEC	✓		Its own files
APL	✓				✓	Various	Various	✓	✓	
APL-DI		✓			✓	IBM	370	✓	✓	DL/I; IMS
APL-PLUS	✓	✓			✓	STSC	Various	✓	✓	
ADF				✓		IBM	370OS	✓		For IMS Applications
ASI INQUIRY	✓	✓				APP Software	370	✓		Queries IMS
ASI-ST						Applications Software Inc.	IBM			

Product			Supplier	Machine			Files / Database
ASRES	✓	✓	Univ. of Georgia	360	✓	✓	Its own files
BASIS	✓	✓	Batelle	Various	✓	✓	Its own files
CAFS	✓		ICL Series	2900	✓	✓	Its own associative Information Retrieval system
COBOL Program Generator			Black/Prime	Prime			
COMPOSE-II	✓	✓	Compusource	Data General	✓		Its own files
CONTEXT C-705	✓		Context System	370	✓		Associative records
CS4	✓		Databaskonsult, Sweden	DEC/IBM			
DATA ANALYZER	✓	✓	Prog. Products	370	✓	✓	Its own files
DATATRIEVE-11	✓	✓	DEC	PDP/11	✓		DEC's files and data base
DMS	✓	✓	IBM	370	✓	✓	DL/I CICS and its files
DMS	✓	✓	IBM	8100	✓	✓	Its own files
DIRECT	✓	✓	Bancohio	Honeywell	✓		Its own files
Display Information Facilities	✓		IBM	S/38	✓		For S/38 DB
D.L.A.	✓	✓	E.M.I. Ltd.	Various	✓	✓	Its own files
DRS-11	✓	✓	Synoco Ltd.	DEC	✓	✓	Its own files
EASYTRIEVE	✓		Pansophic	Various	✓	✓	IMS, TOTAL, ADABAS
EQUS	✓	✓	IBM	S/3, S/32	✓	✓	Its own files
EXTRACTO	✓	✓	Optipro Ltd.	370	✓	✓	Its own files
FLEXTRACT	✓	✓	Faulkner	Various	✓	✓	Its own files
FOCUS	✓	✓	Info. Builders	370	✓	✓	Its own files
Gen. Information Systems	✓	✓	IBM	370	✓	✓	Its own DB
GENASYS			Generation Sciences	IBM			
GIS	✓	✓	IBM	Various	✓		DL/I; IMS
HARVEST	✓	✓	I.D.S.B.	DEC/IBM	✓		Its own files
IBM 3790	✓	✓	IBM	370	✓		Its own files

(Continued)

BOX 2.1 *(Continued)*

Product	Query Language	Report Generator	Graphics Generator	Application Generator	High-Level Programming	Vendor	Machine Type	On-Line?	Suitable for End Users?	Data Base?
IBM BRADS	✓	✓		✓	✓	IBM	5110/20	✓	✓	Its own files
ICES	✓	✓				Univac	Univac	✓		Its own files
IDEA	✓	✓		✓		Data General	Data General	✓		Its own files
IDEAL	✓				✓	ADR	370	✓	✓	DATACOM
										Relational data base
IIS DATA LOGGER	✓	✓				Int. Inf. Sys.	DEC	✓		Its own files
IMDOC	✓	✓				M.A.G.	370	✓		Its own files
IMS FASTON	✓					IBM	370	✓		IMS
INFORMAT	✓	✓				M.R.P.	NOVA	✓	✓	Its own files
IN? QUIRY	✓	✓				Informatics	370	✓		IMS and own files
INSCI	✓	✓				Information Science	Various	✓	✓	Its own files
INSYTE	✓	✓				Remote Comp.	Burroughs	✓	✓	Its own files
INTELLECT	✓					Artificial Intelligence				
IQ	✓	✓				Man. Group	Various	✓	✓	IDS, IMS, TOTAL
IRS	✓	✓				Sigma Data	370	✓		Its own files
ISA/OAS	✓	✓				ISA Corp.	370	✓		Its own files
JPLDIS	✓	✓				Univ. of Georgia	Univac	✓		Its own files
LIRS	✓					Univ. of Georgia	370	✓	✓	Its own files

Product	Supplier	Computer	Database/Files
MANTIS	CINCOM	Various	Total, DL/1 and files
MAPPER	Univac	1100	Its own files
MARK IV	Informatics	Various	DL/I
MAXIMUS	Maximus	Data General & Eclipse 60/66	
MDQS II	Honeywell	60/66	Its own files
MICRODATA REALITY	Microdata	Reality	Its own files
MRS	Infopac	370	Its own files
NCR TOTAL	NCR	NCR	Its own files
IQL	Nat. C.S.S.	N.C.S.S.	TOTAL
NOMAD	Cullinane	Various	Its own relational DB
OADS			IDMS
ON-LINE ENGLISH	Cullinane	370	IDMS and its own files
ORACLE	Distribution Man. Systems	PDP11	Its own files
PRO	Business EDP Services	Burroughs	Its own files
QL SEARCH	QL Systems	370	Its own files
QUERY-BY-EXAMPLE	IBM	370/4300	Its own relational D/B
QUERY 5/3	IBM	S/3	S/3 files
QWICK QUERY	CACI	Various	Its own files
RAMIS II	Mathematica	370	Its own DB
RECALL	Data Man.	370	Its own files
REQUEST	SY. Automation	Various	Its own files
ROBOT	Artificial Intelligence	IBM, Honeywell	
RPG II	IBM	Various	Conventional files

(Continued)

23

BOX 2.1 *(Continued)*

Product	Query Language	Report Generator	Graphics Generator	Application Generator	High-Level Programming	Vendor	Machine Type	On-Line?	Suitable for End Users?	Data Base?
RPG III	✓	✓			✓	IBM	S/38	✓		For S/38 files and DB
S/34 UTILITIES		✓			✓	IBM	S/34	✓		Uses S/34 files
S/38 DBMS					✓	IBM	S/38	✓		For S/38 DB
SL/1		✓		✓		Thorne	370	✓		Defines its own files
SQL	✓					IBM	370	✓	✓	Its own relational DB
STAIRS	✓					IBM	Various	✓	✓	Its own information
SYS/38 QUERY	✓	✓				IBM	S/38	✓	✓	Its own DB
T-ASK	✓	✓				Cincom	370	✓	✓	TOTAL
TCS/1700	✓	✓				Ded. Systems	Burroughs	✓	✓	Its own files
UCC/FCS	✓	✓				U.C.C. Corp.	Various			Its own files
USER/11	✓		✓			Northcounty	PDP/11	✓	✓	
WORK TEN				✓		National Computing Industries	IBM	✓	✓	Uses its own DB

Several query languages and report generators today are suitable for end users, but many application generators at the time of writing are not. As discussed in Chapter 10, application generators *can* be designed for end users and some good ones exist.

Not too much weight should be attached to whether a facility is listed in the "Suitable for End Users" column of Fig. 2.2 or Box 2.1 There will always be some argument about which facilities are truly suitable for end users. *Some* end users learn to employ some of the facilities on the right of Fig. 2.2 to obtain results faster than can be obtained by their overworked DP department.

**ON-LINE OR
OFF-LINE?**

A further categorization of the software in Fig. 2.1 can indicate whether it is on-line or off-line. Some query languages, report generators, and application generators operate interactively at a terminal; some operate off-line with the users or systems analysts filling in forms or coding sheets.

The use of forms gives the user time to think about what he needs. In some cases he may fill in the forms at home or away from his office.

Nevertheless, *on-line* operation can be much more satisfactory if it is well designed psychologically. It can lead the user to do what is required a step at a time. It can check the user's input as he creates it. It can make tutorial explanations available on-line and can assist if the user presses a HELP key. On-line operation can generally be made much more versatile than off-line operation. When some of the product types in Fig. 2.1 are integrated, on-line operation can make a wide range of features available to the user.

**WHAT IS
PROGRAMMING?**

Sometimes the term "application development without programming" is used. This raises the question: "What is programming?" Neither dictionaries nor computer glossaries are much use in answering this.

Most professionals would agree that use of a simple query facility is not programming. Use of a simple language with which *complex* queries can be expressed, such as IBM's QUERY-BY-EXAMPLE or Cullinane's ON-LINE ENGLISH (both discussed later) is not regarded as programming. On the other hand, most professionals would agree that use of a high-level language such as APL *is* programming. APL can express general computer operations with complex logic, whereas QUERY-BY-EXAMPLE or ON-LINE ENGLISH cannot.

Some data-base query languages are expanding their capabilities so that they can update data and express various logic operations. There becomes a blurred distinction between query languages, application generators, and programming.

PROCEDURAL AND NONPROCEDURAL CODE

One might draw a line of distinction by saying that programming refers to *procedural* code; nonprogramming refers to *nonprocedural* code. "Procedural" and "nonprocedural" is a useful and much used language distinction. A procedural language specifies *how* something is accomplished. A nonprocedural language specifies *what* is accomplished but not in detail *how*. Thus languages such as COBOL and PL/1 are procedural. Their programmers given precisely detailed instructions for how each action is accomplished. An application generator whose users fill in forms to tell it what to do is nonprocedural. The user merely says *what* is to be done and is not concerned with the detailed procedure for *how* it is done. Most professionals say that using such a generator is *not* programming.

Most query languages, report generators, graphics packages, and application generators are nonprocedural. However, some high-level programming languages are now acquiring nonprocedural capabilities. NOMAD (Chapter 14) is a high-level language with which some end users obtain fast results from a computer. Most professionals would call it a programming language because it has IF statements and DO loops. However, results can be obtained with brief nonprocedural statements such as

LIST BY CUSTOMER AVERAGE (INVOICE TOTAL).

This is a complete "program." It leaves the software to decide how the list should be formated, when to skip pages, number pages, how to sort into CUSTOMER sequence, and how to compute an average.

Many query languages and report generators are nonprocedural. Some languages combine procedural and nonprocedural code. This is generally desirable because the nonprocedural code speeds up and simplifies the use of the language, while the procedural code extends the range of applications that can be tackled.

In this book we avoid the issue of what is "programming" and concern ourselves with *programmers*. The term "programmer" in this book refers to a person who is a full-time creator of code. This is usually, but not always, procedural code. Our "programmer" is not an accountant, scientist, or systems analyst who programs occasionally to assist in doing his main job. We are concerned with how applications can be created by end users or systems analysts rather than by full-time coders.

INTELLIGENT NONPROCEDURAL FACILITIES

Nonprocedural languages differ in their "intelligence" or ability to provide useful results on the basis of brief statements from the user. As the software continues to improve, nonprocedural facilities will become increasingly *intelligent*. Conventional languages will incorporate intelligent nonprocedural coding capability. There is much scope for research and innovation in intelligent nonprocedural functions.

THE DATA-BASE   Most of the products for application development
CONNECTION   without programmers give greater productivity if
                               they are linked to a data base. The reason is that
the data are then predefined. The application creator does not have to
bother about defining or structuring the data. Report headers referring to
the data may also be predefined.

A separate data administration function decides what data are needed
and how they should be organized. This is a highly professional function
with formal tools and techniques [3, 4]. It is a vitally important function
which some corporations have done badly, but for which there are now
detailed guidelines [3, 4]. The data administrator creates data which multiple different end users and systems analysts (and programmers) employ.

The query languages, report generators, and application generators use
or create the data which are already defined in the data base. To do so, their
software must be coupled to the data-base management system. This may be
a tight or loose coupling. It is generally desirable that a data dictionary is
employed by both the data-base management system and the languages that
link to it.

EFFICIENCY   An argument often voiced *against* application gen-
                               erators and the other facilities of Fig. 2.1 is that
they generate inefficient code and use an excessive amount of computer
time.

It is important to realize that this is true with some and not with
others. It is an important characteristic to examine when selecting such software, but not a blanket argument against its use. *Surprisingly, perhaps, some
application generators create object code which is better than the same
applications programmed in COBOL or PL/1.* The reason for this is that
statements in the generator language result in the use of blocks of code
which have been written in assembler language and tightly optimized. These
assembler blocks are better optimized than the object code, which is compiled from COBOL or PL/1. On the other hand, the worst of both worlds is
a generator that generates COBOL (or PL/1) source code, and this is then
compiled.

Glancing ahead, two tables are given at the start of Chapter 18 which
illustrate performance with application generators designed for machine
efficiency.

Some generators also use less compile time than COBOL or PL/1.
IBM's DMS (Development Management System) commonly takes a sixth of
the compile time of the same functions written in COBOL. The reason for
this is it generates major blocks of code *which are precompiled.*

Some generators work interpretively; some work with compiled code. As elsewhere, *compilation* can give better machine performance than can interpretive operation. Compilation is desirable for repetitive operations.

Applications created for high-volume operation need to be efficient. Some application generators are designed to give efficiency with heavy-duty systems; others are designed for *ad hoc* operation for one of a kind report or low-volume activity.

In some cases an expert on the software is needed to extract good performance from it. The expert may make an application run twice as fast by using a different data-base design. He may save more time by sorting the input or changing the operation sequence. In some cases experts on the software improve its performance by a much larger factor.

When choosing the software it is necessary to decide whether machine efficiency is a selection criterion. If its use is for a few transactions a day, machine efficiency does not matter at all. However, it is also important to use generators for heavy-duty applications as well as for low-volume ones.

FOURTH-GENERATION LANGUAGES

How should we describe the set of languages in Fig. 2.1? They are sometimes called "data-base languages" but some do not use a data base. They are sometimes called "nonprocedural languages," but many contain procedural code. They are sometimes called "fourth-generation languages." The first generation was machine language. The second generation was languages the level of assembler language. The third generation was machine-independent languages of the level of COBOL, PL/1, and BASIC.

Fourth-generation languages is a useful term. However it is sometimes misused. Any new language is likely to be called fourth generation by its promoters even if it does not have the characteristics we have described. *Fourth-generation language* seems to be the best term we have if used with caution. A language should not be called *fourth-generation* unless its users obtain results in one-tenth of the time with COBOL, or less.

REFERENCES

1. J.H. Lehman, "How Software Projects Are Really Managed," *Datamation,* January 1979.

2. James Martin, *Viewdata and the Information Society,* Prentice-Hall, Inc., Englewood Cliffs, NJ, 1981.

3. James Martin, *Managing the Data Base Environment,* Prentice-Hall, Inc., Englewood Cliffs, NJ, 1982.

4. James Martin, *Strategic Data Planning Methodologies,* Savant Technical Report 12, Savant Institute, Carnforth, Lancashire, UK, 1980.

3 PRODUCTIVITY OF APPLICATION CREATION

HUGE GAINS   The most important thing to understand about the facilities in Fig. 2.1 is that *huge* gains in application development productivity have been achieved with them. The best results are far too spectacular to be ignored. Box 3.1 gives examples of successes.

The second most important thing to understand is that these products and these gains in productivity make desirable an approach to application creation which is quite different from the traditional methods. This change in methods is discussed in subsequent chapters.

Figure 3.1 gives numbers of programs installed per person-month in Playtex [4] using COBOL versus using ADF (IBM's Application Development Facility, which employs an IMS data base). For the types of applications shown there is an 80.7-times improvement in the productivity of application creation. For some applications in Playtex, ADF was not used, but these were in the minority.

Whereas some organizations have achieved productivity improvements such as those in Fig. 3.1, others using the same software have not achieved much success. Some have attempted to use ADF (the application generator that achieved the results in Fig. 3.1) and have abandoned it. There are several reasons for this huge difference in experience. First, substantial training is needed to use some application generators. Sometimes the commitment to training is not made. Second, the application generators and other aids are not suitable for every application. They need to be used where appropriate. Sometimes the application, its dialogue, or its screen formats need to be adapted to fit what can be generated. The range of applications for which they are valuable can be greatly extended by using them in conjunction with conventional code where necessary. Third, to achieve high productivity, changes in DP management and methodology are needed, as described later. It is sometimes the group with little experience of conventional DP pro-

BOX 3.1 Huge gains in productivity

Huge gains in application development productivity have been achieved with the facilities in Fig. 2.1. The gains are so great in the best cases that they represent the largest step forward in application creation since the invention of programming. Here are some examples:

- In the Chase Manhattan Bank an end-user department itself created a complex system for on-line analysis of the Chase's management accounting data, in ADMINS 11 [1]. They accomplished this in 4 months with two people and claim that the DP department had estimated that they would take 18 months with 20 people, and cost $1.5 million [2].

- IBM in its own internal DP achieved a 27:1 improvement in development productivity with ADF over what would have been achieved with COBOL and IMS [3].

- Playtex Inc.'s, claim to have increased their rate of code writing from a small number of lines per day per programmer of COBOL to more than 1000 equivalent lines per day using IBM's ADF/IMS. Figure 3.1 gives the number of programs installed per person-month in Playtex using COBOL and using ADF [4].

- The state of Connecticut used IBM's DMS [5] to implement a Medicaid system with one systems analyst on his first assignment, one programmer, one trainee, and a medical social worker. The system was implemented in 18 person-months. Their head of analysis and programming estimates at least 10:1 productivity improvements over CICS on future applications [6].

- The Bank of America has over 500 NOMAD applications running, almost all put up by end users. Half a dozen NOMAD consultants and instructors supported them [7].

- A benchmark version of a management reporting system which had taken 6 months to program in COBOL in Heublein was created in *half a day* with FOCUS [7].

- Karsten, the golf club manufacturer, installed that company's most complex application (on-line order entry) in 6 weeks using IBM's DMS [8].

- End users at the Santa Fe Railroad created applications with Univac's MAPPER, bypassing the DP department, on such a scale that it resulted in Univac's largest computer order ever [9]. The system has about 2,000 display terminals and printers.

- John Deere, Inc., rewrote three existing COBOL applications using IBM's ADF. A new employee inexperienced in programming did the work. He achieved a productivity twice that of the COBOL team on the first application, 32 times that of the COBOL team on the second application, and 46 times on the third [10].

Programs installed per person-month		
Program Type	Using COBOL	Using ADF
Inventory locator	0.3675	20.44
Order billing	0.1365	35.11
Order processing	0.3220	11.11
AVERAGE	0.2753	22.22

Average improvement: 80.71

Figure 3.1 Application development productivity figures from Playtex, Inc. (From [4].)

cedures that achieves the best results, as with the Bank of America or the user groups using Univac's MAPPER in Box 3.1.

When writing this book the author was amazed how many DP organizations were not using the new methods at all. In many cases on-line inquiry applications were being programmed in COBOL or PL/1 instead of using query languages. Many DP managers and teams were unaware of the high-productivity options available to them as described in this book.

OBTAINING INFORMATION WITH COBOL

Consider the following situation. A report is required listing patients in a group of hospitals who are in quarantine wards and who have had a previous stay at the hospital within 1 year of their present admittance. The report should look something like Fig. 3.2.

In many DP organizations at the time of writing this would be given to a COBOL or PL/1 programmer. Figure 3.3 shows a typical COBOL program for this. It contains 364 lines of code.

The same results could be created in 10 minutes by an end user with an appropriate data-base language.

```
                    P R E V I O U S   S T A Y   R E P O R T

      PAGE    1

      HOSPITAL NAME          HOSPITAL ADDRESS                HOSP PHONE

      MAC NEAL               1234 MAIN STREET, CHICAGO IL     3125554376

      WARD NO    TOT ROOMS     TOT BEDS    BEDS AVAIL    WARD TYPE

        01          34           112          018        QUARANTINE

      PATIENT NAME         BED   ADMIT DATE  PREV DATE  PREVIOUS HOSPITAL    PREVIOUS REASON

      O'HARA              0050    062377      1176      MAC NEAL             BUBONIC PLAGUE
      OZIER               0051    052177      1176      ST JOSEPH            BUBONIC PLAGUE
      PARELLA             0056    052777      1076      MAC NEAL             BUBONIC PLAGUE
      WRIGHT              0057    052677      1176      MAC NEAL             BUBONIC PLAGUE
      YANCEY              0058    052977      0976      RIVEREDGE            BUBONIC PLAGUE
      ERIN                0059    051277      1176      MAC NEAL             BUBONIC PLAGUE
      KAPP                0060    061777      1176      MAC NEAL             BUBONIC PLAGUE
      CLAPPER             0070    071877      1176      MAC NEAL             BUBONIC PLAGUE
      LEBEN               0071    080177      1076      ST JOSEPH            BUBONIC PLAGUE
      CAROL               0072    080177      1176      MAC NEAL             BUBONIC PLAGUE
      JOE                 0074    071777      1076      RIVEREDGE            BUBONIC PLAGUE
      KATIE               0077    080177      1176      MAC NEAL             BUBONIC PLAGUE
      PAT                 0078    072677      1076      ST JOSEPH            BUBONIC PLAGUE
      LANOU               0079    072677      1076      MAC NEAL             BUBONIC PLAGUE
      ELLGLASS            0080    072277      1176      MAC NEAL             BUBONIC PLAGUE
      CARLSON             0082    072177      1176      MAC NEAL             BUBONIC PLAGUE
      BUHL                0090    072477      1076      MAC NEAL             BUBONIC PLAGUE
```

Figure 3.2 Sample page of previous stay report.

```
000100 ID DIVISION.
000200 PROGRAM-ID. CHAP5C.
000300 AUTHOR. DKAPP.
000400 DATE-WRITTEN.  APRIL 26 1977.
000500 DATE-COMPILED.
000600
000610 REMARKS.
000700                THE OUTPUT OF THIS PROGRAM IS A LIST OF PATIENTS WHO
000800                ARE IN QUARANTINE WARDS PRESENTLY BUT ALSO HAVE
000900                BEEN IN A HOSPITAL WITHIN THE PAST YEAR.
001000
001100
001200 ENVIRONMENT DIVISION.
001300
001400 CONFIGURATION SECTION.
001500
001600 SOURCE-COMPUTER.    IBM-370-158.
001700 OBJECT-COMPUTER.    IBM-370-158.
001800
001900 INPUT-OUTPUT SECTION.
002000 FILE-CONTROL.
002100
002200      SELECT  PARMETER   ASSIGN TO UT-S-INPUT.
002300      SELECT  PRNTER     ASSIGN TO UT-S-OUTPUT.
002400
002500      EJECT
002600 DATA DIVISION.
002700
002800 FILE SECTION.
002900
003000 FD  PARMETER
003100
003200      BLOCK CONTAINS O RECORDS
003300      RECORDING MODE IS F
003400      LABEL RECORDS ARE OMITTED
003500      DATA RECORD IS PARM-CARD.
003600
003700 01  PARM-CARD.
003800      05  HOSPCONST  PIC XX.
003900      05  IHOSPNAM   PIC X(20).
004000      05  FILLER     PIC X(58).
004100
004200
004300 FD  PRNTER
004400
004500      BLOCK CONTAINS O RECORDS
004600      RECORDING MODE IS F
004700      LABEL RECORDS  ARE OMITTED
004800      DATA RECORD IS A-LINE.
004900
005000 01  A-LINE.
005100      05  PRINT-CTL   PIC X.
005200      05  PRINT-AREA  PIC X(132).
005400 WORKING-STORAGE SECTION.
005500
005600 77  NO-HOSPITAL    PIC X        VALUE '0'.
005700 77  NO-WARDS       PIC X        VALUE '0'.
005800 77  NO-PATIENTS    PIC X        VALUE '0'.
005900 77  TOP-PAGE       PIC X        VALUE '1'.
006000 77  DOUBLE-SPACE   PIC X        VALUE '0'.
006100 77  SINGLE-SPACE   PIC X        VALUE ' '.
006200 77  TRIPLE-SPACE   PIC X        VALUE '-'.
006300 77  END-DATABASE   PIC XX       VALUE 'GB'.
006400 77  SEG-NOT-FOUND  PIC XX       VALUE 'GE'.
006500 77  GET-UNIQUE     PIC XXXX     VALUE 'GU  '.
006600 77  GET-NEXT       PIC XXXX     VALUE 'GN  '.
006700 77  GET-NEXT-P     PIC XXXX     VALUE 'GNP '.
006800 77  LINE-CNT       PIC 99       VALUE 52.
006900 77  PAGE-CNT       PIC 9(4)     VALUE ZERO.
007000 77  CALL-SUCCESSFUL PIC XX      VALUE '  '.
007100 77  END-HOSP-DATA  PIC X        VALUE SPACE.
007200 77  HOSP-NOT-FOUND PIC X(20)    VALUE SPACE.
007300 77  NEW-MONTH      PIC S99.
007400 77  NEW-YEAR       PIC S99.
007500 77  WRDTYPE        PIC X(20)    VALUE SPACE.
007600
007700 01  CURR-DATE.
007800      05  CURRMO     PIC S99.
007900      05  FILLER     PIC X        VALUE '/'.
008000      05  CURRDAY    PIC S99.
008100      05  FILLER     PIC X        VALUE '/'.
008200      05  CURRYR     PIC S99.
008300
008400 01  WS-PREV-DATE.
```

Figure 3.3 A COBOL program of 364 lines of code which produces the report in Fig. 3.2 [11]. (Reproduced from [12] by permission.)

```
008500      05  PREVMO          PIC S99.
008600      05  PREVYR          PIC S99.
008700      EJECT
009800 01  HOSP-I-O-AREA COPY HOSPITAL.
008900
009000 01  WARD-I-O-AREA COPY WARD.
009100
009200 01  PAT-I-O-AREA COPY PATIENT.
009300
009400 01  SSA-HOSP.
009500      05  HOSPSEG         PIC X(8)   VALUE 'HOSPITAL'.
009600      05  FILLER          PIC X      VALUE '('.
009700      05  SEG-SEARCH-NAM  PIC X(8)   VALUE 'HOSPNAME'.
009800      05  HOSP-REL-OP     PIC XX     VALUE 'EQ'.
009900      05  HOSP-NAME       PIC X(20).
010000      05  FILLER          PIC X      VALUE ')'.
010100
010200 01  SSA-WARD.
010300
010400      05  WARDSEG         PIC X(8)   VALUE 'WARD
010500      05  FILLER          PIC X      VALUE '('.
010600      05  SEG-SEARCH-NAME PIC X(8)   VALUE 'WARDTYPE'.
010700      05  WARD-REL-OP     PIC XX     VALUE 'EQ'.
010800      05  WARD-TYPE       PIC X(20)  VALUE 'QUARANTINE
010900      05  FILLER          PIC X      VALUE ')'
010905
010910 01  SSA-PATIENT         PIC  X(9)   VALUE 'PATIENT
011100 01  HEAD-1.
011200
011300      05  FILLER          PIC X(26)  VALUE SPACES.
011400      05  TITLE           PIC X(106) VALUE
011500               'P R E V I O U S  S T A Y  R E P O R T'.
011700
011800 01  HEAD-2.
011900
012100      05  FILLER          PIC X(5)   VALUE 'PAGE'.
012200      05  HPAGE-CTR       PIC ZZZ9.
012300      05  FILLER          PIC X(123) VALUE SPACES.
012400
012500 01  HEAD-3.
012600
012800      05  HHOSPNAM        PIC X(25)  VALUE 'HOSPITAL NAME'.
013000      05  HHOSPADR        PIC X(35)  VALUE 'HOSPITAL ADDRESS'.
013200      05  HHOSPHON        PIC X(10)  VALUE 'HOSP PHONE'.
013300      05  FILLER          PIC X(62)  VALUE SPACE.
013400
013500 01  HEAD-4.
013600.
013800      05  HWARDNO         PIC X(12)  VALUE 'WARD NO'.
013900      05  HTOTRMS         PIC X(14)  VALUE 'TOT ROOMS'.
014000      05  HTOTBDS         PIC X(13)  VALUE 'TOT BEDS'.
014100      05  HBDSAVAI        PIC X(15)  VALUE 'BEDS AVAIL'.
014200      05  HBDAVAIL        PIC X(20)  VALUE 'WARD TYPE'.
014300      05  FILLER          PIC X(58)  VALUE SPACE.
014400
014500 01  HEAD-5.
014600
014800      05  HPATNAM         PIC X(21)  VALUE 'PATIENT NAME'.
014900      05  HBDID           PIC X(6)   VALUE 'BED'.
015000      05  HDATADMIT       PIC X(12)  VALUE 'ADMIT DATE'.
015100      05  HPREVDAT        PIC X(11)  VALUE 'PREV DATE'.
015200      05  HPREVHOS        PIC X(21)  VALUE 'PREVIOUS HOSPITAL'.
015400      05  HPREV-REASON    PIC X(30)  VALUE 'PREVIOUS REASON'.
015500      05  FILLER          PIC X(31)  VALUE SPACE.
015700 01  DETAIL-1.
015800
016000      05  DHOSPNAM        PIC X(20).
016100      05  FILLER          PIC X(5)   VALUE SPACE.
016200      05  DHOSP-ADDRESS   PIC X(30).
016300      05  FILLER          PIC X(5)   VALUE SPACE.
016400      05  DHOSPHON        PIC X(10).
016500      05  FILLER          PIC X(62)  VALUE SPACE.
016600
016700 01  DETAIL-2.
016800
016900      05  FILLER          PIC X(3)   VALUE SPACE.
017000      05  DWARDNO         PIC 99.
017100      05  FILLER          PIC X(10)  VALUE SPACE.
017200      05  DTOTRMS         PIC 999.
017300      05  FILLER          PIC X(11)  VALUE SPACE.
017400      05  DTOT-BEDS       PIC 999.
017500      05  FILLER          PIC X(10)  VALUE SPACE.
017600      05  DBDSAVAIL       PIC 999.
```

(Continued)

```
017700      05  FILLER            PIC X(9)  VALUE SPACE.
017800      05  DWARDTYPE         PIC X(20).
017900      05  FILLER            PIC X(58) VALUE SPACE.
018000
019100 01  DETAIL-3.
018200
018400      05  DPATNAM           PIC X(20).
018500      05  FILLER            PIC X     VALUE SPACE.
018600      05  DBEDID            PIC 9999.
018700      05  FILLER            PIC X(4)  VALUE SPACE.
018800      05  DDATADMIT         PIC X(6).
018900      05  FILLER            PIC X(6)  VALUE SPACE.
019000      05  DPREV-DATE        PIC X(4).
019100      05  FILLER            PIC X(5)  VALUE SPACE.
019200      05  DPREV-HOSP        PIC X(20).
019300      05  FILLER            PIC X     VALUE SPACE.
019400      05  DPREV-REASONN     PIC X(30).
019500      05  FILLER            PIC X(31) VALUE SPACE.
019600
019700 01  NO-HOSP-LINE.
019800
020100      05  ERR-HOSPNAM PIC X(20).
020110      05  FILLER      PIC X(5)       VALUE SPACE.
020200      05  FILLER      PIC X(107)     VALUE
020300                      '****  HOSPITAL NOT FOUND  ****'.
020310
020311 01  NO-WARD-LINE   PIC X(132)   VALUE
020312                     '****  NO QUARANTINE WARDS ****'.
020313
020314 01  NO-PAT-LINE    PIC X(132)   VALUE
020315                     '****  NO PATIENTS WITH PREVIOUS STAY  ****'.
020500 LINKAGE SECTION.
020600 01  DB-PCB-HOSP COPY MASKC.
020800 PROCEDURE DIVISION.
021000 ENTRY-POINT.
021200          ENTRY 'DLITCBL' USING DB-PCB-HOSP.
021300          OPEN INPUT PARMETER  OUTPUT PRNTER.
021500          MOVE CURRENT-DATE TO CURR-DATE.
021600
021700 READ-CARD.
021900      READ PARMETER AT END GO TO END-JOB.
022000      MOVE IHOSPNAM TO HOSP-NAME.
022100      MOVE 45 TO LINE-CNT.
022200
022300      CALL 'CBLTDLI' USING GET-UNIQUE
022400                           DB-PCB-HOSP
022500                           HOSP-I-O-AREA
022600                           SSA-HOSP.
022700
022900      IF STATUS-CODE NOT EQUAL ' '
022900
023000          PERFORM HOSPITAL-NOT-FOUND
023100          GO TO READ-CARD.
023200
023300      MOVE HOSPNAME     TO  DHOSPNAM.
023400      MOVE HOSP-ADDRESS TO  DHOSP-ADDRESS.
023500      MOVE HOSP-PHONE   TO  DHOSPHON.
023600
023700      CALL 'CBLTDLI' USING GET-UNIQUE
023800                           DB-PCB-HOSP
023900                           WARD-I-O-AREA
024000                           SSA-HOSP
024100                           SSA-WARD
024200
024300      IF STATUS-CODE NOT EQUAL ' '
024400
024500          PERFORM WARD-NOT-FOUND
024600          GO TO READ-CARD.
024700
024710      MOVE WARDNO       TO  DWARDNO.
024800      MOVE TOT-ROOMS    TO  DTOTRMS.
024900      MOVE TOT-BEDS     TO  DTOT-BEDS.
025000      MOVE BEDAVAIL     TO  DBDSAVAIL.
025100      MOVE WARDTYPE     TO  DWARDTYPE.
025200      MOVE '0' TO NO-PATIENTS.
025300
025400      PERFORM  CALL-PATIENT THRU CALL-PATIENT-EXIT
025600                            UNTIL STATUS-CODE = 'GE'.
025610
025700      IF NO-PATIENTS EQUAL '0'
025800
025900          MOVE NO-PAT-LINE  TO DETAIL-3
026000          PERFORM WRITE-RTN THRU WRITE-RTN-EXIT
```

Figure 3.3 Continued

```
026100          MOVE SPACE TO DETAIL-3.
026200
026300      MOVE '0' TO NO-PATIENTS.
026400      GO TO READ-CARD.
026600 CALL-PATIENT.
026700
026800      CALL 'CBLTDLI' USING GET-NEXT-P
026900                          DB-PCB-HOSP
027000                          PAT-I-O-AREA
027010                          SSA-PATIENT.
027100
027200      IF STATUS-CODE EQUAL 'GE' GO TO CALL-PATIENT-EXIT.
027300      IF STATUS-CODE NOT EQUAL ' '
027400
027500          MOVE DB-PCB-HOSP TO DETAIL-3
027600          PERFORM WRITE-RTN THRU WRITE-RTN-EXIT
027700          MOVE SPACE TO DETAIL-3
027800          GO TO READ-CARD.
027900
028000      IF   PREV-STAY-FLAG NOT EQUAL '1' GO TO CALL-PATIENT-EXIT.
028100
028200          MOVE PREV-DATE TO WS-PREV-DATE.
028300          SUBTRACT PREVMO FROM CURRMO GIVING NEW-MONTH.
028500          SUBTRACT PREVYR FROM CURRYR GIVING NEW-YEAR.
028700
029000      IF   NEW-YEAR GREATER THAN 1 GO TO CALL-PATIENT-EXIT.
029100      IF   NEW-YEAR EQUAL 0
029200
029300              PERFORM WRITE-PAT-DATA
029400              MOVE '1' TO NO-PATIENTS
029500              GO TO CALL-PATIENT-EXIT.
029600
029700      IF   NEW-YEAR EQUAL      1
029800      AND  NEW-MONTH LESS THAN 1
029900
030000              PERFORM WRITE-PAT-DATA
030100              MOVE '1' TO NO-PATIENTS.
030110
030200 CALL-PATIENT-EXIT.
030300      EXIT.
030500 WRITE-RTN.
030600      IF LINE-CNT LESS THAN 44 GO TO WRITE-PAT-LINE.
030700
030800          MOVE 1 TO LINE-CNT.
030900          MOVE HEAD-1 TO PRINT-AREA.
031000          WRITE A-LINE AFTER POSITIONING TOP-PAGE.
031010
031100          ADD 1 TO PAGE-CNT.
031200          MOVE PAGE-CNT TO HPAGE-CTR.
031300          MOVE HEAD-2 TO PRINT-AREA.
031400          WRITE A-LINE AFTER POSITIONING DOUBLE-SPACE.
031410
031500          MOVE HEAD-3 TO PRINT-AREA.
031600          WRITE A-LINE AFTER POSITIONING DOUBLE-SPACE.
031610
031700          MOVE DETAIL-1    TO PRINT-AREA.
031800          WRITE A-LINE AFTER POSITIONING DOUBLE-SPACE.
031900
032000          IF NO-HOSPITAL EQUAL '1' GO TO WRITE-RTN-EXIT.
032010
032200              MOVE HEAD-4 TO PRINT-AREA.
032300              WRITE A-LINE AFTER POSITIONING DOUBLE-SPACE.
032310
032400              MOVE DETAIL-2 TO PRINT-AREA.
032500              WRITE A-LINE AFTER POSITIONING DOUBLE-SPACE.
032600
032700          IF NO-WARDS EQUAL '1' GO TO WRITE-RTN-EXIT.
032710
032900              MOVE HEAD-5 TO PRINT-AREA.
033000              WRITE A-LINE AFTER POSITIONING DOUBLE-SPACE.
033010
033100              MOVE SPACE TO PRINT-AREA.
033200              WRITE A-LINE AFTER POSITIONING SINGLE-SPACE.
033210
033220 WRITE-PAT-LINE.
033230
033300
033400      MOVE DETAIL-3 TO PRINT-AREA.
033500      WRITE A-LINE AFTER POSITIONING SINGLE-SPACE.
033600      ADD 1 TO LINE-CNT.
033700
033800 WRITE-RTN-EXIT.
033900      EXIT.
```

(Continued)

```
034100 WRITE-PAT-DATA.
034200
034300     MOVE PATNAME TO DPATNAM.
034400     MOVE BEDIDENT TO DBEDID.
034500     MOVE DATEADMT TO DDATADMIT.
034600     MOVE PREV-HOSP TO DPREV-HOSP.
034700     MOVE PREV-DATE TO DPREV-DATE.
034800     MOVE PREV-REASON TO DPREV-REASONN.
034900     PERFORM   WRITE-RTN THRU WRITE-RTN-EXIT.
035000
035100 HOSPITAL-NOT-FOUND.
035200
035300     MOVE '1' TO NO-HOSPITAL.
035310     MOVE IHOSPNAM TO ERR-HOSPNAM.
035400     MOVE NO-HOSP-LINE TO  DETAIL-1.
035500     PERFORM  WRITE-RTN THRU WRITE-RTN-EXIT.
035510     MOVE SPACE TO DETAIL-1.
035600     MOVE '0' TO NO-HOSPITAL.
035700
035800 WARD-NOT-FOUND.
035900
036000     MOVE '1' TO NO-WARDS.
036100     MOVE NO-WARD-LINE TO DETAIL-2.
036200     PERFORM WRITE-RTN THRU WRITE-RTN-EXIT.
036210     MOVE SPACE TO DETAIL-2.
036300     MOVE '0' TO NO-WARDS.
036400
036500 END-JOB.
036600
036700     CLOSE PARMETER PRNTER.
036800         GOBACK.
```

Figure 3.3 Continued

With IBM's QUERY-BY-EXAMPLE [11] the user can display skeletons of records on a screen. In this case he would display the HOSPITAL record, the WARD record, and the PATIENT record, as follows:

HOSPITAL	HOSPITAL NAME	HOSPITAL ADDRESS	HOSPITAL PHONE

WARD	HOSPITAL NAME	WARD NO.	TOTAL ROOMS	TOTAL BEDS	BEDS AVAIL.	WARD TYPE

PATIENT	PATIENT NAME	HOS-PITAL NAME	WARD NO.	BED	ADMIT. DATE	PREV. DATE	PREV. HOS-PITAL	PREV. REASON

He now fills in this skeleton. He enters QUARANTINE in WARD TYPE.

If he wants a listing for any hospital, he can enter any value underlined in HOSPITAL NAME. He enters the same value in each record. Similarly, he enters any value underlined in WARD NO.

He can enter any value in PREV. DATE, underlined. He enters PR and then in ADMIT DATE he enters $\leq$ PR + 365.

The screen now looks like this:

HOSPITAL	HOSPITAL NAME	HOSPITAL ADDRESS	HOSPITAL PHONE
	HOS		

WARD	HOS-PITAL NAME	WARD NO.	TOTAL ROOMS	TOTAL BEDS	BEDS AVAIL.	WARD TYPE
	HOS	**WARD**				QUARANTINE

PATIENT	PATIENT NAME	HOS-PITAL NAME	WARD NO.	BED	ADMIT. DATE	PREV. DATE	PREV. HOS-PITAL	PREV. REASON
		HOS	**WARD**		≤**PR + 365**	**PR**		

The user presses the enter key and obtains the listing in Fig. 3.2. The user can *immediately* adjust the listing if it is not exactly what he wants. He can press a print key to have it printed.

To do this, the user need not learn mnemonics or difficult procedures. Users learn to obtain results from QUERY-BY-EXAMPLE in half a day. The program in Fig. 3.3 took an experienced programmer many days to write and debug and he spent much subsequent time modifying it. The QUERY-BY-EXAMPLE version took 5 minutes and can be done by the *user who needs the data* rather than by a programmer.

Other types of data-base query language also enable end users to obtain information at a terminal without learning any computing skills. With Cullinane's ON-LINE ENGLISH, for example (discussed in Chapter 9), a user can type English phrases to formulate a query. The computer reacts to the phrases and may ask the user to modify them until it can process the query.

MORE COMPLEX REQUIREMENTS

The COBOL programmer may defend his trade by saying that programming is much more flexible. He can specify any type of report format. In fact, however, the best report generators are now very flexible and have the advantage that the *user can adjust* both his query and the type of report when he sees it on a screen. This fast interaction makes the user facilities more flexible in reality than the writing of lengthy programs.

Some end-user facilities have much more power than QUERY-BY-EXAMPLE or ON-LINE ENGLISH. With Univac's MAPPER, for example [9], the user can specify entire applications. Calculations and logic can be expressed in FORTRAN-like statements. The requisite input forms and output documents can be built up on a screen and when the user is satisfied the routines can be catalogued for future use. The results can be transmitted to printers or other terminals.

In a brief terminal session the users can create what they want. Achieving the same results with conventional programming would take weeks or months and then might not be what the user wants.

Fourth-generation *programming* or *procedural* languages, e.g., cincom's MANTIS, can create applications with more complex logic. The change in productivity may not be quite as dramatic as those described in Box 3.1, but is still impressive. It may be necessary to achieve good machine performance and this can be done if the right software is used.

The point of the query illustration above is that conventional programming is clumsy, time-consuming, and difficult to debug, compared with the best of the query languages, report generators, graphics generators, and application generators.

About 70% of the *immediate* needs of *typical* end users can be satisfied with query languages and report generators *if an appropriate data base exists.* or can be created. Much of the remainder can be satisfied with application generators and on-line graphics packages. Unfortunately, no one package of those in Fig. 2.2 is suitable for *all* applications. It is therefore necessary to select *which* software should be used for which applications.

The software is rapidly improving and will become more comprehensive, more powerful, and more user friendly. It is important to understand, however, that software in existence today can do an excellent job of satisfying most end-user needs, and the resulting increase in productivity of application creation is great.

PROGRAMMER PRODUCTIVITY

Programmer productivity is a subject on which much research has been done and many papers written. Almost all the papers relate to programming with conventional programming languages. A slightly unsatisfactory aspect of the subject is that programmer productivity is difficult to measure.

One measure is the *average number of lines of code written per day* over a period that includes debugging and documenting the code. It is necessary to agree on exactly what types of lines are being entered. This varies substantially from one installation to another. A problem with this measure is that it does not adequately compare productivity of writing in two languages of different power. It does not measure the effect of techniques such as eliminating the need to write the Data Division of COBOL because it is generated from a data-base data dictionary. It is not a useful measure for *motivating* programmers because it would encourage them to add unnecessarily to the number of lines in their programs.

A more satisfactory measure would be the time taken to obtain results of a certain type. Unfortunately, it is difficult to quantify the results achieved or to compare numerically, say, the creation of a management report and the creation of a bill-of-materials explosion. Some studies have compared the results by programming them in assembler language and counting the numbers of lines of code. This can be done in an academic research study, but there is not time to do it in a production environment.

The measurements for any one programming language reveal three causes of high variation in productivity. *First,* the best programmers achieve a much higher productivity than poor programmers. *Second,* productivity is higher with small programs than with large ones. It can be improved by modular design, especially with structured data-base facilities in which no one module becomes too large. *Third,* productivity falls with highly complex programs. Good design can reduce the complexity.

VARIATION IN PROGRAMMER SKILL

Good programmers achieve 10 times more the results of poor programmers. Unfortunately for them, their salaries are not proportional to their results. Figure 3.4 shows a typical distribution of productivity of programmers working on low- to medium-sized programs. A major variation in human capability also exists with users of application generator software. The term ADF or DMS *acrobat* is heard describing a person who produces results with these facilities exceptionally rapidly and efficiently. It seems easier to become an ADF or DMS acrobat than a COBOL acrobat. It requires thorough learning and practice with the product. Many competent professionals achieve a high level of skill with these products, whereas becoming the best programmer with conventional languages requires a talent that few people seem to achieve.

The programmer represented by the right-hand side of Fig. 3.4 has a rare talent and should, perhaps, work for those organizations where this talent is most needed—for example, software houses. The programmer toward the left of Fig. 3.4 may be well advised to learn application generators, as he will be able to achieve much faster results with these than with conventional programming. Often, a DMS or ADF "acrobat" has never been exceptionally productive with conventional programming.

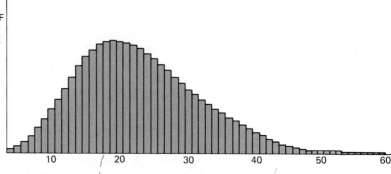

Figure 3.4 Programmer productivity varies greatly from one programmer to another. The best are very good, but difficult to find. Those on
the left should be swung over to work with application generators
rather than programming languages. A small number of briliant programmers achieve results way beyond the right-hand end of this scale.
Most programmers achieve far more lines of code than this on small
stand-alone programs.

**THE EFFECT OF
PROGRAM SIZE**

Lower programmer productivity is achieved with
large programs than with small programs. Figure
3.5 shows a typical distribution. The productivity
achieved with superlarge programs is almost one-tenth of that achieved with
small programs [13].

Fortunately, there are far more small programs than large ones, as
shown by Fig. 3.6. Many organizations have no need to write *any* programs
that are classed as large or superlarge in Fig. 3.6 [13]. Programs of a size
greater than the equivalent of 64,000 lines of assembler language tend to be
written by software houses and computer vendors rather than by user organizations, although there are exceptions to this.

There are several reasons why productivity with large programs is worse
than with small ones. First, the programming team is larger. This requires
more formal interaction between people and gives more scope for miscom-
munication. There is substantial overhead required to fit together all the
pieces of a large program.

The small programs in Fig. 3.6 are often created by one person who has
all the pieces in his head. With large systems, planning and paperwork is
needed to control the development cycle. The various forms of paperwork
with large systems sometimes contain an aggregate of over 50 English words
for each line of source code in the system [16, 17]. In large systems where
the programmer works on one project for more than a year, his or her interest and productivity often decline substantially. On a small program the
programmer can keep working fast to complete the work quickly.

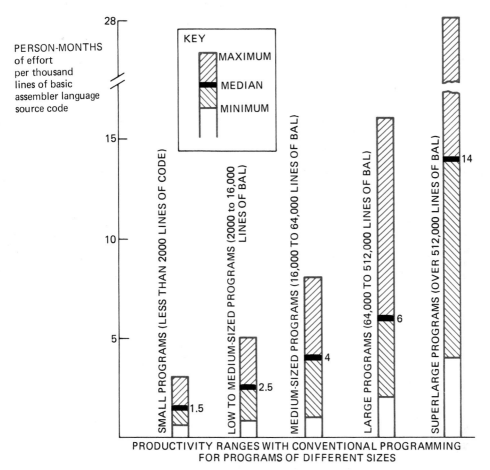

Figure 3.5 Lower programmer productivity is achieved with large programs than with small programs.

A second major factor affecting productivity with large programs is the difficulty of debugging them. The cost of removal of defects in programs typically ranges from 20% of the total costs with small programs to 50% with large programs [13].

The comparison of productivity with large and small programs indicates that development of large programs should be avoided by DP departments wherever possible. Large programs should be split into small programs where possible. They should employ application generators for input, output, and report generation where this can be done. Unfortunately, large programs are often the least susceptible to application generator techniques.

The most dramatic productivity increases reported when using application generators almost always apply to small- or medium-sized programs, not large programs. This is true with the examples in Box 3.1.

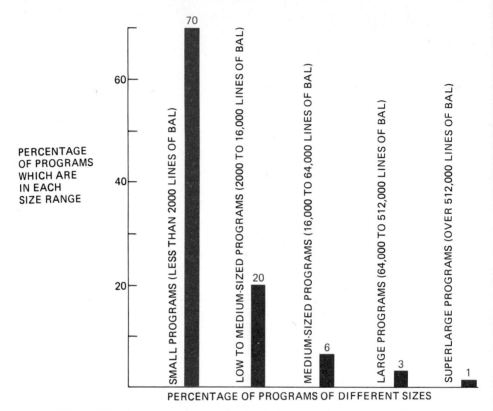

Figure 3.6 Most programs are small. Only a small percentage of programs are very large.

COMPLEXITY Productivity also varies substantially with the complexity of the program. The number of lines of code per person-year in coding operating systems is typically one-tenth of that in coding commercial DP applications [14]. In general the number of interfaces between individuals writing logic code should be minimized. All coders and designers may link to a common data base and be administered for stability [15].

Wherever possible, large or complex programs should be candidates for outside purchase. Operations research routines, simulation, job-shop scheduling, air-line reservation systems, and so on, can often be obtained as preprogrammed packages.

The problems with large or complex programs are often less if fewer people are involved. This can be made possible by using a higher-level language in which one individual can accomplish more of the overall system. For certain types of systems a programming language such as APL is used. APL or NOMAD can reduce the *effective* project size, often reducing it to something manageable without large-project techniques. Large project problems can be avoided in this way with much application development, but generally not with software development such as the creation of operating systems or compilers.

APL is used extensively within IBM for its own data processing. Measurements show that professional programmers using APL can code and test systems for end users with one-tenth to one-fourth of the time and effort required using PL/1 [18]. PL/1 itself has been found to give 25% better programming productivity than COBOL [19].

LIMITS TO PROGRAMMER PRODUCTIVITY   Are there limits to the productivity improvements that can ever be achieved with conventional programming?

This question is addressed in a paper and survey by T.C. Jones [13]. He divides programming productivity improvements into four ranges and discusses what techniques have achieved improvements within these ranges.

1. Methods that may yield up to 25% improvement

2. Methods that may yield a 25% to 50% improvement

3. Methods that may yield a 50% to 75% improvement

4. Methods that may yield more than a 75% improvement

1. Improving Productivity up to 25%

Most of the success stories and firm evidence of productivity improvement with conventional languages lie in this range.

Often, the baseline for comparison is programs that are unstructured, designed in a bottom-up fashion, with no formal reviews or inspections prior to testing, and no use of interactive methods. If this is the starting point, almost *any* step toward structured techniques or interactive development will give results. These results are rarely more than a 25% improvement (if there is no change in language and no move to programmers of greater talent).

Small programs written by individual programmers benefit from interactive methods [20]. Large programs needing many programmers benefit from the better discipline of structured methods [21, 22] and from inspections [23].

In one installation which the author studied, a much-heralded move to interactive programming actually lowered the overall programmer productivity because the programmers made more mistakes. They seemed to be less able to carefully contemplate their code when entering it on a screen than when using off-line coding sheets.

2. Improving Productivity by 25 to 50%

Achieving more than a 25% improvement is more difficult because programming is largely a labor-intensive activity. Real people in real life, Jones concludes, cannot move a great deal faster than they already do. To achieve more than 25% improvement requires techniques that replace human effort in some way.

Jones concludes: "It can almost definitely be stated that no *single technique* by itself can improve productivity at the 50% level for programs larger than trivial ones," except for a change in programming language.

Jones stated that there are a few success stories at the 35 to 40% improvement level, sometimes these related to an unusually backward installation so that the improvement looked better than it perhaps should have. In other cases a good team was made better by this percentage.

3. Improving Productivity by 50 to 75%

Jones concluded that there are only two general ways to achieve programming productivity gains that approach 75%:

(a) Search out those programmers and analysts who are at the very high end of the personal achievement scale (the right-hand side of Fig. 3.4). There are a few isolated stories of abnormally high productivity, such as the programming of the New York Times information system (87,000 instructions) in one year by three people: Harlam Mills, Terry Baker, and an assistant who checked the code. This is a productivity four or five times higher than the norm. It is sometimes quoted as a triumph of structured programming, which it is, but it is more a triumph of selecting brilliant individuals and giving them the fullest support. An IBM executive with the project in his area said: "Baker was supported in a way similar to a great surgeon in an operating room" [24].

The best programmers need to be paid more than average ones. But the increase in results can far exceed the increase in pay. The salary histogram is not as elongated as the productivity histogram in Fig. 3.4, so it pays to seek out programmers on the far right of that chart and avoid those on the left.

(b) Use program generators, very high level languages, shared systems, or other forms of program *acquisition* in place of program *development*.

4. High Productivity Gains

In stark contrast to the surveys of programmer productivity improvement are the results that have been achieved with data-base user languages, report generators, graphics packages, and application generators. With these, productivity improvements of over 1000% are not uncommon. Often, they replace only small application programs. But that is 70% of all applications. The best of the generator languages have the capability to replace most commercial data processing programs that fall into the *small* and *low-medium* categories of Fig. 3.6. Almost all the pressure from end-users is for applications that can be *generated* without conventional programming if a suitably designed data base exists, together with suitable generator software.

VERY COMPLEX APPLICATIONS

Very complex applications are likely to require programmers for the foreseeable future. Application generators are not going to do image processing for NASA, network optimization, design of nuclear reactors, or optimal production scheduling. Sometimes, parameterized packages can be obtained for complex applications. But *some* applications are still going to require programmers and these are often to the right of Fig. 3.5, unfortunately.

What can be done to increase the productivity of creating these applications?

Probably the best approach is to move to the highest-possible programming language. APL users typically achieve a productivity 4 to 10 times higher than COBOL or PL/1 [18, 25]. APL has been used very successfully in operations research, design and engineering, financial planning, and investigating senior management's "What if" questions. NOMAD is very powerful for using a relational data base, generating reports from it, doing statistical analysis, and again, answering "What if" questions.

A nonprocedural language strongly affects productivity by enabling a user to express *what* is required rather than *how* to obtain it. Complex applications, however, often require a procedural language to express complex logic in detail. NOMAD provides a combination of procedural and nonprocedural operations so that the user may achieve the best of both worlds.

There may be an increase in hardware costs due to the languages being interpreted rather than compiled. In many cases, however, the cost of *running* a program is small compared with the cost of creating it.

A study by Kendall [26] found that many programs used more machine cycles *during development* than they used in their entire lives in execution. This is often the case with very large or complex programs because these are not run as frequently as the programs that process routine operations or paperwork, which can usually be *generated*.

In a typical installation 2% of the applications use 50% of the machine cycles; 50% of the applications use only 2% of the machine cycles, in total [18]. For the latter applications, coding efficiency is of little importance compared with programming productivity.

RESISTANCE

In view of the enormous difference in productivity of application creation between conventional programming and the software in Fig. 2.2, why is everybody not using the latter for most commercial data processing?

Perhaps the biggest reason is simply inertia. It takes a long time for a fundamentally new idea to penetrate any field. In this case the idea is somewhat threatening. It suggests that the knowledge that programmers (and, as we will see, systems analysts) so laboriously acquired may become obsolete. It suggests that DP departments could be bypassed by end users finding ways to create their own applications.

BOX 3.2 Great opposition is frequently encountered to the views expressed in this book. Reasons for the opposition are listed below. Most such reasons are invalid compared with the major gains in productivity that can be achieved.

- Programmers, systems analysts, and DP managers want to continue to practice what they are good at. They are afraid that their skills, so laboriously acquired, will be devalued.
- Conservative DP staff refuse to believe that the new methods really work.
- Seminar firms are making much money from teaching structured programming and structured analysis.
- The DP standards manual or corporate DP development "Bible" advocates conventional methods.
- A sentiment exists against "pioneering." Pioneers get killed a lot.
- There is a desire or a directive to avoid language proliferation.
- The new facilities cannot create every type of application, whereas conventional programming can.
- DP managers perceive application creation by end users as an erosion of their authority.
- Application creation by end-user groups is perceived as a formula for chaos.
- There is sometimes an anti-data-base sentiment and many of the new facilities are data-base-oriented.
- Most of the new languages and facilities are not manufacturer-independent.
- The new facility exists on a minicomputer or mainframe from a vendor ruled out by the corporate network strategy, or an IBM-only strategy.
- The perception exists that the facilities in Fig. 2.1 give much worse machine performance (not necessarily true or relevant).
- There is no long-term DP planning with these methods. (Long-term strategic planning is needed and should incorporate these approaches [27]).
- Programmers, or analysts, fearful for their jobs, manage to denigrate the new facilities or methods.

The conventional wisdom in any field cannot be overturned in a hurry. In this case we are expecting to overturn it in the brief space of a few years. But traditional DP methodology and COBOL programming has the momentum of a giant freight train traveling as fast as it can. Nothing will deflect it from its course quickly.

Data processing departments are still struggling to come to grips with structured programming and structured analysis. Ideas as fundamentally sound and nonthreatening as these took the best part of a decade to penetrate the installation community. Now, while the structured revolution is still only half complete, along comes another which is much more threatening. The poor DP professional says: "I'm only just beginning to understand how to make the most of structured techniques. Give me a chance to use them!"

On the one hand, many DP staff do not know about the new techniques; on the other hand, some are saying that they are unworkable, trivial, machine-inefficient, wrong, or mere sales gimmicks.

Common advice in the programming field is: "Use tried-and-tested techniques." "Do not let innovation loose for the sake of innovation" and "Pioneers get arrows in their backs!"

Most programmers want to hang on indefinitely to the language they know. They spent a long time mastering it and new methods represent a threat. If the new methods are easy to learn, they could wholly devalue the programmer's hard-won expertise.

When COBOL was first used in the USSR it employed American compilers running on computers with an IBM 360 instruction set. It was English language COBOL. Today, old programmers still use English COBOL rather than Russian COBOL, writing IF, THEN, ELSE, GO TO, and so on. Such is the reluctance or programmers to change languages.

In some U.S. firms the highest application creation productivity is indeed coming from groups that have bypassed the DP department. In some cases these are end user groups using software such as ADMINS 11 or Univac's MAPPER. In some cases the end users have acquired their own minicomputers. In other firms an organization has been set up by the DP department for exploiting the new techniques and bypassing the programmer shops.

Sometimes end-user groups armed with new languages, such as Univac's MAPPER, are more innovative than DP professionals would dare to be.

Box 3.2 summarizes reasons for opposition to the views of this book.

Many of today's efforts to improve the productivity of application creation are concerned with speeding up conventional programming, with structured techniques, interactive programming, programmer's workbench, composite design, Warnier diagrams, and so on. These are valuable but there is a limit to the extent to which conventional coding can be speeded up.

Daniel McCracken tells a parable about a man with an old car who wanted to go from New York to California in a day. He souped up the engine, changed the transmission, and modified the car any way he could to make it faster. He fitted it with superb police radar detectors, but the attempt to make it sufficiently fast was doomed before it began. When told that he could use a different technology to get to California—take a jet—he said: "Oh those things! They'll never fly!" Many programmers have the same attitude to application generators.

FITTING THE SOFTWARE TO THE APPLICATION

At the time of writing the software for application generation has many shortcomings. It is rapidly improving, but today the software method needs to be selected to fit the application. No one type of software is appropriate for all applications.

The selection process is a key to success. Higher productivity can often be achieved by using more than one type of software for one application area, for example an application generator for DP professionals, certain routines written with conventional programming, and a data-base query language and report generator for end users.

TECHNIQUES ANALYST

It is desirable to have an analyst who is familiar with the capabilities of these diverse languages and software packages, who will decide what language should be used for each application. He may also be responsible for deciding what training is needed. The number of different languages needs to be kept as small as it can be and still maximize productivity. This analyst might be called a *techniques analyst,* TA.

The techniques analyst should be familiar with figures quoted in the industry for typical productivity with different methods. In some organizations he will meet much opposition from DP people who are resistant to changing their methods, standards, and hallowed procedures manuals.

However, numbers such as those in Box 3.1 and Fig. 3.1 are too big to ignore.

SUMMARY

A revolution in application creation is under way. It is somewhat analogous to the revolution that occurred in electronic hardware design when highly integrated circuits replaced transistors. Instead of designing with individual transistors and resistors, the designer uses larger building blocks. This is much more efficient. The line-at-a-time COBOL programmer is like a designer working with individual transistors. A move to higher-level software building blocks is needed.

Given the full costs of specification, coding, debugging, documenting, and maintenance in COBOL or PL/1, management ought to conduct an inquiry whenever a proposal is made to use these to see whether any higher-productivity alternative can be found. COBOL-level blow-by-blow coding should be avoided wherever possible.

To survive the dropping cost of computers, the computer industry must be pushed, kicking and screaming, into the age of application development without programmers.

REFERENCES

1. ADMINS 11 is an application generator used with PDP 11 computers. Manuals are available from ADMINS, Inc., P.O. Box 269, Cambridge, MA 02138.

2. Information from the Corporate Business Department, Chase Manhattan Bank, New York, NY.

3. Information from Barbara Schmidt, IBM, White Plains, NY 10604. "ADF" stands for Application Development Facility. It is discussed in Chapter 16.

4. IBM brochure, "IMS/VS Users Talk about Productivity and Control," G520–3511–0, IBM Corp., White Plains, NY 10604, 1980.

5. DMS, IBM's Development Management Facility, is discussed in Chapter 15.

6. T.A. DiMartino, "DMS/VS at the Department of Income Maintenance, State of Connecticut," Guide and Share *Proceedings,* Application Development Symposium, Share, New York, 1979.

7. D.D. McCracken, "Software Systems in the '80s: An Overview," *Computerworld EXTRA,* September 1980.

8. "DP Dialogue," IBM Corp., White Plains, NY 10604, 1980.

9. The Santa Fe's operation in Chicago, using Univac's MAPPER is a stunning installation to visit and examine in detail. MAPPER is an application generator for end users, described in Sperry Univac Reference Manual RRD–B450.2, 1980.

10. D.H. Holtz, "ADF Experiences at John Deere," D303–SHARE 50, Denver, CO, March 6, 1978.

11. QUERY-BY-EXAMPLE, QBE, is an IBM data-base query language for end users designed by Moshe Zloof, IBM, Thomas J. Watson Research Laboratories, Yorktown, NY. It is discussed in Chapter 9. Dr. Zloof kindly provided the illustration of QBE reflected in Figs. 3.2 and 3.3.

12. D. Kapp and J.F. Leben, *IMS Programming Techniques—A Guide to Using DL/I.,* Van Nostrand Reinhold Company, New York, 1978.

13. T.C. Jones, "The Limits of Programming Productivity," Guide and Share Application Development Symposium, *Proceedings,* Share, New York, 1979.

14. F. Brooks, *The Mythical Man Month*, Addison-Wesley, Reading, MA, 1977.

15. See the discussion of stability analysis in *Managing the Data-Base Environment* by James Martin, Prentice-Hall, Inc, Englewood Cliffs, NJ, 1982.

16. T.C. Jones, "Optimizing Program Quality and Programmer Productivity," Guide 45, *Proceedings,* Atlanta, GA, November 1977.

17. T.C. Jones, "A Survey of Programming Design and Specification Techniques," IEEE Symposium on Specifications of Reliable Software, April 1979. IEEE Order No. 79 CH1401-9C.

18. W.R. Bradshaw, "Application Development Productivity within IBM Information Systems," Guide and Share Application Development Symposium, *Proceedings,* Share, New York, 1979.

19. A.J. Albrecht, "Measuring Application Development Productivity," Guide and Share Application Development Symposium, *Proceedings,* Share, New York, 1979.

20. G.W. Willett et al., "TSO Productivity Study," American Telephone and Telegraph Long Lines, Kansas City, April 1973.

21. P. Freeman and A.I. Wasserman, "Tutorial on Software Design Techniques," IEEE Computer Society, Catalog No. 76CH1145-2, 1977.

22. C.V. Ramamoorthy and H.H. So, *Survey of Principles and Techniques of Software Requirements and Specifications,* Software Engineering Techniques 2, invited papers, Infotech International Ltd., Nicholson House, Maidenhead, Berkshire, England, 1977, pp. 265-318.

23. M.E. Fagan, "Design and Code Inspections to Reduce Errors in Program Development," *IBM Systems Journal,* Vol. 15, No. 3, 1976 (Reprint Order No. G321-5033).

24. Joe Fox, *Software Management,* Prentice-Hall, Inc., Englewood Cliffs, NJ, 1981.

25. R.S. Robinson, "Financial Planning Applications of APL in J. Ray McDermott," in *APL in Practice,* Rose and Schick, eds., Wiley & Sons, Inc., New York, 1980.

26. R.C. Kendall, "Management Perspectives on Programs, Programming and Productivity," *Proceedings,* Guide 45, Atlanta, GA, November 1977.

27. J. Martin, *Strategic Data Planning Methodologies,* Prentice-Hall, Englewood Cliffs, NJ, 1982.

4 PROBLEMS WITH CONVENTIONAL APPLICATION DEVELOPMENT

INTRODUCTION   Productivity, alone, would be a powerful reason for moving from conventional programming to more automated forms of application creation. There is, however, another reason which is often more powerful: in many situations the conventional development process *does not work*.

Time and time again one finds stories of a system being cut over after years of development effort and the end users saying it is not what they want, or trying it for a while and then giving up. Frequently, after using a system, laboriously created, for a few weeks the users say they want something different.

A common reaction to this unfortunate situation is to say that the requirements were not specified sufficiently thoroughly. So more elaborate procedures have been devised for requirements specification, sometimes resulting in voluminous documentation. But still the system has been unsatisfactory.

The fact is that many of the most important potential users of DP do not know what they want until they *experience* using the system. When they first experience it, many changes are needed to make them comfortable with it and to meet their *basic* requirements. Once comfortable with it, their imaginations go to work and they think of all manner of different functions and variations on the theme that would be useful to them. And they want these changes *immediately*.

MORE RIGOROUS   Many DP organizations have realized that their
SPECIFICATIONS   application creation process is not working to the
satisfaction of the users, and have taken steps to correct this. Unfortunately, the steps they take often make the situation worse.

Steps are often taken to enforce more formal procedures. Application creation, it is said, must be converted from a sloppy *ad hoc* operation to one that follows rules like an engineering discipline.

The U.S. Department of Defense recognized that it had software problems and *mandated* certain actions in response to them, in DoD Directive 5000.29. A major concern in creating this directive was that the programs created did not meet the users' requirements. The directive specified more formal requirements documentation prior to the design, coding, and testing. A Computer Resource Life Cycle Management Plan was specified, as shown in Fig. 4.1, and depicted certain milestones that are to be attained and documented. The milestones are to be used to "ensure the proper sequence of analysis, design, implementation, integration, test, deployment and maintenance" [1].

This approach formalizes the conventional wisdom of programming development and can work well *if and only if* the end users' requirements can be specified in fine detail before design and coding begins. With some systems they can, and with others they cannot. The requirements for missile control can be specified completely beforehand. The requirements for management information systems cannot be specified beforehand and almost every attempt to do so has failed. The requirements change as soon as an executive starts to use his terminal.

The point that this book makes is *not* that conventional application development with a life cycle like Fig. 4.1 should be abandoned, but rather that *it only works for certain types of systems.*

The types of systems for which it does not work are becoming more common and more important in running corporations and other complex organizations. For these, a new type of development cycle is needed, often linking into formal data administration, as discussed later in this book.

FAILURES

In one large insurance company a system was developed for claim processing which would put terminals in all the branch offices. It took about three years to develop at a cost of about $4 million. To ensure that the end users were well understood, an end-user manager was moved into a high position in the development process. When the first terminals were cut over, to everybody's horror the users gave up using them after a short period. They perceived the system as unsatisfactory compared with their previous method. The system was eventually abandoned.

A Department of Defense study was conducted of 10 major automated systems. It concluded that all ten had *unstable and changing* requirements, indicating the need for techniques that could adapt quickly to changing requirements.

IBM designed a system to automate two Japanese newspapers—Asaki and Nikei. What do editors of newspapers really want at their terminals?

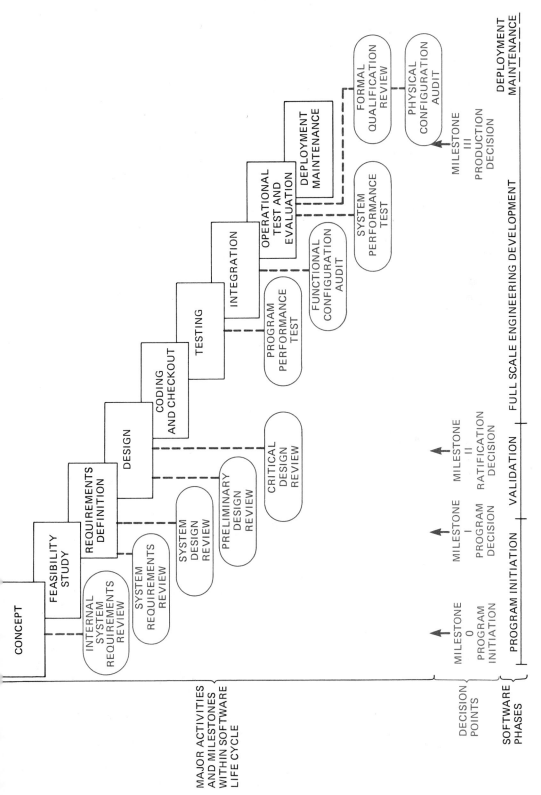

Figure 4.1 A traditional system development life cycle. The reviews and milestones shown here are those required in the U.S. Department of Defense. (Redrawn from [1].)

They did not know. When the system was first installed it was not useful to the editors and IBM lost about $2 million on the software development effort [2]. Undaunted, newspaper automation continued. Years later, after a great effort, a requirements document of *2400 pages* was produced. It was created to automate several U.S. newspapers. It was so thorough that management thought *nothing* could go wrong. But unfortunately, when the document was used to settle questions, the developers and their customers interpreted it differently! Both worked in good faith, but the difficulty of specifying the requirement so that both parties understood the subtleties (needed for programming) was too great [2].

The difficulty of writing adequate requirements specifications has resulted in some spectacular court cases. In the early 1970s two major airlines sued their computer suppliers who were to provide the application programs, after $40 million had been spent, because the application programs were not about to work. At the time of writing a European bank is in court for a $70 million claim over application software. The U.S. Air Force spent more than $300 million in a futile attempt to automate an Advanced Logistics System (ALS) [2].

For every big failure that hits the headlines there are a thousand small ones where ordinary end users abandon their terminal or complain that it does not do what they want. There should be nothing surprising in this by now. It is a solvable problem on the majority of ordinary systems. The best solutions involve the software in Fig. 2.1, the use of prototyping, a change in the role of the systems analyst, an appropriate methodology of data-base design, and a new approach to creating what end users need.

Although these methods work well for most ordinary data processing, they are not appropriate for highly complex, technical systems such as those for refinery operation, satellite image processing, air traffic control, or moon launches. With these, a formal requirements specification, a development life cycle like Fig. 4.1, and tight controls are needed.

It is, then, necessary to distinguish between systems that need dynamic user-driven modification of requirements after the system is initially implemented and systems that need complete, formal, requirements analysis and specification before implementation. Much commercial and administrative data processing and systems oriented to human needs fall into the former category.

USER-DRIVEN VERSUS PRESPECIFIED COMPUTING

We will use the terms *user-driven computing* and *prespecified computing*. Box. 4.1 shows characteristics of these two types of computing.

Note that *user-driven* computing does not imply that users themselves create their applications. Sometimes they do this, but usually the applications are created by an analyst working hand in hand with the users and employing application

BOX 4.1   The distinction between prespecified computing and user-driven computing. Much of what has been *prespecified* ought to be *user-driven* with today's software.

PRESPECIFIED COMPUTING

- Formal requirements specifications are created.
- A development cycle such as that in Fig. 4.1 is employed.
- Programs are formally documented.
- The application development time is many months or years.
- Maintenance is formal, slow, and expensive.

Examples: Compiler writing, airline reservations, air traffic control, missile guidance, software development.

USER-DRIVEN COMPUTING

- Users do not know in detail what they want until they use a version of it, and then they modify it quickly and often frequently. Consequently, formal requirement specification linked to slow application programming is doomed to failure.

- Users may create their own applications, but more often with an analyst who does this in cooperation with them. A separate programming department is not used.

- Applications are created with a generator or other software in Fig. 2.1, more quickly than the time to write specifications.

- The application development time is days or at most weeks.

- Maintenance is continuous. Incremental changes are made constantly to the applications by the users or the analyst who assists them.

- The system is self-documenting, or interactive documentation is created when the application is created.

- A centrally administered data-base facility is often employed. Data administration is generally needed to prevent chaos of incompatible data spreading.

Examples: Administrative procedures, shop floor control, information systems, decision support, paperwork avoidance.

generators so that he can quickly create and modify terminal dialogues or reports.

Most computing that ought to be *user-driven* is being developed as *prespecified* computing today. A drastic change in the management of application development is needed, as discussed later, together with the introduction of the new software and techniques. It is not clear how much computing ought to be user-driven rather than prespecified. When the power and efficiency of application generators increases substantially, it is likely that most commercial data processing *ought* to be created by user-driven methods rather than with the long development cycle of traditional DP. To do so will require firmly managed corporate data administration. There is scope for much argument about what ought to be prespecified.

It is not *only* user-driven computing that should employ the new software. The productivity of developing *prespecified* computing of certain types is greatly improved by the use of application generators such as IBM's DMS or ADF, or the use of higher-level languages such as APL and its diversity of incremental facilities (Chapter 13).

Prespecified computing needs the methods discussed in this book, wherever possible, because the old methods are too slow and expensive in personpower. *User-driven computing* needs the new methods because the old methods *do not work.*

MANAGEMENT INFORMATION   Perhaps the most notorious class of systems that do not work is management information systems. In spite of repeated failures, these remain one of the most important classes of data processing.

Using the traditional development approach, the MIS designer would go to managers and ask them what information they would like to have. It took long and painful experience to discover that most managers do not really know. To know what information he needs, an executive must be aware of each type of decision he will (or should) make, and how he will make it. Some executives play it safe and ask for everything. Some designers have tried to provide everything on bulky reports that tend to hide rather than reveal the few pieces of information that are pertinent.

In some cases an executive with a strong personality makes firm statements about the information he or his department wants. A systems analyst at last sees a clear directive and an unambiguous statement of requirements is created. The project life cycle then rolls on, but by the time the programming and testing are finally done, the executive in question has moved on. His replacement does not like the system. Systems that are highly personalized almost never survive the departure of the user they were created for.

STRUCTURED ANALYSIS   The system development cycle is represented somewhat differently from Fig. 4.1 by the advocates of structured analysis. Figure 4.2 shows de Marco's

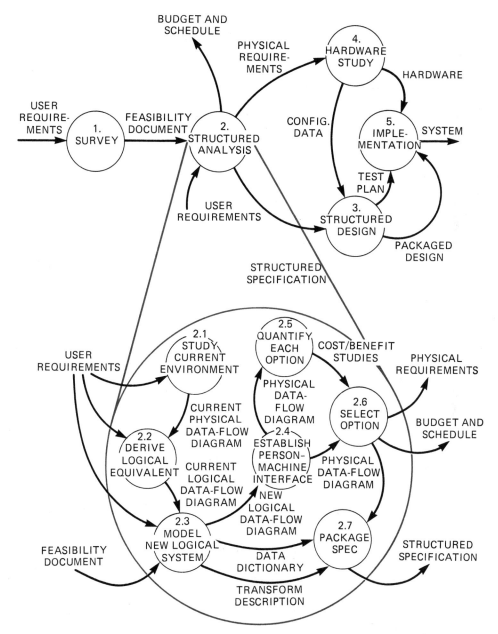

Figure 4.2 The structured analysis version of the DP development cycle. (From [3].)

representation of the process [3]. Structured analysis replaces the Victorian-novel form of system specifications with a more formalized set of charts and representations. It uses data-flow diagrams (Fig. 4.2 is itself a data-flow diagram) to show how data move from one process to another. The circles in figures like Fig. 4.2 are processes. The arrows are data flows. The analysis uses top-down design, in which a circle like process 2 can be expanded as shown.

With this methodology the requirements analysis phase takes *longer* and needs *more personpower* than with conventional analysis. The payoff is that the coding, testing, and documentation in a language like COBOL is generally faster. More thorough and more structured analysis lessens the number of fundamental programming errors that are made.

Other forms of structured analysis exist, some of which appear to give better results than that in Fig. 4.2. They are undoubtedly an improvement on the Victorian-novel type of system specification. However, they do not solve the fundamental problem that many systems, especially interactive ones, need to be tried out by the users before the users can be really sure what they can use, or what will work as computerized procedures.

To solve this problem, prototyping is needed, as we will discuss later. But prototyping in conjunction with the software of Fig. 2.1 changes the entire systems development process.

The procedures for factory control or office paperwork flow should be entirely different with interactive data-transmission data-base systems from those that existed before. Most structured analysts document what existed before.

USER CHOICE

It is useful to distinguish between these systems where the user has a choice as to whether he employs the system and those with no choice. When payroll is automated, there is no choice. The system is switched on and everyone is paid via the system whether they like it or not. With an airline reservation system the user has no real choice about whether or not he uses the system. However, with management information systems, decision support systems, shop floor control, planning and budgeting, information retrieval, and so on, managers will decide whether they employ the terminals. Often, they must be wooed to use them because they are familiar with a different way of working.

Some such systems only have their big payoff when *most* users are using them because much information should pass *among* users via the system. Electronic mail is not useful if only one person has a set; the same is true with some types of information systems because it is the interchange that is valuable. A user takes items from his work queue and moves items to work queues of other users.

Many of the potentially most valuable information systems live or die depending on whether the end users fully adopt them. Their designer cannot afford to misunderstand the users' requirements, but again, *the requirements usually change fast once the terminals are in use.* The traditional development life-cycle of defining requirements in great detail before coding is not likely to work with such systems. Instead, the users should be involved in developing and modifying their own system, working with systems analysts who now assume much of the role of a consultant or interactive application creator.

Great successes can be observed with this new form of system development. In some cases analysts working with the users create and adjust their applications. In some cases the users do it themselves with languages such as Univac's MAPPER. An organizational culture grows up around this form of system creation. The users learn that they *can* obtain applications quickly and *can* make changes to them. It saves them much paperwork and frees much of their time for more important activities. In GTE Automatic Electric the users created a monthly newsletter about the new applications they themselves were creating with MAPPER, showing how it was being used to solve corporate problems and give better customer service. Users of many types joined the club of persons who created and modified their own applications, or at least used applications which their associates had created.

PROBLEMS WITH THE SPECIFICATION PROCESS

When the traditional systems analyst and a potential end-user community first come face to face, they come from widely different cultures. It is rather like a Victorian missionary first entering an African village. Unlike the missionary, they have to produce a very precise document—the specification of requirements.

The missionary is steeped in computer terminology and analysis methods. The villagers' culture is accounting, plans and budgets, or production control—cultures with a complex folklore. They use different languages. Somehow they are supposed to communicate with no ambiguities or misunderstandings. If the missionary is skillful at communicating and can offer the villagers a promise of better things, they can begin to learn each other's conceptual framework. However, there is no way that either can understand the nuances and subtleties of the other's way of thinking.

In an attempt to clarify and formalize the process, specifications are written for the applications which must be programmed. This can take person-years to complete, and results in a set of documents that are inches or even feet thick. For his own protection, the missionary needs the villagers to sign this document.

THE SPECIFICATION DOCUMENT

The specification document is extremely important in the traditional DP life cycle. It guides the programmers and is supposed to answer the numerous questions that will arise about the system. In practice we ask too much of it. There is really little hope that it can provide perfect communication between the programmers and the end users.

The specification document usually has the following unfortunate characteristics. It is so long that key managers do not read it all. They read the summary. It is incredibly boring and this causes it to be skip-read by many people who should read it fully. It contains technical terms, systems analysis charts, and various forms of professional shorthand, all of which the end users do not fully understand. It contains words which have very precise meanings in the user areas but which programmers do not understand, and often most systems analysts do not appreciate their nuances.

The end users fail to comprehend things that are *obvious* to the computer staff, and vice versa. A user may have signed off on a data field in *month–day–year* format and cannot be expected to realize that records cannot be sorted into time sequence with this field. A programmer cannot be expected to know that *benefit-effective-date* is different from *benefit-posted-date,* although that is obvious to the end user. A DP professional may not realize that an oil well has many different definitions or that the oil it accesses spreads underground to areas with different ownership. A user may have signed off on a document referring to *rating basis* without understanding that the systems analyst meant something entirely different by that. The DP professional might read phrases like the following over and over again without knowing what they mean: "indicates the date on which a given qualification was verified in the context of the structure within which it existed." (A real example! Its meaning is obvious to the end users in question.) There are endless such examples.

Much of the vital specification document is misinterpreted on both sides. Often, its readers *think* they understand it but in fact do not.

Sometimes much trivia or motherhood is added to the document. Both sides understand this. It increases the comfort level but has zero value.

Specification documents are bad enough with batch processing; with interactive systems they tend to be worse because they cannot capture the dynamic quality of the user interaction. How many users will know what to do when confronted with a new screen? What happens when the user keys in something stupid? What is the effect of response time? Will the user prompting be effective? Is the dialogue too long-winded? Most users cannot obtain a feeling for what using a dialogue will be like in use when they read its specification.

USER SIGN-OFF   The users are coerced to sign-off on the specification document. They know that until they do that the detailed design and programming will not begin.

DP hopes that the need to sign off will encourage the users to check the document very carefully and find any errors before programming starts.

SPECIFICATION FREEZE

It is important in the traditional development cycle to *freeze* the specifications when programming begins. Usually, the sign-off represents this freeze. The sign-off is invariably a moment of apprehension on both sides. The users are not sure whether it is really what they want. They often feel that their views on the system are changing as they learn and think more about it. Half way up a learning curve the specifications are *frozen*.

DP is apprehensive because they are not sure that they understand all the users' needs. They are about to put much effort into the implementation and any imperfections in the specifications will prove expensive.

BUGS

Not surprisingly, the specification document contains errors.

In most installations there are more bugs in specifications than in program coding. In one typical case a large corporation found that 64% of its bugs were in requirements analysis and design—in spite of a formal sign-off by the user departments.

Even worse, *45% of these bugs were discovered after the acceptance tests for the finished applications were completed.*

This corporation had a formal development life cycle not unlike Fig. 4.1, and was following its installation standards meticulously. It was using a formal method of structured analysis in creating the specifications.

If there is not a formal structured method of system specification, the situation is usually worse. Figure 4.3 shows the distribution of bugs in a large bank before it moved to structured analysis: 56% were in the requirements document; 27% were in design and most of these were related to misinterpretation of the requirements document.

The bugs in the requirements specification are much more time consuming and expensive to correct than are those in coding. Figure 4.3 illustrates this. Ninety-five percent of the cost of correcting bugs in this bank was for the bugs in requirements and design. The ratios in Figure 4.3 are typical of many installations.

THE UNCERTAINTY PRINCIPLE

The uncertainty principle in physics says that the act of observing subatomic events *changes* those events. There is an uncertainty principle with data processing. The act of providing what an end user says he needs *changes* his perception of those needs.

The mere act of implementing a user-driven system changes the requirements for that system. The solution to a problem changes the problem.

As the system comes live, it will affect the rest of the department in a variety of unforeseen ways. It suddenly becomes possible to move work

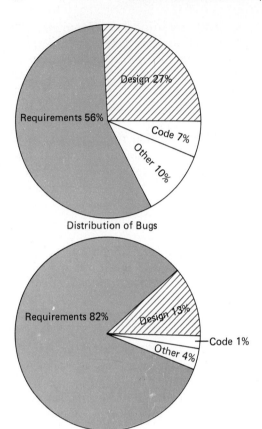

Distribution of Bugs

Distribution of Effort to Fix Bugs

Figure 4.3 In a typical installation with a traditional development methodology, more bugs occur in requirements specification and design than in coding. The bugs in requirements specification are much the most expensive ones to correct. (From [3].)

from one person's screen to another. Salespeople can suddenly provide a service that was previously so difficult that they ignored it, and demands for that service boom. A manager suddenly sees information that was previously hidden from him, so he makes changes in the department. Some users do not like the system and insist on using their previous methods. Others want new types of reports or want the computer to do calculations not in the system requirements.

The system has many unforeseen psychological effects. It may make some employees feel unwanted and resentful. Some become prima donnas with the new terminals. It changes the organizational interaction and power patterns.

END-USER LEARNING CURVE   End users have a long learning curve to climb in assessing how they should use today's data processing. They cannot climb far on this curve as long as it remains at the talking stage. It is only when they have a terminal and use it on their own work that they begin to understand the reality of the computer's challenge and limitations. Their imagination slowly begins to realize what they *could* do with that screen. After implementation the users have a common basis for discussion of the system. They argue at lunch about what it does well and badly, what it ought to do better, and how it could benefit them in different ways from what it is doing now. They would like to modify its behavior *quickly*.

In many cases the functions of a user-driven system when first installed are less than one-tenth of those they feel they need a few months after installation. These new functions are more valuable because they are based on experience. But the rigid development cycle prevents them from making the changes they want.

The system makes it possible to have more finely structured inventory reorder points. The reordering rules can now be changed easily to better adapt to seasonal peaks. It becomes possible to deal with problems on the shop floor that were quietly ignored before, but to do so needs additions to the data base, or different patterns of data entry.

It is often the case that the end user does not know what he wants until he gets it. When he gets it he wants something different.

A NEW TYPE OF DP IMPLEMENTATION

What is needed to deal with these problems can now be seen in operation in a small fraction of installations. It represents a new type of DP implementation. At its best it is very impressive compared with the traditional DP development cycle.

Its characteristics are as follows:

- It uses the types of software in Fig. 2.1.

- Application creation is *fast*.

- Applications can be modified *quickly*.

- Where possible, users create their own applications. Often, a systems analyst creates the application working at a terminal with the end user much of the time.

- Where possible, users modify their own applications; again a systems analyst working with the end user may do this.

- Where conventional programs are written, this is not done without prototyping. Prototypes largely replace the use of lengthy written requirements documents. Where possible the prototype is converted into the application directly.

- The process is incremental and interactive as opposed to the single great leap forward associated with requirements documentation and a specification freeze.

- The process usually uses data-base facilities and needs tight data administration controls with computerized tools.

PROTOTYPING   The concept of prototyping is particularly important.

With most complex engineering a prototype is created before the final product is built. This is done to test the principles, ensure that the system works, and obtain design feedback which enables the design to be adjusted before the big money is spent. A chemical plant is built in a pilot form before the plant is finally designed. The hull shape of a boat is tested. A new airplane is simulated in a variety of ways before it is built.

Complex data processing systems need prototyping more than most engineering systems because there is much to learn from a pilot operation and many changes are likely to be made. Prototypes would help to solve the problems we have discussed of systems not working in the way the end users really need.

The reason why DP prototypes were not generally used until the 1980s was that the cost of programming a prototype was about as high as the cost of programming the live working system. The software in Fig. 2.1 now enables prototypes to be created relatively cheaply.

A system analyst working with an end user can create and demonstrate dialogues for data-base queries, report generation, and manipulation of screen information. The analyst discusses an end user's needs with him and then creates a specimen dialogue on a terminal. This might take him an hour or a week, depending on the complexity and the language that is being used. Initially, he ignores questions of transaction volumes and machine performance.

The end user is shown the dialogue and quickly trained to use it. Usually, he has some suggestions for changes he would like and the analyst makes these. The user may add subtotals or extra columns. He may want to perform certain calculations. The analyst may show him the different types of charts that could be created: scatter plots, bar charts, charts with regression lines, linear versus log scales, and so on. The user remembers a different type of customer or some union rule that was forgotten.

As the analyst and user continue their discussion of what is needed, the running prototype is now a focus of the debate which helps to ensure that they are both talking about the same thing. The screens are printed and the end user takes them home to think about them. The analyst works further, improving the screen interaction, adding new features, and improving the displays.

Finally, the user is satisfied, excited, and says: "When can I get it?"

In some cases he can have it very quickly. The data base exists and the prototype can become the final application. In other cases he cannot have it yet because design work is needed to achieve machine efficiency, security, auditability, telecommunications networking, or to create the data base.

In the latter case the prototype becomes, in effect, the requirements document for application programming.

In a sense the system created by the life cycle of Fig. 4.1 is a prototype. It is not *meant* to be a prototype and is not regarded as such, but it has all the imperfections of a prototype. These imperfections are expensive to correct and so often remain in the system.

THREE TYPES OF APPLICATION DEVELOPMENT

We thus have three types of application development:

1. Traditional development with a life cycle like that in Fig. 4.1. This has the problems which this chapter has discussed.

2. Use of an application generator as a prototyping tool. The end user interacts with the prototype and the systems analyst modifies it until it is a suitable model for application programming. The prototyping tool alleviates as much of the need for separate requirements documentation as possible. Modules of code may be created by the prototyping tool to alleviate the need for programming *all* of the application.

3. Use of an application generator (or other software in Fig. 2.1) to develop the entire application. The prototype becomes the application. No separate use is made of professional programmers.

The third of these development approaches can be used for much but not all commercial data processing. For many data processing applications there need be little concern with machine efficiency because they do not run frequently. Only a small proportion are high-volume applications.

In a typical installation 50% of the applications consume 2% of the machine time. Only 2% of the applications consume 50% of the machine time [4]. The latter 2% might be coded with high machine efficiency.

Again, typically, 90% of the applications cost more to develop and compile with conventional programs than to run for their entire lifetime [4]. Money saving for these programs requires concentration on the development cost rather than on the running cost.

For the heavy-duty applications, high machine efficiency is needed. This can be achieved in one of three ways:

1. First, some of the languages in Fig. 2.1 can achieve high machine efficiency. As we stressed in Chapter 2, in some cases the code generated is better than that generated with COBOL or PL/1, because the generator uses blocks of code that have been tightly optimized with assembler language.

   A specialist who knows all the tricks with an application generator can sometimes achieve much more efficient results than the average analyst. The analyst may create a heavy-duty application in DMS or ADF and then hand it over to a DMS or ADF "acrobat" for optimization.

2. There may be certain routines which are time-eaters. These can be isolated and programmed in a more efficient language if the generator has suitable EXITS.

BOX 4.2 Three types of application development

	Conventional Application Development (Like Fig. 4.1)	Application Generator Used as a Prototyping Aid Followed by Programming	Application Development Without Professional Programmers
Requirements Analysis	A time-consuming, formal operation, often delayed by long application backlog.	The user's imagination is stimulated. He may work at a screen with an analyst to develop requirements.	The user's imagination is stimulated. He may develop his own requirements, or work with an analyst.
System Specification Document	Lengthy document. Boring. Often inadequate.	Produced by prototyping aid. Precise and tested.	Disappears.

User sign-off	User is often not sure what he is signing off on. He cannot perceive all subtleties.	User sees the results and may modify them many times before signing off.	No formal sign-off. Adjustment and modification is an ongoing process.
Coding and Testing	Slow. Expensive. Often delayed because of backlog.	The prototype is converted to more efficient code. Relatively quick and error-free.	Quick. Inexpensive. Disappears to a large extent.
Documentation	Tedious. Time consuming.	May be partly automated. Interactive training and HELP response may be created on-line.	Largely automatic. Interactive training and HELP responses are created on-line.
Maintenance	Slow. Expensive. Often late.	Often slow. Often expensive. Often late.	A continuing process with user and analyst making adjustments. Most of these adjustments can be made very quickly— in hours rather than months.

3. The entire application may be reprogrammed for efficiency. The generator version is used to guide the programming team instead of written requirements documentation. Sometimes the generator creates only part of what is needed, so a hybrid of generator input/output and written specifications is needed.

Box 4.2 lists typical characteristics of these three approaches to application development. In many large corporations all three types of development are likely to coexist. A good DP executive will organize his operation so that they can coexist. In some corporations the DP department uses only the traditional development life cycle, and the end users have bypassed the DP department using the tools of Fig. 2.1 to create their own applications more quickly and satisfactorily.

The mature DP executive should *welcome* end users creating their own applications and not fight it. He should regard it as his job to provide them with the software tools, data bases, networks, and consultant systems analysts that they need.

REFERENCES

1. U.S. Department of Defense, "Management of Computer Resources in Major Defense Systems," Directive 5000.29.

2. Joe Fox, *Managing Software,* Prentice-Hall, Inc., Englewood Cliffs, NJ, 1981.

3. Tom de Marco, *Structured Analysis and System Specification.* (New York: Yourdon Press, 1979), p. 26. Copyright © 1978, 1979 by Yourdon inc. Reprinted by permission.

4. F.A. Comper, "Project Management for System Quality and Development Productivity," Guide and Share Application Development Symposium, *Proceedings,* Share, New York, 1979.

5. W.R. Bradshaw, "Application Development Productivity within IBM Information Systems," Guide and Share Application Development Symposium, *Proceedings,* Share, New York, 1979.

5 CASE STUDY OF A MEDIUM-SIZED INSTALLATION

INTRODUCTION Figure 4.1 shows the development life cycle in large installations where much thought has been given to managing the traditional DP environment. Many DP installations are less formally managed and do not yet have such detailed standards, reviews, and milestones. This chapter is a case study of a less formally managed installation which is typical of thousands of today's medium-sized DP operations.

A much better form of DP development is now available, but it would require a painful wrench away from both the methods and management of today's data processing organization.

The study is of a medium-sized bank whose business expanded at a high rate during the 1970s. It has assets of over $1 billion. It has more international business than most banks of its size and this is a major revenue earner.

The top executive officers have been with the bank for many years and are cautious and conservative in their decision making. They have little direct contact with the computer department and prefer to leave the DP policy to younger middle management, except when required to take major decisions regarding hardware to the Board of Directors. The bank, however, does rely heavily on its computer.

HISTORY A computer was first installed in the 1960s and a major development plan was implemented at that time to produce such systems as current accounts, savings, loans, and trust. On-line inquiry systems were implemented in the mid-1970s and at that time a commitment was made to move to data-base operations. A customer data base was developed and worked moderately well. This initial success was followed by great confusion and argument about how to proceed further with data base. For five years the subject was studied, but the only development was of conventional files. There were constant changes to the structure and content of the data base and the promise of data base was not fulfilled. Nobody understood the principles of stable logical data-base design. There was no data dictionary, no data modeling tool, and in fact no data-base administrator.

COBOL was used for all application development with the exception of a few programs written in assembler language. We could find no good reason for the use of assembler language for applications, although it was needed for the creation of a teleprocessing monitor (because of dissatisfaction with the manufacturer's teleprocessing software).

A massive backlog of application development built up. Requests for new or modified applications grew faster than the fastest rate of application development. The backlog is quoted as being 3 years, but some important application areas such as trust accounting have been waiting 6 or 7 years. The end users are becoming increasingly annoyed and dissatisfied with the slow development of systems and DP's refusal to listen to further user requests. This problem is being tackled by increasing the number of COBOL programmers and conventional systems analysts working with files.

Structured programming was introduced sporadically. There was no means of measuring productivity improvement and there were doubts as to whether any had in fact occurred. Some programmers, especially new ones, did not use the structured techniques, and this caused confusion when they were called upon to maintain programs. Even the programmers who did use structured programming differed greatly on how they thought it should be done.

To make matters worse, a new computer was introduced in the late 1970s and the DP department was faced with transferring all existing systems to the new machine. No new applications were developed during this conversion period which lasted 9 months.

The new machine permitted on-line application development. This improved the rate of coding and debugging by about 5 to 10%. It did not speed up the documentation, maintenance, or systems analysis.

Maintenance consumed a substantial proportion of the programming effort but nobody knew exactly how much. A third of the programmers were employed full time on maintenance in a separate maintenance section and others sporadically maintained programs in their area.

Staff shortages and rapid turnover made the problems worse. In one year the attrition rate was 40% of the total DP department. Attrition has grown steadily throughout the last 10 years. The cost of training a new programmer and bringing him up to acceptable level of productivity was very high. It was worse with the systems analysts.

The staff turnover worsened the problems that resulted from the absence of a data dictionary, data-base administration function, or top-down data resource planning.

END USERS To the end users DP was a major mystery. They were given no DP familiarization course. Nobody explained to them how they could help in the DP development process. They were often hostile to DP. With the exception of two key individuals, they rarely took the initiative and rarely became involved in helping the systems analysts. This hindered the systems staff and made their jobs more difficult. The systems staff usually took the initiative and designed what they *thought* the required system was. This was handed to programmers and much effort was spent before mismatches were detected.

Because of the high rate of new business generation, senior management, and usually lower management, had little or no time to think about effective computer systems. They took no interest in DP, and assumed that it was someone else's job.

Senior management did not understand the potential of data-base operation or the concept of managing information as a resource.

When complaints from end users reached their ears because of the extreme slowness of application development, and the mismatch in systems developed, senior management were quick to criticize DP.

The president of the bank emphasized that the bank's predominant problem in DP was shortage of staff.

HOW *COULD* THESE APPLICATIONS BE CREATED? This story is sadly typical. This type of development process will come under more pressure and be more harmful as computing hardware continues to plunge in cost.

Let us now ask the question: To what extent *could* the banks applications be created without programming?

Figure 5.1 lists today's applications together with their numbers of programs and approximate transaction volumes.

Some of these applications could be stand-alone systems, running on a minicomputer. They have low transaction volumes. Others need a large mainframe and would benefit from data-base techniques.

Figure 5.2 was created by a leading systems analyst who left the bank and is now familiar with high-level application development facilities. The applications are divided into two groups. The first uses a data-base management system chosen because it has powerful application development languages and uses an IBM mainframe. The other used a minicomputer also chosen so that applications can be created quickly. A variety of other application development software could have been chosen instead.

A general-purpose information retrieval system is indicated in Figure 5.2 to give customer and general on-line information. The use of this could be expanded into all types of information which the bankers use. Logical files from the data base would be restructured for access via the information retrieval system. This has been done extensively in the Continental Bank in Chicago.

Application System	Approximate Number of COBOL Programs	Level of Maintenance	Average Transactions Per Day
Current account checking system	40	High	10,000
Domestic savings account system	30	Medium	1,000
Trust accounting system	100	High	2,000
Payroll system	20	Medium	100
Time deposit system	30	High	2,000
Customer information system	60	High	2,000
Domestic loans system	20	Low	100
Auditing support system	16	Medium	10
Mutual funds system	20	High	200
On line information retrieval system	20	Medium	2,000
Domestic mortgage system	30	Low	100
General ledger system	16	Medium	1,000
Credit and collection system	10	Low	100
Safe deposits registration system	16	Low	5
Stationery and supplies control system	8	Low	20
Cable and mail control system	16	Low	200
TOTAL:	452		

Figure 5.1 The application systems of the bank at the time of study.

Some conventional (e.g., COBOL) application programs would still be needed, but not many. Figure 5.2 indicates 25 COBOL programs instead of the 452 programs in use today.

The applications that still need COBOL tend to be those with complex updating needs. The trust accounting system, for example, requires four input files. The updating of the daily trades of stock, bonds, and securities is a fairly complex task which requires these to be matched against customer accounts. As the software for application development improves, complex updates will presumably be handled by the new facilities and the small residual need for conventional programming will diminish further.

Most of the applications in the bank could today be developed completely without COBOL, in a matter of days rather than months or years. More than one language would be necessary. Various application packages would be used. Good data-base development would be needed. Some of the reports in the bank, which a person skilled with an interactive report generator for a data base could create in an hour or so, in fact took 5 months of systems analysis, application programming, debugging, and documentation.

Although most applications *could* be developed without COBOL, this does not always mean that they *should* be. A planned evolution to the new methods is necessary. Sometimes use of the new tools needs to be preceded by data-base design and planning.

The bank has a list of about 20 more application systems which need developing. These are also amenable to development without conventional programming, with a few exceptions, as in Fig. 5.2.

Application System	Example of Application Development Language*	Approximate Number of COBOL Programs
Data Base		
Current account checking system	ADF/DMS + COBOL	2
Domestic savings account system	ADF/DMS + COBOL	2
Trust accounting system	ADF/DMS + COBOL + RG	15
Time deposit system	ADF/DMS + COBOL + RG	2
Customer information system	DB QUERY/STAIRS	0
Domestic loans system	ADF/DMS + RG	0
Auditing support system	ADF/DMS + Package	0
Mutual funds system	ADF/DMS + COBOL + RG	2
On-line information retrieval system	DB QUERY/RG/STAIRS	0
Domestic mortgage system	ADF/DMS + RG	0
General ledger system	ADF/DMS + Package	0
Minicomputer		
Payroll system	PACKAGE	0
Credit and collection system	DFU/SDA + RPG	0
Safe deposits registration system	DFU/SDA	0
Stationery and supplies control system	DFU/SDA	0
Cable and mail control system	DFU/SDA + COBOL	2
	TOTAL:	25

*ADF, IBM's Application Development Facility; DMS, IBM's Development Management System; RG, Any good report generator; STAIRS, IBM's information retrieval system; DB QUERY, Any good data-base query language; DFU, IBM's System 34 Data File Utility; SDA, IBM's System 34 Screen Design Aid.

Figure 5.2 Application development aids that could today be used for the applications in Fig. 5.1.

HOW SHOULD THE DP OPERATION BE MANAGED?

It is clear that fundamental changes are needed in both the methods and the management of the bank's data processing. Some of the changes would be painful, however, and there is every indication that the current DP regime would resist them furiously. The necessary changes are unlikely to happen unless top management takes a strong hand to the tiller. Unfortunately, the managers do not understand this, and are avoiding any involvement with their own DP organization. They are too busy doing an excellent job of developing the bank's business and are proud of the growth rate they are achieving—a growth that puts DP into steadily deeper water.

To change the development process, the following actions are needed. Several of them should proceed simultaneously:

1. Obtain top management's support for a thorough overhaul of the DP organization. Make top management understand that their help will be needed at certain points.

2. Appoint a person to investigate thoroughly the tools that are available for application development without conventional programming (Box 2.1).

3. Appoint a data administrator, and ensure that he is appropriately trained.

4. Select a data-base management system that has a good query language, report generator, and a powerful application generator such as IBM's ADF or DMS, or Cullinane's ADS. (The bank's existing DBMS is not adequate in this regard.)

5. Select a data-base modeling tool such as DDI's DATA DESIGNER and train two or three people in its use.

6. Initiate a first data-base project, for example, redesign of the customer data base, this time doing a thorough job of logical design with the data-base modeling tool. Employ a data dictionary.

7. Conduct a top-down design of the data resources needed in the organization (as described in the author's *Strategic Data Planning Methodologies* [1]. The planning must involve top management. *User* analysts should be trained and should participate in it.

8. Possibly select a minicomputer with powerful application creation aids and report generators for low-volume applications of importance to the end users. Proceed with its implementation and the creation of selected applications.

9. Plan and model the main data bases that the organization needs (following the guidelines of the top-down data planning). Involve the end users thoroughly in this design (as described in the author's *Managing the Data Base Environment* [2].

10. Select applications with high maintenance activity and convert them to data-base operation using the new development facilities.

11. Plan and prioritize new application development, following the guidelines of the top-down planning.

12. Establish an information center mode of development, as described in Chapter 6.

13. Establish an end-user training course to train the users in DP concepts.

14. Select *early adaptors* to the new methods wherever they exist among end users. Train them to generate their own information from the systems, where useful, by means of data-base query languages, report generators, and in a few cases by means of user programming. As the early adaptors accept this means of operating, spread the techniques among other users.

15. Train the systems analysts in the use of the application generation facilities. Train them in the different type of analysis that is necessary for efficient development of applications in a data-base environment. Make them understand that it is now their job to generate the applications, reports, terminal screens, and dialogues, wherever possible without involving programmers.

16. Train the analysts to act as consultants to the end users, aiding them in using the new facilities and working with them to improve their screens, dialogues, and reports.

17. Upgrade programmers where possible to analysts who create applications.

18. Implement a generalized information retrieval system and train user management to employ it wherever possible. Build up the types of information that are available by this means.

19. Survey the banking application packages which are available, including packages for support of management decisions, for example, trust or customer portfolio management.

20. Have top management direct user management to participate fully in the new application development process.

REFERENCES

1. James Martin, *Strategic Data Planning Methodologies,* Prentice-Hall, Inc., Englewood Cliffs, NJ, 1982.

2. James Martin, *Managing the Data Base Environment,* Prentice-Hall, Inc., Englewood Cliffs, NJ, 1982.

6 THE CHANGE NEEDED IN DP MANAGEMENT

INTRODUCTION   The change in methodologies that this book describes encounters great emotional resistance in many installations. There are several reasons for this. First, to many DP people the whole idea of application creation without programmers still seems strange and alien to the God-given order. Second, programmers, not surprisingly, resist the idea and concoct scornful arguments against it. Higher DP executives can be alarmed by it also and sometimes envision their empires dwindling if end-user departments learn to create their own applications.

DP professionals who have done so much to automate other people's jobs are remarkably reluctant to have their own job automated. A major reason for resistance is that DP organizations have struggled to achieve discipline in the DP development process. This process used to be an unruly free-for-all until standards and guidelines were established relatively recently. The standards and methods have assumed the force of law, have been taught to all DP staff in an organization, and are regarded as a vital necessity in the crusade against unstructured methods, unmaintainable codes, nonportable programs, and lack of scientific discipline. The installation standards, religiously adhered to, have frozen the methodologies of large installations at a time when the technology is plunging into new forms.

One typical corporation with many computer installations in many countries spent much effort in the 1970s perfecting a project management system. This incorporates installation standards, guidelines, and some software for project control. It is referred to as the installation "Bible." No DP manager will admit that he does not use it; to do so would be detrimental to his career.

If the Bible is followed literally it prevents DP managers and analysts from using most of the methods we advocate in this book. It insists on having elaborate formal specifications for all applications. These are typically 1 inch thick or more. It is not possible to do prototyping and remain within the project management system. The interactive use of report generators and application generators results in applications being created and adjusted to fit the users' needs much better than what is usually specified in the formal specifications. Again, when detailed specifications are created it is rarely possible to purchase a preprogrammed application package which fits them. Furthermore, the Bible would prevent end users from creating their own applications.

Some organizations have standards specifying that only certain languages may be used. They exclude all the languages in Box 2.1. The U.S. Department of Defense took action to reduce the proliferation of languages and increase the transfer of software among new systems. DoD Instruction 5000.31 listed seven languages which it called HOLs (high-order languages) and restricted application development to these [1]. Whichever language is selected, 100% of the programming must be done in it except possibly for optimized subroutines written in assembler or machine language. All seven of the HOLs are procedural and should be regarded as *low-level* languages compared with NOMAD or most of the other languages in Box 2.1. The DoD Instruction thus prohibits high-productivity techniques.

Other government departments are still issuing application development directives which lock their vast organizations into conventional procedural techniques. Often, such directives have been developed with high-powered academic participation and much exhortation about making programming more professional. As a recent paper about the Department of Defense programming directives states: "The theme pervading all of these steps is to elevate software policy, practices, procedure and technology from an artistic enterprise to a true engineering discipline" [2]. These directives prevent the use of the new methods with which more flexible organizations have speeded up their application creation by a factor of 10 or more.

The installation standards, then, so laboriously created in many organizations, are full of trip-wires that prevent the productivity increases which new methods and end users are demanding. It is not easy to reverse the standards because so many people have been trained and drilled in their use.

A WALL BETWEEN The traditional techniques for application develop-
USER AND ment tend to build a wall between the application
PROGRAMMER *user* and the application *creator*. The programmer
is kept away from the end user. Figure 6.1 shows
aspects of the wall. First there is the formal development life cycle, of which Fig. 4.1 is typical. Written requirement specifications are created. This takes much time but, as discussed in Chapter 4, is rarely adequate.

The specifications must be *frozen* at the start of the design and coding

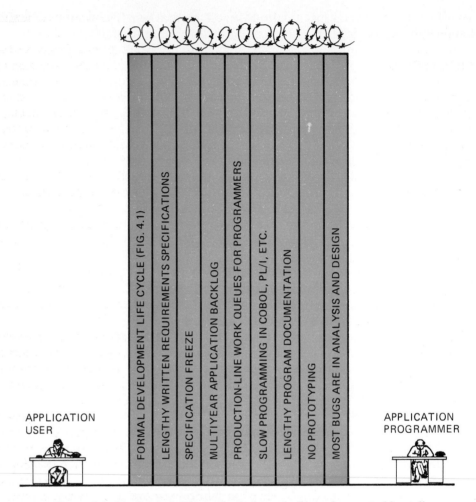

Figure 6.1 Traditional DP methods have built an impenetrable wall between the application user and the application creator.

phase. Often they are frozen when the ideas about what the system ought to do are still fluid. The user often does not know what he wants until he sees it on a terminal and uses it. This is becoming increasingly so as we move to more complex applications. We have now done the simple, easily standard-ized applications—payroll, invoicing, and the like—and are faced with more subtle and valuable applications, such as decision support systems, oper-ations control, and financial planning. With these applications a rapid rate of adjustment is needed as the end users begin to change their methods of working. With many such applications, *prototypes* should be created quickly to see if the users like them. The prototypes should be rapidly changeable.

In this environment it is vital that the application creator works hand in hand with the application users. The systems analyst who learns to understand the users' needs should himself create the application and work with the user to adjust it interactively. For most applications this can be done with the new software for generating applications, graphics, reports, and data-base queries. In a few cases the systems analyst will need to call on the services of a programmer to create complex algorithms, but not (with good software) to create the end-user interface.

The programming in languages such as COBOL or PL/1 takes a long time. The programmer must document his code. In typical installations which are well controlled with a development standards manual, there are about 10 pages of program documentation to each 1000 lines of code. In some installations documentation never gets done.

Often, a production line is established for use by programmers. Jobs for coding wait in a queue until a programmer is free. This maximizes the use of programmers—a scarce resource—but further adds to the overall elapsed time.

The user sees a multiyear delay before work starts on the application he needs. When work is under way, the time between specifying requirements and obtaining results is so long that during it the requirements have changed.

In one typical corporation there is a backlog of 70 applications. In the previous 12 months only 19 applications were created. The acknowledged demand for new applications is growing faster than applications are being created. However, there is also an *unacknowledged* need for applications. Many end users, now beginning to understand what computers could do for them, do not formally notify DP of their need because of overload on DP and the multiyear backlog. There is a large invisible backlog.

The DP creation process is further slowed by errors that have to be corrected. As indicated in Fig. 4.2, most errors are in requirements analysis or interpretation and design. The use of structured analysis of certain types relieves this somewhat with prespecifiable applications, but not with user-driven applications.

Errors in analysis become less of a problem when analysts can create the applications themselves, quickly, and show them to the end users. Relatively fast end-user feedback enables the analysts to make adjustments while they are still familiar with that they created. This fast cycle of application creation, and feedback, using the new application generation software, makes prototyping and adjustment a natural procedure.

The validation process changes. Validation of the *data* should be via the data administration function, which is discussed later. Validation of the function may be done by a DP audit or validation process, but can often be made an end-user responsibility.

Program bugs are reduced by the move to higher-level application creation facilities. Errors are also reduced by removing, where possible, the traditional interaction between systems analyst and programmer. Too often the analysts' program specifications are misinterpreted. When the analyst *creates* the application directly, this cause of errors is removed.

To build this wall between application user and application creator is the worst thing we could do. It is becoming more serious as we evolve to more user-driven applications. New methods of application creation are vital to the future of the computer industry. This future lies with vendors, who make possible application creation without the wall of Fig. 6.1.

SOLVING THE WRONG PROBLEM   Much of today's research into the development process is oriented toward improving existing methods: improve programming with the move to structured programming; improve systems analysis with the move to structured analysis; formalize the life cycle of Fig. 4.1 and provide tools for documentation and review; add yet more reserved words and instruction types to COBOL; adapt languages and compilers for better structured programming; and so on.

In a sense these activities (although highly valuable because much conventional programming will remain) are solving the wrong problem. The important problem is how to migrate from conventional programming and the life cycle of Fig. 4.1 to development methodologies that are fast, flexible, interactive, and employable by end users; methodologies in which interactive prototyping replaces formal, voluminous specifications which must be frozen; methodologies with which end users can create and continuously modify their own applications.

If a hammer is not achieving much success in fixing screws, the solution is not to obtain a better hammer. The problem is that the wrong methodology is being used. More appropriate tools are now available for DP development. In some cases DP managers still want to use the old development life cycle even with the new tools. This is rather like hammer enthusiasts driving in screws by hitting them hard with the handle of the screwdriver.

THE INFORMATION CENTER CONCEPT   The installation Bible is not going to be abandoned overnight, nor should it be. What is happening instead is that *alternative* means of creating applications are coming into existence, and coexist with the traditional methods.

In some cases the end users have created the alternative method, without DP approval. User departments acquire their own minicomputer or use software that permits fast application creation. Sometimes they use time-sharing services with languages such as NOMAD or a partition of a mainframe with languages such as MAPPER. DP executives in some organizations have tried to stop this uncontrolled spread of minicomputers and languages. In other cases they have allowed it to happen, only too glad to get some of the end users off their backs. The *uncontrolled* spread of minicomputers, however, can store up trouble for the future because multiple versions of incompatible data come into existence, as well as multiple machines that cannot be linked into networks.

A valuable approach is the *Information Center* concept. The information center is a group within the DP organization designed to serve end users directly and speedily. The group is aware of which data bases exist and sometimes sets up other data bases. It makes this information available to end users, employing the types of languages described in this book. Information center consultants work with the end users and create, where possible, the applications they want. The consultants help to create the decision support systems, personal computing facilities, information retrieval systems, and organizational support systems. A major reason for establishing this mode of operation has been the extreme dissatisfaction expressed by end users about the way DP has been responding to their information needs.

The consultants encourage the users to employ the information facilities that already exist. They sit at terminals with the users to create the catalogued query procedures, report generation routines, or graphics generation routines. They train users to employ these facilities.

Where more complex applications are needed, the information center consultants decide how they can be created, selecting where possible an application generator or language that avoids the formal programming development cycle of Fig. 4.1.

The rapid methods for application generation and report generation enable prototypes to be built and tried out with the end users. The prototypes will be adjusted to fit the users' needs and often completely changed. It is common for end users to say: "I don't know what I want until I see it."

Prototyping allows new frontiers to be explored. Sometimes a system is created which users will never employ. This can be done quickly with the application generators and not too much time is wasted. The lessons learned enable better design next time.

There is much to be said with some user-driven systems for creating *pilots* which are somewhat experimental–if they can be created quickly and cheaply. An attitude of "Let's try it and see how it works" develops. Some of the pilots may be scrapped or changed, but they lead to an understanding of what is useful.

The end users need much training and handholding in adapting to new systems. The information center consultant can work closely with users, showing them how to employ the facilities. In some cases substantial use is made of computer-based training. IBM's IIS (Interactive Instruction System) are used extensively in some installations for training end users. It is sometimes used for prototyping. It is used to simulate an end-user terminal dialogue before detailed programs are generated.

Chapter 19 discusses *Information Center Management.*

INFORMATION RETRIEVAL

Some corporations make extensive use of information retrieval systems. It is almost impossible to tell what information some executives will need. With information retrieval systems such as IBM's STAIRS or ICL's CAFS (Content Addressable File System, an associative storage machine), a mass of information can be stored centrally and made easily available to all types of executives (with suitable security control). In some corporations, the policy followed when the information needed by executives has not been predictable has been to set up an information retrieval infrastructure in which any type of data can be made available quickly. This becomes more practical with today's storage costs and on-line information retrieval software and hardware. The best dialogues for information retrieval make it easy for executives or their staff to find information from the mass of data that is stored. These data can be formatted and reports created. As the software improves, graphics capabilities will enable the data to be charted.

Such information retrieval facilities can satisfy most end-user requests for information in certain areas. One large corporation used to have three analyst/programmers working full time for the personnel department, generating ad hoc reports. A personnel information retrieval system was installed and the end users were taught how to generate the reports they wanted. The requirement for analyst/programmers dwindled to zero. In this case the personnel data discs were loaded only for 6 hours per week. The end users needed some help at first, but rapidly learned to solve their problems without technical assistance, and became extremely enthusiastic about the system.

In a large U.S. bank, terminals were steadily installed in users' offices. Most of the data that bank officials might need were stored on an information retrieval system, including all checks processed for the last 42 days, all customer data, stock and bond data, and much financial data. Users were trained to find the needed data. The same terminals were used for a variety of office-of-the-future applications, such as electronic mail, electronic work queue management, calendars, work tracking, and so on. The technical staff who acted as consultants to the end users were thus concerned with spreading the office-of-the-future culture as well as helping users solve their own data processing and retrieval problems.

SELLING THE FACILITIES TO USERS

Such facilities have a different characteristic from much early DP in that users can accept them or reject them. When computers are used to create information services or office automation services, end users have a choice about whether they use the new facility. User acceptance spreads gradually. Office-of-the-future services, such as internal electronic mail, mail filing, in-basket automation, and work tracking, have a large payoff only when *most* office workers are cooperating in using them. The information center staff therefore has an important *selling* job to do, persuading office workers throughout the organization to adapt to the facilities that now exist.

MAINTENANCE　　　Organizations that have moved aggressively into information center operation claim that most end-user demands can be met by the information center. This can be done relatively quickly, so end-user dissatisfaction with DP is greatly relieved. In typical corporations with substantial well-designed data bases in existence, 70% of end-user needs can be met with query languages and report generators. In many cases less than 10% of the end-user demands for new applications require conventional DP development with formal programming specifications and languages such as COBOL or PL/1.

Unfortunately, this does not mean that the conventional DP staff can quickly dwindle to 10%, because in most organizations a high proportion of them are working on *maintenance* of old programs.

The term *maintenance* is used to refer to the rewriting of old programs to make them accommodate new requirements or make them work with new terminals, operating systems, computers, or data structures. Maintenance, if not consciously controlled, tends to rise as the number of programs grows. This is especially so in a file (as opposed to data-base) environment where files become used by more than one program. A seemingly trivial modification sets off an expensive chain reaction of changes that have to be made to multiple programs.

Figure 6.2 shows how maintenance programming has tended to grow in typical installations, becoming a higher proportion of the DP budget and

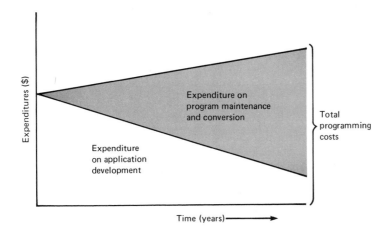

Figure 6.2 New application progress is often deferred by the rising cost of modifying existing programs and files. Some corporations now spend more than 80% of their programming budget just keeping current, and only 20% forging ahead.

greatly worsening the application backlog. In many organizations, sometimes those moving fastest into on-line and interactive systems, the ratio of maintenance activity to new application development has reach 80%. Large corporations often have some systems or application areas where 100% of the programmer effort is spent on maintenance. An average breakdown of maintenance is 15% on conversions, 21% on systems maintenance, and 64% on application maintenance (statistics from IBM).

It is often thought by systems analysts that existing programs that work well can be left alone. In reality, the data such programs create or use are needed by other applications and are almost always needed in a slightly different form, unless thorough logical data-base analysis has been performed.

The maintenance mess has become a nightmare in some large corporations. It is alarming to reflect what it would be like 20 years from now if more and more applications and systems were added with conventional methodologies. Under appropriate conditions, microbes can multiply exponentially like today's computers. But if they multiply when shut in an enclosed laboratory dish, they eventually drown in their own excrement. One top DP executive compared this to his maintenance problems. New growth, he said, was being stifled by the use of old COBOL and PL/1 systems. If new techniques were not widely accepted and used, the programming team would eventually drown in its own maintenance.

SOLUTIONS TO MAINTENANCE

The solutions to the maintenance problem are:

1. Thorough logical data-base analysis [3].

2. A well-designed data-base environment (many have not been well designed) [3].

3. Use of high-level application generators, query languages, and report generators rather than COBOL or PL/1, preferably operating as data-base facilities. The application-creation facilities should be chosen such that they are self-documenting and applications can be modified quickly and easily.

4. Avoidance of programmed modifications to purchased application packages.

5. Avoidance of hardware configurations and changes that may look cost-effective from the hardware viewpoint, but cause conversion problems.

6. Redevelopment of old applications with application generators to eliminate the need for COBOL and PL/1 reprogramming, where possible. This is by far the best solution where practicable. Some generators are designed to facilitate this conversion and can use the files or data bases of the old applications, or convert them directly.

The cost of recreating an application with the very high level languages and facilities is often less than continuing to maintain it in COBOL or PL/1.

Some corporations have adopted a policy of recycling old applications into the development process to make them fit into the new data-base and application generation environment. The purpose of this is to lower the long-term maintenance costs and enable changes to be made faster.

A major market for software vendors is the automated conversion of programs with expensive and slow maintenance to an environment that is on-line, data-base, and uses application generators which permit fast, easy modification. With the best application generators, most modifications to applications wanted by the end users can be completed in an hour or so.

An important selection parameter for very high languages is their ease of maintenance. It is often difficult to understand and modify another person's APL code, for example, but it is easy to understand and modify NOMAD or DMS code. In some installations 80% of all changes to applications created with DMS are made within 1 hour.

SUMMARY

Box 6.1 summarizes the problems with conventional DP development and their solution with the information center approach.

BOX 6.1

Problems with conventional DP development	Solutions with information center operation
• Very long applications backlog, causing DP unresponsiveness and severe end-user dissatisfaction.	• Immediate interaction with end users, with fast creation of results. The backlog for the conventional programmers is bypassed.
• Low applications development productivity.	• Use of query languages, report generators, and application generators give 10 to 50 times higher productivity than does COBOL or PL/1 programming.
• Conventional programming builds a wall between the application creators and application users (Fig. 6.1).	• Information center consultants interact directly with end users.
• There is minimal end-user involvement.	
• Formal specification writing is very time consuming.	• Formal specifications are usually not written.
• Substantial programmer time is used in documentation.	• Report and application generators are used which are self-documenting.
• Prototyping is not done.	• Prototypes are easily created and quickly modified.

(*Continued*)

Box 6.1   (Continued)

Problems with conventional DP development	Solutions with information center operation
• Specifications must be frozen early in the development cycle.	• No freeze is necessary. The development is fast and flexible.
• Requirements specification documents are long and very time consuming to produce.	• Requirements specification documents are generally not created.
• Requirements definition is often poor. The end users often do not know what they want until they see it.	• The results are worked out with the end user and can be quickly modified to suit his needs.
• Typically, two-thirds of all bugs are in design and analysis. These are expensive to correct.	• Design errors are quickly adjusted with end-user participation.
• The quality of the programming code is often poor.	• The generators generate good-quality code.
• The talents of good systems analysts are often poorly used.	• The systems analyst has scope for exercising his full skills. He has a more creative, less frustrating job.
• Much unnecessary redundancy exists in the code and applications that are written.	• Redundancy can be avoided with appropriate data-base planning methodologies.
• The impact of change is severe.	• The impact of change is minimized.
• A crippling future maintenance burden is created.	• The applications are relatively quick and cheap to maintain.

REFERENCES

1. U.S. Department of Defense Instruction 5000.31, *Interim List of D.D. Approved High Order Programming Languages.*

2. B.C. De Roze and T.H. Nyman, "The Software Life Cycle—A Manage-

ment and Technological Challenge in the Department of Defense," *IEEE Transactions on Software Engineering,* Vol. SE–4, No. 4, July 1978.

3. James Martin, *Managing the Data Base Environment,* Prentice-Hall, Inc., Englewood Cliffs, NJ, 1982.

7 PREPROGRAMMED APPLICATION PACKAGES

INTRODUCTION   At first sight it might appear that the best way to avoid programmers is to install preprogrammed application packages. More and more of these are becoming available. They represent one of the largest sources of revenue to the software industry. During the 1970s the total independent software industry revenue for application packages grew from almost 0% to 4% of the total of computer users' expenditures on programs. The percentage will rise during the 1980s, perhaps to 10% or higher.

NIH SYNDROME   In many large corporations the percentage use of preprogrammed application packages is low. The percentage is larger in small corporations. Corporations with fewer than 100 employees are often entirely dependent on application packages and have greater flexibility in adapting to the packages than do large organizations. One giant multinational corporation that we studied used no application packages until 1979, and then used them only in a few isolated areas. This firm spends hundreds of millions of dollars each year on application development, but only a few thousand on packages.

Typical reasons given for not using packages include "our organization is unique," "the packages do not fit our requirements," and "we do it differently." In some cases the differences are genuine. In some there is the *NIH syndrome*—an opposition, not overtly stated, to using anything Not Invented Here. In other cases, particularly in small corporations, it pays to change the administrative methods and paperwork to fit the packages.

Substantial problems have been experienced with application packages and it is necessary to watch out for the pitfalls; nevertheless, we feel that most corporations are not making as much use of packages as they should.

PACKAGES ARE IMPROVING

As the market for packages increases, software houses can afford to spend more money on them and make them better. They design them with more parameters which can be selected and varied. Parameterization is the key to making packages fit into organizations with as little change in procedures as possible.

In the early 1970s the largest use of application packages was probably that for airline reservations. The predominant package was IBM's PARS (Program for Airline Reservation Systems) and IPARS (International PARS). Various additions to these were created and marketed by certain airlines. PARS and IPARS had a major effect on IBM's sale of hardware to the airlines. At the time, this degree of application packaging success was not repeated with any other industry. The reasons why it worked with airlines were that the reservation application was very precisely defined and essentially the same for all international airlines, there was already substantial cooperation between airlines because this was necessary for booking multi-airline journeys, the application was very complex and expensive to develop, and IBM made the package the basis of its worldwide marketing and teleprocessing design for airlines.

Although airline reservations may look the same across the world, production control, budgeting, planning and so on, differ from one corporation to another. On the other hand, inventory control, invoices, purchase orders, and such are sufficiently similar from one organization to another that packages with a good choice of parameters for varying their actions could satisfy these applications in a vast number of corporations. Nevertheless, such packages had remarkably little success until the late 1970s, when the concern about DP costs swung increasingly from hardware to application development. It was easy to underestimate the differences and complexities in these and other applications.

Now there are many thousands of software packages available. Their variety is tremendous. The total revenues from standard packages are increasing at about 30% per year and the prices of packages are dropping as competition and market size grows. That growth rate may increase as the quality, diversity, and general acceptance of packages increases. Box 7.1 gives examples of some of the types of packages that are available.

TRAINING AND ADAPTABILITY

The installation of an application package often needs adjustments by the puchaser and sometimes by the vendor. Teamwork between the purchaser and the vendor is *sometimes* essential for success. This teamwork requires the following essentials.

1. Willingness of the purchaser to make adjustments in his methods so that the package is fully usable

BOX 7.1   Typical examples of available application packages

Accounting
  Banking
  General
  Tax
  Trust
Accounts Payable
Accounts Receivable
Airline Reservation
Application Development Aids
Architecture

Banking Systems
Bill-of-Material Processing
Bond and Stock Management

Check Processing
Commercial Loans
Computer-Aided Design
Computer-Aided Instruction
Computer Management Aids
Construction
  Accounting
  Job Costing
Conversion Aids
Correspondence Control Systems
Customer Information File (CIF)

Data Management Systems
Demand Deposits
Distribution Systems
Document/Text Processing

Education
Engineering
  Electrical
  Mechanical
  Space

Financial
  Control/Planning
  General
  Management
Forecasting and Modeling

General Ledger
Government

Federal
Local
State
Graphics
Health Care
Health Insurance
Hospital Management
  Accounting
  Administration
Hotel Management
  Accounting
  Reservations

Information Storage and
  Retrieval
Instalment Loans
Insurance
  Accounting and Billing
  General
  Life and Health
  Property and Liability
Inventory Control
  Management
  Manufacturing

Job Accounting
Job Costing
Job Performance Measurement
  Systems

Letter Writing/Mailing Systems
Liability Insurance
Library Systems
Life and Health Insurance
Loans
  Commercial
  Instalment
  International
  Mortgage

Mailing/Correspondence Lists
Management Sciences
Manufacturing
Mathematical/Statistical
Medical and Health Care

BOX 7.1 (*Continued*)

Modeling	Resource Management
Mortgage and Loans	Route Scheduling
Order Entry	Sales and Distribution
	Savings Systems
Payroll, General	Scientific
Performance Measurement	Securities Management
Personnel Systems	Statistical and Modeling
Petroleum Industry	Stock Portfolio Management
Preprocessors, Computer Language	
Production Control	Tax Accounting
Project Control and Planning	Teleprocessing Systems
Property and Liability Insurance	Text/Document Editors
Process Control	Time-Deposit Accounting
	Trust Accounting
Query Languages	
	Utilities Accounting
Real Estate Management	
Remote Job Entry	Word-Processing Systems
Report Generators	Work in Progress

2. Willingness of the vendor to make adjustments to the package, for a fee, when needed

3. Willingness of both to work together as a team, with appropriate personal resources, to make what adjustments are needed

4. The vendor's commitment to training

Sometimes the sum paid to the vendor for training and adaptation of the package is greater than the cost of the package itself.

Perhaps the biggest problem with purchased packages is underestimating the adjustments that are needed. The user sometimes assumes that the software will run itself.

The input and output of a package is often unfamiliar to users. Substantial training and familiarization is needed in its use. The user department may have a number of adjustments to make. The vendor, who has much experience with the package, should give advice on how to make the installation as successful as possible.

It is often desirable to operate an earlier system (often manual) in parallel with the package until the package has settled into full operation and all the necessary adjustments have been made.

The vendor sometimes forgets or underestimates the uneasiness of a new user or difficulty in learning and adjusting to the package. Considerable patience and handholding is needed as the package is being phased into use.

MAINTENANCE   Perhaps the biggest unforeseen danger with application packages is the difficulty of maintenance. Most business applications change substantially with time and the package has to be modified. Often the customer has to make the modifications.

If the modifications have to be made in a language such as COBOL, PL/1, or FORTRAN, this requires much work. To facilitate maintenance, excellent documentation and clean design of the package are needed. These characteristics need to be examined when the package is bought.

In some cases the maintenance programming that is necessary is more expensive and takes more time than creating and maintaining the entire application would have taken with an application generator. Potential users should compare the cost of application generation with the cost of purchasing and maintaining packages.

SOURCES OF   There are five types of sources of software:
SOFTWARE

1. Computer manufacturers
2. Software houses
3. Software brokers
4. Time-sharing companies
5. User groups and individual users

1. Computer Manufacturers

Until the 1970s, IBM and other manufacturers provided software free in order to sell machines. When IBM "unbundled" and began to charge for its software, this gave the whole software industry a boost. Now it is clear that a substantial part of computer manufacturer's revenue will be from application software.

Manufacturers offer a bewildering array of application products. Prospective users should apply the same rigorous evaluation procedure to them as to software from other sources. Some application packages from manufacturers are "silent salesmen" which will force the user to add more memory, more terminals, or use a particular data-base management system such as IMS. Nevertheless, it can be much more economical to use such packages than to write your own.

Packages are *essential* for many small customers. The accounting package on the IBM System/34, for example, contains about 80 programs for statements, trial balances, and so on. It costs $30 to $40 per month. To write what a typical customer needs in this area would be likely to cost about $50,000 to $100,000.

Manufacturers pass on to customers the benefits of packages developed internally, by their own field employees and by customers. IBM has two categories for the latter type of software products.

(a) Field-developed programs (FDPs)

(b) Installed user products (IUPs)

An FDP is a product that has been developed by IBM in the field, but not as part of a planned software product. It is available through IBM to its customers.

An IUP is similar, but is written by IBM customers. IBM agrees to maintain it with limited support. Naturally, the type of product is carefully analyzed by IBM before it appears on the market.

2. Software Houses

Software houses are moving away from contract programming, which was once their lifeblood, toward the development and mass distribution of packages. The best-selling packages have been *extremely* profitable.

Some of these popular packages have been created by small companies formed by one or a group of individuals who know a particular application area extremely well. A substantial number of individuals have become millionaires through doing this. The software industry therefore has many small firms as well as large ones. Some of the very small firms have excellent products but shaky management. Some of them may not be in business 5 years from now.

Programmers are noted for being colorful and unpredictable and they sometimes form companies in their own images. A programming manager recently described a career programmer as one who returns after lunch. Sometimes they form companies designed to provide a quick killing and quick retirement. Their customers should protect themselves by *insisting that source code and good documentation of the product is held in escrow* so that it can be made available to customers if the firm ceases to function.

3. Software Brokers

Because excellent products are being created by cottage corporations, there is a need for software brokers. Most new small software corporations cannot handle their worldwide marketing. Often, they do not want to be bothered with the administration necessitated by success. A software broker, like a publisher, handles sales, service, and administration and pays royalties to the software creators. It may help the creator in legal matters and protect him from taxes on worldwide sales. Like a rock star, the software creator can burst into fashion, have sales that rocket for 2 years, then fade and lose a potential fortune in taxes unless a corporate structure protects this fortune.

The software broker can also protect users of software by helping to ensure quality, good documentation, and no loss of source code. Brokers may convert good packages so that they run with multiple machines, operating systems, terminals, and data-base management systems. Some software brokers provide installation and maintenance of the packages.

4. Time-Sharing Companies

Time-sharing organizations make software available via teleprocessing. Accessing software in this way is dropping in cost and becoming easier because public data networks are spreading. Many countries around the world now have easy access to time-sharing computers in North America and to a lesser extent in Europe.

For some applications, time sharing is a way to try out a package before making a commitment to buy it. Sometimes the use is perceived as being temporary or intermittent, so time sharing may always be cheaper than purchase. Some corporations end up spending much more money for time sharing a package than they would have spent if they had purchased it. For infrequently or intermittently used packages, the cost of time sharing should be compared in detail with that of leasing or buying the package.

A rapidly growing area of time sharing is the use of public data banks. Use of this information may be combined with the use of software that manipulates it, searches it, or generates reports.

5. User Groups and Individual Users

User groups are increasingly playing an important part in information exchange and making available programs to members. They also play a role in liaising with manufacturers not only on software but on hardware as well.

Some individual users who have developed an excellent application keep it proprietory; others make money by selling it. In the 1970s one nationalized airline sold the software it developed and made more profit doing so than it did from flying airplanes. (If only it could have given up its addiction to flying airplanes, it would have been highly profitable!)

When obtaining a package or program from a user group or individual user, be sure to investigate such details as support, documentation, and quality of the product. User groups vary considerably, and care should be exercised when purchasing application development products.

An important role of user groups and industry associations ought to be to develop standards. Standards are needed so that data can be exchanged between corporations without conversion and so that packages can be used throughout an industry. An insurance broker ought to be able to access many insurance companies through its terminal rather than having a different terminal for each insurance company, for example. Purchase orders, invoices, and other documents ought to be standardized and exchanged directly between application software in different firms.

INFORMATION ABOUT APPLICATION PACKAGES

Information about packages can be obtained from computer vendors, software houses, industry groups, and periodicals. Organizations such as Datapro and Auerbach provide listings and surveys of packages. They often include detailed surveys from users who have used the products, and their findings are valuable. A good indication of the use and acceptance of a particular product is the number of users and the date of first installation. For example, a product introduced 5 years ago with 1,000 users could be considered very successful, whereas a similar product with five users should alert you to the need for further research.

The *International Directory of Software* [1] provides a detailed, 1105-page summary of a great many packages.

DEVELOP OR BUY

A careful analysis is required by the application under consideration before a decision is made whether to develop the application programs or to buy a package.

There are several considerations other than cost:

- Consider the functional characteristics of the application itself. How complex is it? What is the priority of implementation? What is the time scale for development?

- A long development backlog may be a good enough reason to consider a package. In-house projects may take several years to develop and may go seriously over budget by the end of it. An application software package should be implemented in a month or two at a fixed price.

- Often, for a variety of reasons, some aspects of an in-house development project never reach a programmer's coding pad, whereas the content of software packages is well known and defined.

- Do the application data have close links to other applications, for example in a data-base environment? Can the data-base administrator accommodate the package with some form of bridge between it and the data-base systems?

- Sometimes senior management resists the whole idea of purchasing applications from outside sources. One way around this problem is to present the clear economic advantages and point out that the programming staff will be free to concentrate on more important areas of application development.

- Documentation, which is so often neglected with in-house development, can be a necessary prerequisite for the purchase of a software package. It is also a good indication of the quality of the product itself.

PITFALLS

Box 7.2 lists some of the main pitfalls with packages. One pitfall results from insufficient care being taken to fit the package to user needs. There may be subtleties that were not perceived in the rush to purchase the package.

Sometimes the package does a good job when first installed but user needs change, or the system changes, and substantial maintenance is required. Some packages are designed for maintenance and some are a nightmare to maintain.

Some package users have modified the package when it was first installed and later have found it expensive to maintain the combination of the package and in-house changes. The vendor often develops the package in ways that invalidate home-made modifications. Because of such troubles, some DP organizations have decreed that packages *cannot* be tinkered with by in-house programmers; if changes are needed, they must come from the package vendor.

BOX 7.2   Pitfalls with application packages

- The package is insufficiently parameterized and does not fully meet the needs.
- DP modifies the package when it is installed and subsequent maintenance becomes almost as expensive as with in-house application programs.
- Expensive maintenance becomes necessary later when the hardware, operating system, terminals, or network are changed, or when user requirements change.
- The package is difficult to maintain because of poor documentation, or lack of hooks for user-created code.
- The package does not fit in with the corporate data-base implementation and strategy.
- The software house that owns the package ceases operation.

Possibly in the future packages will be written with application generators so that they are easy to modify by users. This would be very valuable for certain applications.

Many corporations have a corporate-wide data-base plan with which the proposed package is incompatible. Many packages use their own files, not data bases. Increasingly, package vendors are adapting them to use data-base management systems, but even then their fields and records do not conform to those of the data administrator. Some corporations have solved this by modifying the data their packages use so that the data conform to the corporate data structures.

In some cases a package can exist in isolation, but often it must pass data to other information systems. Sometimes it must link into a data-base environment. Some package users have modified their packages so that the field structures are the same as those in their corporate or data-base data dictionaries. It is often preferable to avoid modifying the package and use external conversion routines which convert the data to the data-base form. This type of link between packages and a data base is shown in Fig. 7.1.

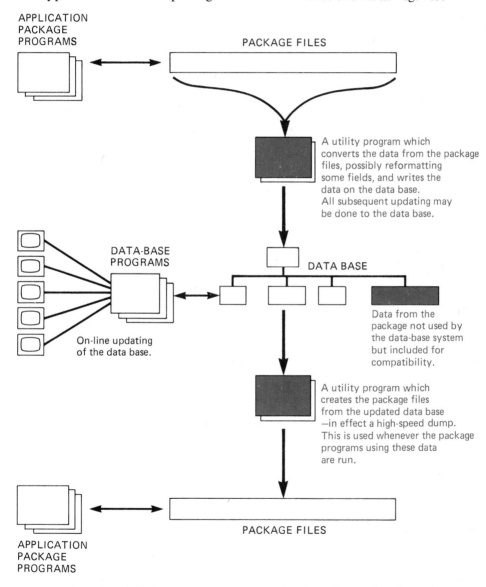

APPLICATION
PACKAGE
PROGRAMS

PACKAGE FILES

A utility program which converts the data from the package files, possibly reformatting some fields, and writes the data on the data base.
All subsequent updating may be done to the data base.

DATA-BASE
PROGRAMS

DATA BASE

Data from the package not used by the data-base system but included for compatibility.

On-line updating of the data base.

A utility program which creates the package files from the updated data base —in effect a high-speed dump. This is used whenever the package programs using these data are run.

PACKAGE FILES

APPLICATION
PACKAGE
PROGRAMS

Figure 7.1 Utility programs may be written to make purchased application packages link to a data-base environment.

Some manufacturers' application packages are written for that manufacturer's DBMS alone. IBM's impressive set of applications for production control, COPICS, is written for IMS only, as are many other IBM packages. Cullinane has created a conversion tool, called ESCAPE, so that these and other programs can be automatically converted to run with an IDMS data base. Only in a few cases have package creators tried to fully accommodate the needs of a data administrator.

A particular danger is that of the software house ceasing to exist and the source code disappearing with it. As commented earlier, users should insist that the source code is well documented and is held in escrow in case the software house goes out of business.

ACQUIRING A PACKAGE

Selecting an application package should be approached systematically, with a formal, logical procedure. Box 7.3 lists suggested steps in acquiring a package.

If a very detailed list of requirements is drawn up, it may be difficult to obtain a package that fits them. Some compromise is often needed in fitting the application to package. It is desirable to minimize future maintenance problems, so a thorough listing should be made of how application needs may change in the future.

BOX 7.3   Steps in the acquisition of an application package

- List the present and future requirements of the application in detail.
- Survey *all* available packages for that application.
- Examine their documentation.
- Check whether the packages are sufficiently parameterized.
- Check whether the packages have adequate aids to maintenance.
- Draw up a short list of suitable packages.
- Examine the vendors. Will they provide adequate service?
- Talk to users of these packages.
- Can each package link into the corporate data-base plans?
- Conduct benchmark tests if performance is critical.
- Allow end users to use the packages on a temporary basis if the end-user interface is critical.
- Write an appropriate contract.
- Monitor the use of the package selected.

Information on related packages should be gathered from all available sources: Datapro reports, Auerbach reports, software directories (e.g., Ref. [1]) consultants, user groups, sales personnel, trade journals, and so on.

The documentation of the package should be examined thoroughly. Is it well documented? Is it sufficiently parameterized? Will it need modification, now or in the future? Is it easy to modify? Is it designed for maintenance? What may be the future cost of maintaining the package?

A short list of possible packages may be drawn up based on the answers to these questions. A number of packages will not reach the list, for reasons such as price, availability, disc space, machine configuration, and not fitting the users' needs.

The vendor of the package may be examined to see whether it is likely to give suitable service. Will the vendor be prepared to make modifications? Will the vendor help install the package? What future development of the package is planned? Could the vendor go out of business or cease to support the package? Would this matter? In some cases the purchaser is prepared to take over the support and maintenance of the package.

It is particularly valuable to talk to users of a package before acquiring it. The vendor should be asked for a list of users. Users should be asked about any delays, numbers of bugs encountered, response times, vendor service, and so on. They should be asked how they would like to see the package improved.

Can the package fit into the corporate data-base plans? Does it use a DBMS? Does it have a data dictionary? Is it designed to be adapted into data-base environments? If not, does that matter?

Where performance is critical, as with high-volume runs, different packages may be benchmarked employing users' data. Where end-user interface is critical, selected end users may be allowed to use the package, or different packages, for a period, to see whether they find them user-friendly and effective. There is often a great difference between user reactions to packages for the same application.

Corporate lawyers may become involved in negotiating the contract. They should ensure protection in the event of the vendor ceasing to operate. Sometimes it is desirable to drive a hard bargain to ensure adequate support. The legal process is necessary but should not be taken to extremes. One software house selling a package in New York for $12,000 estimated that the firm it was selling to had spent more than that on legal fees in acquiring the package and the lawyers caused a harmful delay of many months.

The vendor's help may be needed in installing complex packages. A plan should be drawn up for this. A considerable period of vendor advice and handholding may be needed when the package is first in operation.

After a period, the operation of the package should be reviewed. Statistics may be collected on performance, or errors. Any operational inefficiencies should be identified and corrected with the help of the vendor. In some cases an agreement with the vendor, and possibly a contract, may be made for improvement of the package.

The performance of the vendor should be analyzed and recorded if additional packages might be purchased from the firm in the future.

REFERENCE

1. *International Directory of Software 1980/1981*, CUYB Publications Ltd., London, 1980.

8 LANGUAGES FOR END USERS

DP moves forward in a series of revolutionary changes. The coming of the commercial computer in the late 1950s was one such change. Another was the coming of discs and the change from batch to on-line processing. Another was the spread of terminals, telecommunications usage, and networks. As important as any of these will be a change in software which permits end users to create their own applications.

Enthusiasts sometimes say that this will happen through *programming languages* such as BASIC, or some future *programming* language. This is a naive view. The use of these languages is growing fast. Some end users find APL particularly valuable, others MANTIS. Subsets of these can be used without programming. But only a small proportion of all users are likely to *program* in the normal meaning of the term in the foreseeable future. They will create applications with different types of software.

There are now examples of on-line application generators and graphics generators which are both extremely easy to use and powerful in the results they achieve. In some corporations spectacular results are being achieved with these for user-driven applications, as described in Chapter 11. In many cases end users are doing this with no involvement by their DP department.

End users bring a vital skill to the development of computer systems— their knowledge of the application and its environment. It is desirable to harness this as fully as possible. Their understanding of what they need from computers grows slowly, a step at a time. It is an evolutionary process.

Box 8.1 summarizes reasons why users should be given the capability to generate their own applications.

BOX 8.1   Reasons why end users should "do their own thing" with computers

- Only the end users truly understand the subtleties of their own applications (especially if they are complex).
- The end users should be made *responsible* for how they employ computers.
- End users can obtain the applications they want earlier, thereby relieving the extreme frustration with DP that some end users feel.
- Spontaneous demands for information may be satisfied quickly.
- End users should be encouraged to use their imagination about what computers can do for them.
- The total number of people working on application development can be much larger.
- An understanding of what is needed comes slowly with the experience of using the system. A facility is needed with which users can make many modifications to their system quickly.
- Complex administrative procedures tend to evolve a step at a time, each step being a reaction to current problems and pressures. Computerized procedures should evolve in the same way.
- End users are much brighter than many DP professionals admit; the best of them can be highly inventive in their use of computers.
- The traditional development life cycle (Fig. 4.1) does not work for user-driven systems.

CATEGORIES OF COMPUTER END USERS   There are five categories of end users, as shown in Fig. 8.1.

First, there are *indirect* users, who obtain computerized information via a third party. These include airline customers who phone an airline, and executives who make use of a third party to obtain information for them.

Direct users may be on-line or off-line. Off-line users employ paper listings or reports. On-line users employ a terminal. We subdivide on-line end users into those who use applications but do not create them, and those who create applications.

Until recently, very few end users created applications. End users who *do not create* applications include the vast mass of terminal users: bank tellers, airline agents, order-entry clerks, salespersons with a terminal, and so on. They also include those who use a data-base query language. Nonpro-

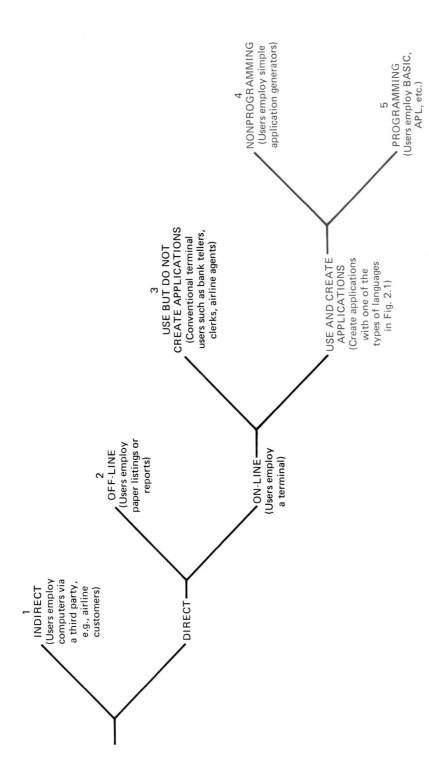

Figure 8.1 Categories of end users.

gramming end-users employ facilities for creating applications without normal programming, for example screen dialogues or fill-in-the-blanks techniques.

The end users who *create* applications are shown in red in Fig. 8.1. They are subdivided into programming and nonprogramming end users. Programming end users employ a language such as APL or NOMAD. They are sometimes referred to as "DP amateurs." This term does not have a derogatory connotation. It implies that their profession is other than DP or programming. The number of end users who can program is growing, but is likely to remain a small special minority.

Data-base languages and report generators are being used increasingly by end users. An extension of these can make them into application generators for end users. Substantial improvement is needed in this type of software. It is very important for the future of the computer industry that application generators for non-DP-skilled end users should improve and come into widespread use. They will be used for user-driven applications, not heavy-duty applications.

It is also possible for *off-line* users to create applications with tools that involve filling in forms. This is so much less satisfactory than on-line application creation that it has not been included in Fig. 8.1.

Chapter 9 discusses data-base languages for end users. Chapters 10 to 13 discuss end users who create their own applications.

CLASS 4 USERS   The conventional wisdom in the DP industry is that end users cannot create their own applications. One finds DP professionals, software developers, seminar lecturers, and even computer manufacturers' product-line planners who dismiss as absolute nonsense the idea of application creation by end users.

The best case histories of end-user application creation have a very different story to tell. Not only is it practical; in addition, it can pervade an entire organization and the results (with user-driven applications) are far better than would have been achieved with typical traditional DP development. The end users in question are not geniuses or freaks; they are a typical cross section of white-collar workers who are often hard-pressed for time.

The end user who programs is the exception rather than the rule. Some users, particularly those working for planning departments of various types, find that skill invaluable. They create their own cash flow models, planning algorithms, actuarial routines, or decision-support aids. Sometimes APL enthusiasts train their whole department to program. It is relatively easy to use the simpler operations of APL, as shown in Chapter 13.

A major thrust of the computer industry at present should be toward the class 4 users of Fig. 8.1. The software firms that create the best products for class 4 users will make a great deal of money in the 1980s. The DP manager who creates a vigorous thrust into this form of computing is likely to have a major effect on his corporation in a period of 3 years or so.

The majority of white-collar workers spend much of their time carrying out the set of activities shown in Fig. 8.2. If they can automate these, they can save much of their own time and can improve communication and the quality of decision making. Most of the automation of the activities in Fig. 8.2 can be done without programming (in the conventional sense of the word).

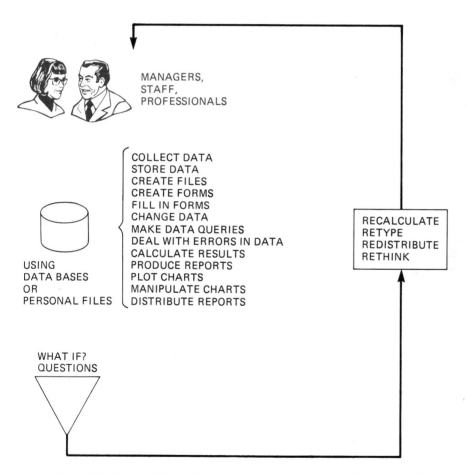

MANAGERS,
STAFF,
PROFESSIONALS

COLLECT DATA
STORE DATA
CREATE FILES
CREATE FORMS
FILL IN FORMS
CHANGE DATA
MAKE DATA QUERIES
DEAL WITH ERRORS IN DATA
CALCULATE RESULTS
PRODUCE REPORTS
PLOT CHARTS
MANIPULATE CHARTS
DISTRIBUTE REPORTS

USING
DATA BASES
OR
PERSONAL FILES

RECALCULATE
RETYPE
REDISTRIBUTE
RETHINK

WHAT IF?
QUESTIONS

Figure 8.2 Many white-collar workers require terminals to carry out these types of activities. With the best of today's end-user software, these can be done by the end users themselves without programming.

VARIETIES OF END USERS   Society had endless varieties of people, with enormously differing interests and skills. The same is true of computer end users. It is desirable that they have available a wide variety of techniques for using the computing power which is now spreading to the users. A type of dialogue structure that is good for one user is not necessarily good for another. Some end users will learn to program; most will not. Some end users will learn mnemonics; most will not. Some end users will be happy with simple menu-selection dialogues; others will find these slow and restricting.

We sometimes make the mistake of talking about "end users" as though they were all the same. In fact, they are as diverse as all people are. While the new software gives one class of users terminal dialogues of extreme simplicity, other software offers the capability to use sophisticated languages. To all these groups, usability should be the prime consideration. Value to users is of more concern than machine performance.

The role of the end user is being changed by a variety of technologies: microelectronics, desktop computers, minicomputers, distributed processing, better terminal dialogue facilities, and end-user-oriented data-base facilities. Because of these technologies, the numbers of end users are growing fast.

Today, because of the backlog with conventional application development techniques, many DP managers perceive the pressure from end users for applications as being excessive. *In reality, however, most end users have barely begun to realize the potential of computing for improving how they do their job.*

As the services that can be created by an information center approach become operational, a major task will be the training of end users to employ these services and understand their potential. In the years ahead an enormous change has to be brought about in the working methods of all office staff. A major role of the systems analyst or information center consultant will be *selling* the new facilities to the end users, showing them how to make good use of them, and adapting them to the users' real problems.

Many white-collar workers require terminals to carry out the types of activities shown in Fig. 8.2. Where the software is human-factored well enough, these tasks can be done by the users themselves without programming.

THE TWO-DAY TEST   In the early days of computers, only programmers and computer operators had an *active* role in using the machines. When the spread of terminals began, it was thought that only users with detailed and lengthy training would use them. Ten years later terminal dialogues had improved so that the layperson could use terminals with no training or practice, examples being viewdata systems [1] and bank customer terminals. However, it was generally thought that end users could not *create* applications—that only programmers could do that. Now it has become clear that end users can and should create certain types of applications. Only in this way can their unique knowledge be fully harnessed. We distinguish between *routine* applications and *user-driven* applications.

The key to *user* creation of applications is the existence of terminal dialogues that are psychologically appropriate. This software now exists and is improving rapidly. It is quite different from the software traditionally used by the DP professional. It needs to be sufficiently easy to use so that the typical manager can employ it effortlessly to make more intelligent decisions. In a few organizations the use of such software has greatly improved the effectiveness of computers.

Unfortunately, almost every query language and report generator on the market is advertized as being "suitable for end users." Some are tried out and gain little acceptance. Some are used by systems analysts, not end users.

BOX 8.2   The two-day test to determine whether products are suitable for end users

To pass the 2-day test, a product should have the following properties:

- *Most* end users can learn to use it effectively in a 2-day course. Some can learn it much faster.

- At the end of this course they are *comfortable* with it and can use it on their own.

- At the end of the course they can start getting *useful* work out of it. This emphasis on useful work is important. There is no point in learning gimmicks that have little relevance.

- After the course the end users can leave the product for a week and still be able to use it. (Most users would forget mnemonics or fixed entry sequences in a week.)

- End users will not necessarily have to return to another class on the product.

- Users can expend or refresh their knowledge of the product at the terminal by using HELP features and computer-aided instruction.

  (In some cases the 2-day course may cover a useful subset of the product's features and more can be learned later when the users have had experience with it).

One language was advertised with the phrase "Learn to write computer programs in five minutes!" But in many organizations it did not prove to be suitable for or accepted by the end users. We suggest that a test be applied to such products, the *2-day test*. This is described in Box 8.2. If the users can learn to be *comfortable* with the product and carry out *useful work* with it in 2 days and not necessarily need to return to classes on it later, then we can put it in the END USER column of Fig. 2.1.

Some products are complex and the 2-day course may cover only part of their capability. It is a good idea to package products so that a useful subset can be taught and employed. When users are experienced in using this subset and find it valuable, they will be more receptive to learning advanced subsets.

An important aspect of the 2-day test is that users should be able to leave the product for a week or more and concentrate on other matters, and when they confront the product again, should be able to use it. This is not likely to be the case if the product requires them to remember codes, mnemonics, formats, or fixed sequences of entry.

Having said this, it must be noted that *some* end users *do* make good use of products that would not pass this test. Some use programming languages, for example. But they are more dedicated users than most. For the masses the 2-day test applies.

INTEGRATED SET OF PRODUCTS　　When end users are first confronted with a terminal on which they can obtain or manipulate data, the facility ought to be simple to use. Some data-base query languages, as we discuss in Chapter 9, are very easy to use—easy enough to encourage the most faint-hearted user. Some electronic mail and information retrieval systems are very easy to use.

The naive user tends to go through phases of fear, fascination when he begins to make something work, then euphoria. While he is confident and euphoric, he should be introduced to the next step up in system capability.

A good query language ought to lead to a data-base updating capability, report generation, and graphics generation, using the same style of dialogue and syntax. An electronic mail facility ought to lead to tools that enable a user to process an electronic in-basket or work queue. With these facilities a second level of sophistication is reached, as illustrated in Fig. 8.3.

A user might be left some weeks to master the techniques, or some of them, at this second level before he is introduced to further complications. Ideally, he should be able to grow to the third level in Fig. 8.3: application generation and the general ability to use the system to support decisions.

Again, ideally, the syntax and style of the dialogue ought to be the same in progressing from the second to the third level. Unfortunately, this is not true with much of the software listed in Box 2.1. The vendors have not

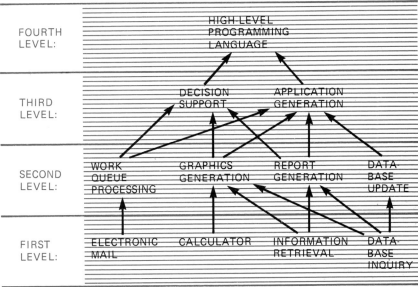

Figure 8.3 Ideally, end users should learn to use the first-level facilities, then progress to the second level, then the third level. Only a few will progress to the fourth level. Many products do not have this range of capabilities.

completely put their act together. A data-base query language is often no more than a query language. The same vendor may have an application generator but it has no relationship to the query language. IBM's QUERY-BY-EXAMPLE has no resemblance to its GIS (Generalized Information System) and that has no resemblance to DMS (Development Management System) or ADF (Application Development Facility). Cullinane's products for users of its IDMS data base are equally unrelated (at the time of writing). Ideally, everything in Fig. 8.3 ought to be provided by related products with similarly structured end-user dialogues. Some products on the market do encompass many of the facilities in Fig. 8.3.

Some products begin their evolution as a query language and have features added which take them into other areas of Fig. 8.3. Sometimes these are human-factored well, with a major emphasis on use by naive users, but they do not have sophisticated application generation capability.

Other products begin their evolution as high-level programming languages such as APL or NOMAD. Non-procedural features are added. Facilities are improved for querying data bases, generating reports and graphics, and handling electronic mail. This evolution gives the sophisticated users much capability because of the power of the programming language, but it is sometimes not as easy for beginners or casual end users to employ.

The ideal language set ought to have all the capabilities shown in Fig. 8.3 and have elegant human factoring for the lower three levels. The lower levels ought to be extremely easy for the beginner to use. Commonality of syntax and dialogue style ought to make it natural for users to progress from one subset of Fig. 8.3 to another.

REACTIVE SYSTEMS   As microelectronics continues its downward plunge in cost, it becomes possible to put increasing amounts of computing power at user locations. This may be in the form of minicomputers, microcomputers, intelligent terminals, or controllers. Microelectronics provides elaborate computing resources which interpret user input or create elegant color graphics displays on the user's screen.

It is no longer necessary to share a distant computer with many other users, and access it by means of a low-bandwidth line. Each user can have substantial computing power *to himself.* The further microelectronics drops in cost, the more this will be true. Telecommunications will be used for accessing data rather than for accessing computing power. If users can have substantial computing power at their fingertips at low cost, system design efforts should be directed to making a person's time on the computer as profitable as possible.

The term *reactive system* has been used by Alan Kay of the Xerox Palo Alto Research Center [2] to refer to systems in which a substantial processor has, as its sole job, catering to a single user. It can afford to do relatively large amounts of processing when the user is doing the simplest of tasks. It can format data on the screen and add text so that it is easy to understand. It can check the user's spelling and flash any items not in the dictionary. It may contain an interpreter or incremental compiler. It can assemble and maintain multiple forms of color graphics display and allow the user to interact with them. It can afford to do extensive processing to figure out what the user wants to say or what information he is trying to obtain, and can interact with him to deduce or refine his intended input. As the price/performance ratio of microelectronics drops, a primary concern must be end-user efficiency rather than machine efficiency.

End users will increasingly be given facilities that make it easy for them to obtain the information they need from distant data banks, manipulate the information, format it into meaningful graphics displays and reports, and create data-related applications.

DIALOGUE   When end users communicate with a terminal,
STRUCTURE   the structure of the dialogue they employ is very
                  important. Computer manufacturers have "human
factors" experts. However, most of the time they are concerned with such

factors as the feel of the keyboard, the positions of the switches, and the glare on the screen. Much more important is the structure of the dialogue. What does the machine say to the user? Can he understand it? Is he confused by any part of it? Does he know how to respond or how to initiate an interchange?

Psychological structuring of the dialogue is a complex subject. Guidelines can be established [3, 4], but it cannot be reduced to an exact science. It is more akin to *style* in writing than to the layout of instruments in an airplane cockpit, although it has elements of both.

Many of the early terminal dialogues required the operators to remember mnemonics and fixed sequences of input. Sometimes this was done to create a dialogue with a small number of characters, because every character has to be transmitted over the communications links. Often it was done because the dialogues were created by programmers, who spend their lives using mnemonics and assumed that terminal users could use them also.

It is important to understand that most potential end users do not think like programmers, and are remarkably poor at remembering mnemonics, fixed sequences, and formats. If they are full-time terminal operators, spending their entire working day using the terminal, they can be expected to remember such things, but most future end users are doing some other job and use terminals only occasionally. The rate at which they forget mnemonics, fixed sequences, and so on, is *much* greater than most programmers realize.

MNEMONICS AND　　In the dialogues used on airline reservation sys-
FIXED SEQUENCES　tems, NN2 means "two seats are required," HS2
　　　　　　　　　　means "two seats are available," ORD means
"Chicago." In a factory shop floor system the author looked at recently, the foreman has to type "PX748K123" to check the status of job 123. In the new standard for access to public data networks (CCITT Recommendation X.28) DER means "out of order," NP means "unobtainable," OCC means "number busy." It is unnatural and difficult for the average potential end user to learn such mnemonics.

Even worse, in many dialogues for dumb terminals, the user has to remember a fixed input format. He must key in a string of fields which must be the right length and in the right sequence. In a typical airline reservation system, the operator wishing to inquire about seat availability on a flight has to key in

```
021Y06MARLAXJFKNN1
```

0 is the segment entry; 21 is the flight number; Y means tourist class; 06MAR is the date (it is amazing how many different ways of entering dates there are); LAX is Los Angeles and JFK is Kennedy Airport, New York;

NN1 means that one seat is required. If the user omits any field, changes the sequence, or uses a wrong length field (e.g., 6MAR), the message will be in error. The error may be detected by the computer or the message may be processed erroneously.

AVOIDANCE OF
MNEMONICS

In most commercial dialogues it is possible to avoid completely the use of mnemonics and formats which the user has to memorize. The aforementioned request for seat availability on a flight, for example, could be handled as follows. The operator indicates that he is interested in seats, either by pressing a key labeled SEATS on the terminal or by selecting SEATS from an application menu on the screen. The following display then appears:

```
SEAT AVAILABILITY REQUEST
PLEASE ENTER THE FOLLOWING INFORMATION:

FLIGHT NUMBER (if known):
CLASS OF SEAT:
NUMBER OF SEATS REQUESTED:
DATE OF DEPARTURE:
DEPARTURE CITY:
DESTINATION CITY:
```

The cursor jumps rapidly to the successive entry positions.

If the user enters the flight number, he may omit the departure city and destination city. The computer (possibly a small distributed processor close to the user) displays the cities at which that flight stops and asks the user which he requires.

```
PLEASE TYPE 1 AFTER THE
DEPARTURE AND DESTINATION CITIES:

NEW YORK:
LONDON:
ATHENS:
TEHRAN:
NEW DELHI:
```

Casual end users who approach a terminal only occasionally should never be forced to remember mnemonics, codes, sequences of entry, and fixed formats.

**BACKTRACKING
AFTER MISTAKES**
Another major failing with some dialogues is that the user can reach a point where he does not know what to do next. The terminal may have done something that surprises him. He may have pressed a wrong key. Now what does he do? There is no obvious means of recovery. Guessing, he makes another entry, but that only puts him in worse trouble.

A senior civil servant once took me into his office to demonstrate, proudly, his new terminal. I asked him if he could obtain a slightly different result and he said "yes." However, the device produced an unexpected response. He tried repeatedly to get the dialogue back onto the correct track, but it eluded him. Eventually, the only way he could continue the demonstration was to put down the telephone handset, redial the computer, reload the program, and enter the dialogue from the beginning. A month later the terminal sat in his office largely unused.

All terminal users will do things wrong and get surprises at the terminal. The dialogue should be structured so that when that happens, the user has an obvious and natural way to recover. The simplest way is a key labeled "BACK," or an option labeled "BACK" which can be selected with a light pen or cursor. The dialogue should be designed so that the user can backtrack simply whenever he needs to. If he makes a mistake or takes a wrong path, he can return simply to where he was before that happened. The backtracking should happen in the peripheral machine, usually without any transmission to or involvement of the higher-level computer.

Sometimes the user enters data to be filed or to update records in a distant machine. These data may be entered erroneously. Any accuracy checks that can be applied in the local machine should be applied before the data are transmitted to the higher-level computer.

**SIGN-ON
PROCEDURES**
On some systems users never get as far as grappling with the application dialogue. The sign-on procredure defeats them.

A typical sign-on using the ARPA network proceeds as follows:

TERMINAL: LOGIN

USER: JM   (identification of the user)

TERMINAL: PASSWORD

USER: BEAR   (user password for the network)

TERMINAL: UNIX MESSAGES . . .   (terminals print a string of unwanted messages)

TERMINAL: %

USER: STTY HAZ

TERMINAL: %

       USER: TELNET

TERMINAL: TELNET VERSION

TERMINAL: #

       USER: CHAR

TERMINAL: CHARMODE

TERMINAL: #

       USER: ECHO OFF

TERMINAL: #

       USER: CONN BBN

TERMINAL: ATTEMPTING CONNECTION
                 CONNECTION OPER
                 BBN TELEX

TERMINAL: @

       USER: LOGIN UCLA

TERMINAL: PASSWORD

       USER: 2470 WW (password for UCLA system)

TERMINAL: LOGIN COMPLETE

TERMINAL: @

       USER: (attempts to establish what application he will use)

The system designer or network expert can give a logical explanation of why all these steps in the sign-on procedure are needed. To the uninitiated user they seem like the incantation of some secret society. It might as well have been devised by a witch doctor. Perhaps it is fine for technicians and university professors, but the computer industry now has to lure all manner of reluctant end users to sit down at the terminals. A sign-on procedure such as the one above will make them stay away in droves. With some terminals it is almost equally difficult to sign *off!*

There is no need for such hocus pocus, especially with intelligent terminals. The sign-on procedures should be designed to be simple, natural, and *obvious* (and include suitable security procedures).

DESIRABLE PROPERTIES OF SOFTWARE FOR CASUAL END USERS

By *casual* end users we mean a user who employs a terminal only occasionally. It is not his main job. He does not sit at the terminal most of the day as an airline agent does. Box 8.3 lists a set of desirable properties of software designed to be employed by such end users.

It is sadly true that many dialogues being written today look as though they were designed by programmers for programmers. It is important to understand that dialogues suitable for programmers are quite different from dialogues suitable for casual end users.

A harassed professional or executive may feel that he is too busy to spend more than a half-hour learning how to use a terminal. At the same time, he is intelligent and can react powerfully to an easily understood dialogue. He will be impatient if he receives many error messages or if he loses his way in the dialogue. He will assume that the terminal is not designed for him if it produces unintelligible strings of characters. We may characterize a large group of potential users as:

Highly intelligent

Requiring a high information bandwidth

Too busy for a training course

Highly impatient

Nonrugged

Requiring worthwhile results

BOX 8.3 Desirable properties of software dialogues for end users in categories 3 and 4 of Fig. 8.1

- The means of establishing contact with the computer and signing on should be simple, natural, and *obvious* (with appropriate security routines).

- The user should be required to know as little as possible in order to get started.

- The dialogue should completely avoid forcing the user to remember mnemonics.

- The dialogue should completely avoid forcing the user to remember formats or entry sequences.

- The dialogue should never put the user in a situation where he does not know what to do next.

- The dialogue should provide a simple, natural, and *obvious* means for the user to recover from any mistakes or surprises. A good facility is that of *backtracking* to the point before the surprise occurred.

- The response times should be fast enough to avoid frustrating the user.

- The software should have good HELP functions with which any facility can be explained.

- The software should be self-teaching, with computer-aided instruction at the same terminal.

BOX 8.3 *(Continued)*

- It should be human-factored well enough that the end user for whom it is intended can become skilled with it and obtain valuable results after a 2-day training course.

A vitally important aspect of the future of the computer industry is the search for dialogue structures that such persons will enjoy using. We now have enough examples of excellent dialogue design to make inexcusable the bad dialogues still being created.

The same executive or professional who has rejected a stumbling dialogue on a typewriter-like terminal can be captivated by a well-designed graphics dialogue that encourages him to explore. This can be observed in many applications. For example, some of the attempts to give computer assistance to portfolio managers in banks and brokerage houses failed in the early 1970s. The dialogues written for time-sharing systems with dumb and rather slow terminals were sufficiently difficult to preclude obtaining worthwhile results. Today, similar employees in several major companies are making very powerful use of graphics dialogues for the same application.

MACHINE LITERACY   Literacy is the skill of communicating ideas and thoughts fluently to ordinary people. In this age we need to extend literacy from the printed page to a variety of electronic media. Programmers and systems analysts are only occasionally literate. Their's is a different skill. But now they have to design end-user dialogues for enabling machines to communicate with ordinary people. A form of machine literacy is needed. This is a change in culture, and cultural changes are always resisted.

The computer industry has never excelled in literacy, as evidenced by its manuals, its love of complexity and jargon, and its alphabet-soup mnemonics. Now the future growth of the computer industry depends on the extent to which ordinary people find the machine dialogues attractive, usable, and worthwhile. It depends upon machine literacy.

Dialogue style is vitally important for crossing the hurdle of getting end users to employ the facilities in Fig. 8.3 and for steadily improving their capability with them.

REFERENCES

1. James Martin, *Viewdata and the Information Society,* Prentice-Hall, Inc., Englewood Cliffs, N.J., 1982.

2. Alan Kay, "Personal Computing," ACM National Conference, August 1975.

3. James Martin, *Design of Man–Computer Dialogs,* Prentice-Hall, Inc., Englewood Cliffs, N.J., 1973.

4. Guidelines for dialogue structuring are explored in the series of courses on the terminal–user interface in: James Martin, *Advanced Technology Library,* Deltak, Oak Brook, Ill. 60521.

9 DATA-BASE USER LANGUAGES

INTRODUCTION   Most corporations now store vast amounts of computer data. These data could be extremely valuable in many types of decision making if end users at terminals could request and search for the data they need.

For this purpose a wide variety of data-base query languages exist. Some are simple, so that an unskilled user such as a clerk can compose a query. Some can carry out more complex searching and report-generating functions, but more skill and training is needed to use them.

For many end users the use of data-base query languages is how they start instructing a computer to go to work for them. They may progress from the use of these facilities to software at the higher levels shown in Fig. 8.3.

ON-LINE?
INTERACTIVE?   Some query languages are designed essentially for off-line use. The user fills in query forms, submits them to the computer center, and expects a reply in a few hours or on the following day. Some are designed for on-line use, in which the user composes his query at a terminal and expects a reply in seconds or, at most, minutes. On-line use places constraints on the data-base organization in that it must be designed to give suitably fast response times. Nevertheless, on-line use can be far more effective than off-line use when the user has the capability to carry on a dialogue with the system. The system can help him to specify complex queries, and he can narrow down his search step by step until he finds the information he is looking for.

HEURISTIC
SEARCHING   It is often the case that the answer to a single off-line query does not provide the information that was sought. The user needs to try a new query or

adjust the previous one. Often, an initial query is too broad and would result in hundreds of responses or an entire file search. Interactive operation allows the query to be modified so that it is more reasonable before the full search is executed. On some systems the user may adjust his query 20 to 30 times before he finds the information he wants. The successive modification of queries to home in on information being sought is sometimes referred to as *heuristic searching* of a data base.

SPONTANEITY   Executives who understand that data-base information is available to them sometimes develop many spontaneous ideas for using it. To put the data base to good use for decision making, however, they usually need to receive the information *quickly* — tomorrow they will have a different problem.

As Fig. 9.1 indicates, a vice-president may have to wait weeks or months if a program written in a conventional language is needed to process his information request. With a data-base interrogation language usable by the information staff at terminals, he may receive the information he wants in minutes. Spontaneous ideas involving information usage are encouraged.

As indicated in Fig. 9.2, the fact that the data base can be interrogated directly by the information staff takes a load off the data processing department.

Using a conventional programming language:

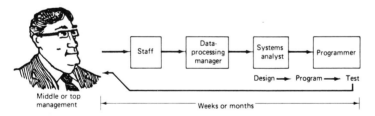

Using a data-base interrogation language.

Figure 9.1 An executive can evaluate spontaneous ideas if he receives sufficiently fast responses to his requests for information.

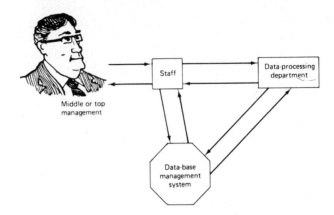

Figure 9.2   The fact that the management staff can interrogate the data base directly takes a load off the data processing department.

STANDARD DATA-BASE STRUCTURE?

Some end-user data-base facilities operate with standard data-base management systems such as IBM's IMS or Cullinane's IDMS. Others operate with their own special structures, often relational structures, which are separate from the organization's major production data bases.

In some cases data bases are built specially for end-user activities. These may be built by end-user departments themselves. Often they are spin-offs from an organization's major production data bases. In selecting a structure and organization for the data in such data bases the predominant concern is convenience and speed of use by end users. Often, the spin-off data base has a different structure from its parent and may be built with a different data-base management system.

INFORMATION RETRIEVAL SYSTEMS

Sometimes a data base is built solely for the purpose of being searched so that queries can be answered. This would be the case with *information retrieval systems*. These were originally used to store library abstracts or legal documents in such a way that users can search them rapidly to find the information they need.

After initial successes with document retrieval it became realized that *information retrieval software,* such as IBM's STAIRS, for example, was valuable for many of the types of information that are needed in running an organization. Some corporations load their information retrieval system periodically with data from their major production systems (which may use data bases or files).

Searching through a large amount of information in order to answer queries can take many machine cycles or disc accesses. It is desirable to find data organizations that speed up this process. Special hardware is becoming available that automates much of the searching process. An example of this is ICL's CAFS (Content Addressable File Store). Content addressing is a technique for retrieving information by its attributes and characteristics. The ICL machine searches data in 12 parallel channels simultaneously. Each channel handles data read from a one-disc track. Hardware units can scan the data looking for field values that meet specified search criteria. When data are found that meet these criteria, they are sent through the channel to the CPU.

FORMS-ORIENTED LANGUAGES

In a common type of off-line query language, the user fills in forms to indicate what he wants. Informatics' MARK IV system is of this type [1]. Figure 9.3 gives a simple example of a MARK IV query. The form that it represents can be filled in very simply and quickly and then keypunched and processed. The user employs a simple data dictionary to tell him the names of the data items that he can list on his form.

MARK IV employs many different forms including forms for defining data structures, defining transactions used to update the files, defining logical and arithmetic operations to be performed on the data items, defining in detail the layout of reports to be generated, defining tables to be used, and cataloguing the processing requests.

MULTIPLE LANGUAGES

There are a relatively small number of types of data-base management systems. However, the data-base languages that use these are proliferating. Many user languages plug into IBM's IMS or Cullinane's IDMS, for example.

There is much to be said for standardizing within a corporation on one type of data-base management system for routine DP applications. An organization might adopt CODASYL, IBM's DL/1, or some other form of data-base *schema* representation as its internal standard. In addition to this, it is often desirable to have a more flexible data-base system for user-driven applications. This is described as a class IV system in Box 17.3. A relational data base is often used, linked to nonprocedural relational languages.

When a standard type of data-base management system is used for routine DP, different end-user data-base languages may profitably employ it. The data-base language software is usually loaded and scheduled as though it were an application program. Different types of end users need different types of languages. Some of the interesting forms of data-base user dialogues come from independent software houses rather than large manufacturers, and this represents a major business opportunity for software houses in the future. Craftsmanship and ingenuity in dialogue design may be more likely to come from talented independents than from major manufacturers.

MARK IV, produced by Informatics Inc., is a data-base management system which permits information requests to be specified very quickly by filling in forms. MARK IV can handle complex data bases using the DL/1 language, and process complex information requests. The following is a simple illustration.

An accountant has received a request from his boss for the total year-to-date activity on one vendor's account. Taking an Information Request form, the accountant writes in a Request Name. Any name that fits in a Request Name. Any name that fits ①. He writes TODAY in the Report Date box (to get today's date on the report) ②.

No other information is required in the heading area of the form. MARK IV provides automatic default conditions for everything left blank. In this example, MARK IV will produce a detail report, single spaced, on standard 8½" by 11" paper.

To be able to request information from a file of data, the file has been defined previously to MARK IV. The file definition provides the accountant with the names of the pieces of data which make up the file. Other qualities of the data, such as size, are also provided. MARK IV stores this definition, and a printed glossary of the names is available any time for any users of the file.

Therefore, when the accountant wants to refer to the data in the file, he just looks at the glossary for the Accounts Payable file and uses the names that were assigned to the pieces of data in the file. For instance, the piece of data which is the vendor number is called VENDOR, and since the vendor in which he is in-

terested is ABC Manufacturing (vendor number 2386), he "selects" that vendor by writing VENDOR EQ (equal) D (for Decimal) 2386 in the Record Selection area of the form. When looking at the Accounts Payable file, MARK IV will pick out only the data about vendor number 2386 ③.

And, since only activity for 1972 is of concern, the accountant writes A (for And) INVYEAR EQ D 72 to select only the activity concerning ABC Manufacturing Company that has taken place in 1972 ④.

If no such special selection criteria are required, then the Record Selection portion of the form is left blank. The default condition for this is that MARK IV will report on the total contents of the file.

Now that the accountant has specified the selection criteria, he can specify the data he wants to see on the report itself. He wants to see the vendor's invoice number, invoice date, invoice amount, check number, check date and amount paid. He writes the names for those pieces of data, one to a line and in the sequence he wants them to appear across the report, in the Report Specification section of the form ⑤.

To get a total of the activity being reported, the accountant simply enters a G (for Grand) in the column marked Total on the same lines as INV-AMT and AMT-PAID. MARK IV will provide a grand total of all the INV-AMTs and AMT-PAIDs in the report ⑥.

Finally, to give a meaningful title to his report, the accountant writes his own title in the section of the form labeled TITLE ⑦

④

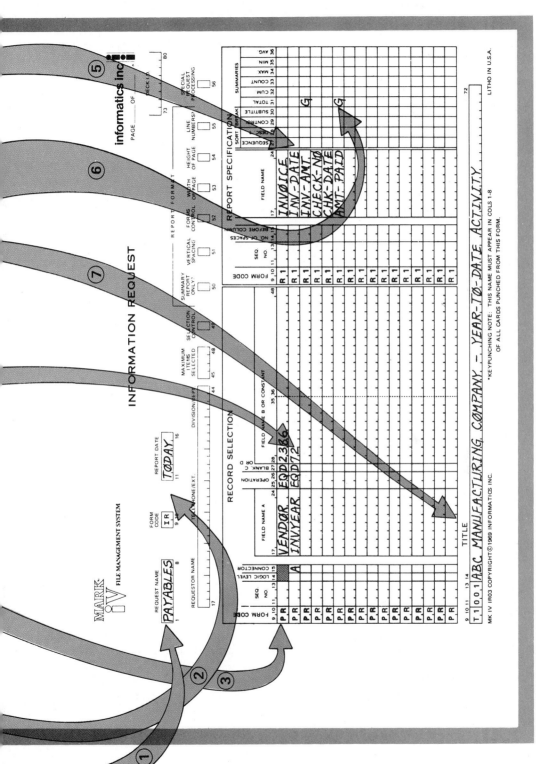

Figure 9.3 Typical Mark IV information request form. (Courtesy of Informatics, Inc., Canoga Park, Calif.)

(Continued)

The accountant will give his filled out Information Request form to someone in the data-processing organization who will have the form keypunched, put it on the computer, and deliver the resulting report as soon as it is available.

The report produced by this request is shown below:

```
04/28/72      ABC MANUFACTURING COMPANY - YEAR-TO-DATE ACTIVITY      PAGE 1

------------------------------------------------------------------------------
          INVOICE    INVOICE    INVOICE    CHECK      CHECK      AMOUNT
          NUMBER     DATE       AMOUNT     NUMBER     DATE       PAID
------------------------------------------------------------------------------
          51-03917   01/12/72        3.47  002571     02/15/72         3.47
          51-07242   01/14/72       60.43  002571     02/15/72        60.43
          51-11275   01/21/72      152.40  002571     02/15/72       152.40
          51-12336   01/27/72      104.53  002571     02/15/72       104.53
          51-14514   02/03/72       14.44  002819     03/15/72        14.44
          51-17180   02/14/72      102.42  002819     03/15/72       102.42
          51-20992   02/29/72       63.00  002819     03/15/72        63.00
          51-21541   03/02/72      189.12  002819     03/15/72       189.12
          51-23730   03/07/72       19.72  003093     04/17/72        19.72
          51-24226   03/10/72    1,092.46  003093     04/17/72     1,092.46
          51-28859   03/27/72      605.00  003093     04/17/72       605.00
          51-29331   03/31/72    5,486.00  003093     04/17/72     5,486.00
          51-31155   04/11/72       19.09
          51-33126   04/21/72      187.55
          51-34568   04/25/72       28.90

                                                                 7,892.99
```

Other MARK IV forms enable the professional analyst programmer to execute more complex processing and reporting operations.

Courtesy of Informatics Inc., Canoga Park, Calif.

Figure 9.3 Continued.

There are various data-base user languages that plug into IBM's DL/1 or IMS data bases. Mark IV (Fig. 9.3) is one of them. Another is GIS/2 (Generalized Information System). [2]. Both are intended primarily for off-line operation, although GIS is often used from terminals. Some data-base languages are intended primarily for use at terminals, for example ASI's INQUIRE using DL/1 or IMS.

Many data-base languages look as though they were written by programmers for programmers. Some are now beginning to emerge that are suitable for use at terminals by an end user with very little training. DEC's DATATRIEVE language, like others, uses English-like commands. DATATRIEVE is a command interpreter that both interprets and acts on each statement received. The language is built like an extension to COBOL. It can be learned easily, but the manual [3] warns that, ideally, its reader is a programmer or data administrator.

Substantial research has been done on the psychological factors affecting an end-user data-base language, and a variety of languages have been designed in a research environment to demonstrate ease of use. These include:

RENDEZVOUS [4]

SQL [5]

INGRES [6]

QUERY-BY-EXAMPLE [7-9]

QUEL

SQUARE

CUPID [10]

FORAL LP [11]

**SEPARATE
END-USER
DATA BASES**

All of the languages listed above use *relational* data-base structures (FORAL LP uses binary relations) rather than the structures of conventional data-base management systems such as IMS, IDMS, and TOTAL. In a relational data base the logical structure of the data is in the form of simple two-dimensional tables [12]. These are easier to comprehend and to manipulate than the more complex structures of DL/1 data bases, CODASYL data bases, and others.

Various software products are designed to facilitate the flexible manipulation of data packaged together with a relational data base and a user friendly nonprocedural language. This is the case with IBM's SQL (pronounced "sequel") [5].

With distributed processing an attractive feature is the ability to create data bases for end users in a peripheral machine so that users can manipulate or search them without affecting the central data base or the work load on the central machine. Such features may then reside in the peripheral machine, whereas the data base itself does not.

There is often concern that end users employing a data base will harm its integrity if they are allowed to modify it, and even if not, may cause performance problems that will interfere with other processing. The performance problems may be especially severe if the users' language triggers *secondary key* operations or *join* operations in a relational system.

Because of these concerns, it is often good design to place the users' data manipulation activities and information systems in a peripheral computer with separate files. This separate computer handles the data manipulation language (Fig. 9.4). In some cases the peripheral computer is a small minicomputer with good data manipulation capabilities, and is relatively easy to install. Sometimes it contains a small relational data-base management system; sometimes it stores data in file rather than data-base form.

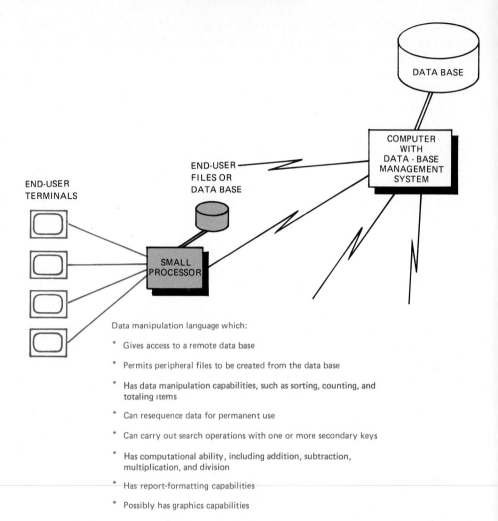

Figure 9.4 Some systems need languages that can create peripheral files from a remote data base and allow end users to manipulate and search those files peripherally, without endangering the integrity or performance of the remote data-base system.

AUTOMATIC NAVIGATION

We have commented that the move to higher productivity in application creation must come from the use of high-level building blocks, like an electronic engineer moving from design with transistors to design with chips containing many logic operations. The use of nonprocedural data-base languages is an example of this.

Much has been written about "navigation" through a data base, meaning that the programmer accesses the data with a step-by-step procedural code, a record at a time. High-level data-base languages provide *automatic navigation* to the target data. This means that the user specifies *what* he wants, not *how* to get it—the system works out *how* to get it. A nonprocedural language is used and the user need know no details of how the data are stored or physically accessed. This can simplify the use of a data base to such an extent that end users rather than programmers can achieve complex operations.

High-level data-base languages can manipulate collections of records, not merely single records, in a single statement. Relational data-base systems are designed for this type of operation, with relational languages. In some systems the high-level data-base statements can be mixed with programming statements in COBOL or PL/1. In other systems they form a separate data-base query or report-generation facility.

DYNAMIC
MODIFICATION

Users or systems analysts employing user-driven data-base systems often need to make changes in the data-base structure. Some types of data-base systems (those described as class IV in Box 17.3) are designed to give such flexibility. A new data item may be added to a relation, or old ones deleted. New relations may be added or dropped.

Some systems support such contraction or expansion of relations without bringing programs or transactions to a halt (unless the data required by the transaction have been dropped). Processing can then proceed as usual while data-base changes are being made.

Other data bases do not allow dynamic restructuring. Restructuring has to be done off-line.

GIS

IBM's GIS (Generalized Information System) is designed for operations on a data base structured using the DL/1 data description language. The following example consists of 14 lines of GIS code. To produce the same report in COBOL would require about 250 lines of code [13].

Figure 9.5 shows a DL/1 data base and a GIS query using that data base. Suppose that a marketing manager has been conducting a new advertising campaign. He is concerned after an intensive burst of advertising that certain warehouses may be running out of stock of product number 75438. From the data base in Fig. 9.5 he receives monthly reports of sales and advertising expenditure. These do not tell him about the sales of the 13 days of the current month which may have been critical. He can obtain a stock status report on any product when he wants it, using a previously written inquiry program. This confirms his fear that certain warehouses may be running short. He can also check the replenishment schedule for the warehouses, and

A DL/1 schema data-base description:

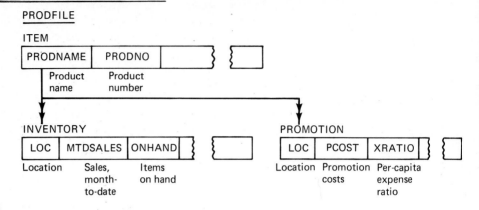

A GIS query using this data base:

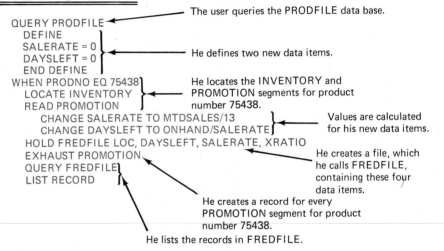

Figure 9.5 Use of GIS.

he sees that the next delivery to some warehouses is not scheduled until late next week. His staff assistant asks the data processing manager for an urgent report showing how many days of stock are left at the current rate of sale.

The results could not be obtained sufficiently quickly using COBOL or any other conventional programming language. The GIS specialist enters the query shown in Fig. 9.5. He creates a new file, which he calls FREDFILE, and creates two new data items in it. The first, called SALERATE, shows the average rate of sale of product number 75438 over the past 13 days. The second, called DAYSLEFT, shows how many days' worth of stock are left if the item continues to sell at that rate. The printout that results from the query in Fig. 9.5 is as follows:

LOC	DAYSLEFT	SALERATE	XRATIO
ATLANTA	3	805	4.0
BOSTON	10	512	2.7
CHICAGO	15	441	1.0
HOUSTON	20	325	0.8
MILWAUKEE	12	622	2.1
NEW YORK	3	2113	2.1
SAN FRANCISCO	25	401	0.7
ST. LOUIS	4	407	3.7

On seeing the result, the GIS specialist decides to add a title to the report and sort the output to show the warehouses that are running out fastest at the top of the list. He enters:

```
QUERY PRODFILE 'DEPLETION REPORT FOR PRODUCT NUMBER 75438,
PRODNAME
    SORT FREDFILE DAYSLEFT
    QUERY FREDFILE
    LIST RECORD
```

This time he obtains the following:

DEPLETION REPORT FOR PRODUCT NUMBER 75438, BEDWARMER

LOC	DAYSLEFT	SALERATE	XRATIO
ATLANTA	3	805	4.0
NEW YORK	3	2113	4.1
ST. LOUIS	4	407	3.7
BOSTON	10	512	2.7
MILWAUKEE	12	622	2.1
CHICAGO	15	441	1.0
HOUSTON	20	325	0.8
SAN FRANCISCO	25	401	0.7

The marketing manager holds a conference and decides that some of the product should be moved from the Houston warehouse to the Atlanta warehouse, from Boston to New York, and from Chicago to St. Louis. The advertising expenditure in San Francisco is stepped up.

The GIS specialist improves his routine and his report format in anticipation of its being used again and stores it. Decision making is rarely a one-step process. The decision maker is likely to come back with a series of refinements, a progressive reexamination of successive results. The ability to store GIS routines, report formats and interim files, and to modify them later is therefore important.

GIS has facilities for more elaborate logical and arithmetical operations. Its output can be edited and formatted as required. The user can query many segments at once, taking different data items from each, and can create many temporary or permanent files. These files, unlike that in the example, could be very large files. It does, however, need a specialist to use it, not a casual terminal user without training.

EASY-TO-USE DATA-BASE LANGUAGES
Although languages such as GIS are easy for a programmer to use, most (but not all) end users avoid them because of their seeming difficulty. However, other query languages with equivalent data manipulation capabilities have the characteristics listed in Box 8.2.

As we commented, many of the better data-base languages use *relational* data bases. Psychologists Greenblatt and Waxman [14] compared three such languages by teaching them quickly to undergraduate students and then testing their use of them. The results they achieved were as follows:

	QUERY-BY-EXAMPLE	SQL	Relational Algebra-Based Language
Mean age of student	19.3	24.8	20.9
Mean high school average	90.8	82.8	87.4
Mean college GPA (grade A = 4.0)	3.3	3.4	2.9
Training time (hours:minutes)	1:35	1:40	2:05
Mean total exam time (minutes)	23.3	53.9	63.3
Mean correct entries (%)	75.2	72.8	67.7
Mean time per query (minutes)	0.9	2.5	3.0

The students took from 1½ to 2 hours to learn these languages. The time to formulate a query was substantially shorter with QUERY-BY-EXAMPLE, and the accuracy was slightly higher. Typical queries were of the level of complexity of the QUERY-BY-EXAMPLE query used in Chapter 3, which needed 364 lines of COBOL to program (Fig. 3.3). The average time to formulate such a query was less than a minute.

QUERY-BY-EXAMPLE
It is desirable that a naive user approaching a terminal be required to know as little as possible

in order to get started. He may have to know a little more in order to use the subtleties of the language, but this should also be *minimized.*

He may approach a data base knowing very little about the names of the records or fields, or how to access them. Using QUERY-BY-EXAMPLE, I have taken a secretary who had never touched computers or terminals before, and explained in the simplest terms what a data base is. Within half an hour she was using the language, and exploring and manipulating the data stored.

The user sitting at the terminal is presented with the skeleton of a table on the screen, thus:

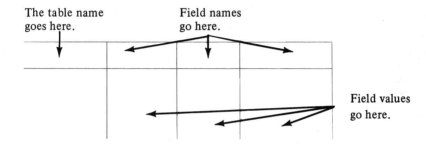

The user may fill in the spaces for table name, field name, or field value in order to express a query. He can also modify the data, or insert or delete new items.

P. stands for "print." If the user writes P. in one of the spaces, he wants the machine to fill in that space.

He might want to know what fields are in the EMPLOYEE record, so he types:

EMPLOYEE	P.	P.	P.

or, in a shorter form:

EMPLOYEE P.		

The terminal may respond, increasing the number of columns as necessary:

EMPLOYEE	EMPLOYEE #	NAME	SALARY	DEPARTMENT

The SALARY field heading may not appear if the user is not authorized to see salaries.

If he wants to know what employees work in the TIN BENDING department, he types:

EMPLOYEE	EMPLOYEE #	NAME	SALARY	DEPARTMENT
		P.		TIN BENDING

Their names are then listed in the NAME column.

He may not be sure of the correct title of the TIN BENDING department, so he puts a P. in the DEPARTMENT value column:

EMPLOYEE	EMPLOYEE #	NAME	SALARY	DEPARTMENT
				P.

The terminal will then list the names of all the departments, and the user can select the one he needs.

If the user wants to know the salaries of all the employees in the TIN BENDING department, he enters two P.'s:

EMPLOYEE	EMPLOYEE #	NAME	SALARY	DEPARTMENT
		P.	P.	TIN BENDING

To obtain all the information in the EMPLOYEE record about employees in the TIN BENDING department, he can write:

EMPLOYEE	EMPLOYEE #	NAME	SALARY	DEPARTMENT
P.				TIN BENDING

The machine will then fill in the whole skeleton for the TIN BENDING department.*

The user may be interested in SALARY values, but he does not know which record contains salaries. He can write SALARY in the empty skeleton and a P. in the table name position:

P.	SALARY		

It does not matter which column heading SALARY is written in. The machine displays the name of the tables, or names of several tables, that contain a field called SALARY.

Even more basic, the beginner might simply print P. in the table name position:

P.			

The machine then displays the names of *all tables that the user is allowed to see* (within whatever security constraints exist).

UNKNOWLEDGEABLE BEGINNERS   It will be seen that the user can approach this dialogue from the standpoint of uncompromising ignorance. He need not even know the names of any tables or fields in the data base. Yet 5 minutes after first sitting at the

---

*The software implementation of QUERY-BY-EXAMPLE at the time of writing does not contain all the features of the language described by Zloof [7, 9].

terminal, he can be making enquiries, even enquiries that would be fairly complex in other languages, such as: "List all employees with a training in cost accounting who joined the company before 1975 and are earning more than 20,000."

EMPLOYEE	EMPLOYEE #	NAME	SALARY	DEPT	YEAR OF HIRE	TRAINING
P.			$>$ 20000		$<$ 1975	ACCOUNTING

Here he is using the operators *greater than* and *less than* ($>$ and $<$). He may use any of the following inequality operators: $\neq$, $>$, $>=$, $<$, $<=$; $\neq$ can be replaced by $\neg$ or $\neg=$.

The user may have more columns than he needs on the screen (especially if the width of the display exceeds the width of the screen). He may blank out some of the column headings and reenter his request. The result omits the unwanted columns.

UPDATES

The user may be permitted to update certain fields. The update operator is "U.". If he wants to increase WEINBURG's salary to 21,000, he may type "U.", and "21,000" as follows:

EMPLOYEE	EMPLOYEE #	NAME	SALARY
U.		FLANAGON J E SNOOK S WEINBURG G	21000

As with any data-base user, dialogue security is important. If access to the data base is made easy, security must be made tight.

ARITHMETIC

The user can employ arithmetic operators. For example, he may want to increase WEINBURG's salary by 10%. He can do this as follows:

EMPLOYEE	EMPLOYEE #	NAME	SALARY
		WEINBURG G	20397

EMPLOYEE	EMPLOYEE #	NAME	SALARY
U.		WEINBURG G	20397 × 1.1

The machine responds by placing in the SALARY field the updated amount—22436.70.

EXAMPLES　　　　　With some of the more elaborate types of query, the user gives an *example* of the results he wants. In doing so he may type a value that is not an actual value but a made-up value. He indicates that it is a made-up example of a value by underlining it.

To illustrate this, suppose that the user was not permitted to know WEINBURG's salary, but nevertheless wanted to update it by 10%. He would type an example of what the salary might be (e.g., 500). It does not matter how far the example is from actuality. The update is done as follows:

EMPLOYEE	EMPLOYEE #	NAME	SALARY
U.		WEINBURG G	500 × 1.1

The machine indicates that the salary field has been updated.

This is rather like the use of algebra. To solve the same problem with algebra, we would say "Let the salary of WEINBURG = X. Change it to X × 1.1." X (underlined) could be used as the example above instead of 500. In practice, most users are not told to use X because it appears like algebra and the average bookkeeper or secretary wants nothing to do with algebra!

This is a potential powerful form of dialogue because algebra is powerful. X, or an example, could refer to many fields that should be changed with the same instruction. Thus everybody in the TIN BENDING department could be given a salary increase of 200 as follows:

EMPLOYEE	EMPLOYEE #	NAME	SALARY	DEPARTMENT
U.			500 + 200	TIN BENDING

"200" is real, it is not underlined. "500" is a guess, it is underlined. These two types of entries, real and imaginary, can be placed anywhere in the skeleton. This is like saying, "Let the salary of an employee in the TIN BENDING department be x. Update it to $x + 200$."

Partial underlines are also permitted. For example "WONG" or "WX" might be typed in the NAME column. This would mean that W is real, the other letters are imaginary. It would refer to all names beginning with "W." Similarly "WENDY" is an example referring to all names beginning with "WE." If he does not know WEINBURG's initials, he might type "WEINBURG X." Similarly, "20000" means all numbers ending with "000."

MORE COMPLEX QUERIES

More complex queries are possible, in which the user enters more than one row into the skeleton. The rows are linked by *examples*.

The user might have the following query: "Find the names of all employees who earn more than WEINBURG." He can guess a value for WEINBURG's salary, say 700. He then makes an entry requesting the names of employees who earn more than this value 700:

EMPLOYEE	NAME	SALARY
	WEINBURG	700
	P.	> 700

"WEINBURG earns x. Print the name of employees who earn $> x$." Thus:

EMPLOYEE	NAME	SALARY
	WEINBURG	X
	P.	> X

The user might want to ask the question: "What employees earn more than their manager?" Using the following table:

EMPLOYEE	NAME	MANAGER	SALARY

The user types an example of the result that he wants. Print the names of employees who work for <u>FRED</u>, let us say, and earn more than <u>700</u> (also an example), when <u>FRED</u> earns <u>700</u>:

EMPLOYEE	NAME	MANAGER	SALARY
	P.	<u>FRED</u>	> <u>700</u>
	<u>FRED</u>		<u>700</u>

The names of employees who earn more than their manager will be printed.

The cautious user may want to check that the result is what he wanted, so he might display the salaries in question. If WEINBURG's name is in the result, he might verify it by entering:

EMPLOYEE	NAME	MANAGER	SALARY
	WEINBURG	<u>Z</u>	P.
	<u>Z</u> P.		P.

The name of WEINBURG's manager will be printed and the salaries of both of them.

The user might want to ask "Does anyone earn more than the salaries of WEINBURG and FLANAGAN combined?" Let us imagine that WEIN-

BURG earns <u>2000</u> and FLANAGAN earns <u>3000</u>:

EMPLOYEE	NAME	MANAGER	SALARY
	WEINBURG		<u>2000</u>
	FLANAGAN		<u>3000</u>
	P.		$>$ <u>(2000 + 3000)</u>

IMPLICIT "AND" AND "OR"   To display all employees in the TIN BENDING department with a salary between 2000 and 3000, the skeleton is filled in as follows:

EMPLOYEE	NAME	SALARY	DEPARTMENT
	P. <u>FRED</u>	$>$ 2000	TIN BENDING
	<u>FRED</u>	$<$ 3000	

This request contains an AND condition:

(SALARY $>$ 2000) AND (SALARY $<$ 3000).

The AND condition is implicit in the way the skeleton is filled in. Similarly, an OR condition can be implicit. For example: "Display all employees earning more than 2000 who work in either the TIN BENDING or MILLING departments":

EMPLOYEE	NAME	SALARY	DEPARTMENT
	P.	$>$ 2000	TIN BENDING
	P.	$>$ 2000	MILLING

LINKS BETWEEN TABLES   The query a data user has often cannot be answered by reference to one type of record. It requires data in more than one record. With QUERY-BY-EXAMPLE it would require more than one table.

Often, managers perceive their data processing installation as being inflexible because their queries cannot be answered. The data to answer them is scattered through more than one type of record. Data-base management technology seeks to solve this problem by providing appropriate links between records. The *relational algebra* of a relational data-base system provides a powerful way of doing this [12].

The QUERY-BY-EXAMPLE user can display two or more different skeletons on the screen at once. He fills in both of them and then presses the ENTER key (or equivalent), indicating that this is one entry.

The skeletons we have shown above do not show who is the manager of the TIN BENDING department. Suppose that this information is given in a separate table, as follows:

DEPARTMENT	DEPT NAME	LOCATION	MANAGER

The user wants to know the salary of the manager of the TIN BENDING department. He enters the following query, using the example "FRED" to link the two tables:

DEPARTMENT	DEPT NAME	LOCATION	MANAGER
	TIN BENDING		FRED

EMPLOYEE	NAME	SALARY
	FRED	P.

The machine will print the salary of the manager of the TIN BENDING department.

The language is designed on the excellent principle that the thinking process the user follows is that which he would use to find the same information without a computer. Suppose that he had to answer the foregoing query with a set of printed tables. He would first look up the name of the manager of the TIN BENDING department and then look up his salary.

Suppose that the manufacturing of a product requires operations to be done in several departments as shown in the shop floor routing record:

SHOP FLOOR ROUTING	PART #	OPERATION #	OPERATION TYPE	DEPARTMENT

One location has several departments in it, and the query must be answered: "What parts have operations performed in the location XYZ?" Using manual tables, the user might look up what departments exist in the location XYZ, and then what parts have operations in those departments. With QUERY-BY-EXAMPLE he would do the same, as follows:

DEPARTMENT	DEPT NAME	LOCATION	MANAGER
	MILLING	XYZ	

SHOP FLOOR ROUTING	PART #	OPERATION #	OPERATION TYPE	DEPARTMENT
	P.			MILLING

FUNCTIONS

QUERY-BY-EXAMPLE has a number of built-in functions. These are represented by mnemonics such as the following:

SUM:	the sum of the values
CNT:	a count of the values
AVG:	the average of a set values
MAX:	the maximum value
MIN:	the minimum value
UN:	unique values (i.e., the values in a set excluding duplicates).

The average salary in the TIN BENDING department is found as follows:

EMPLOYEE	EMPLOYEE #	SALARY	DEPARTMENT
		P. AVG	TIN BENDING

The department whose manager has the maximum salary can be found as follows:

DEPARTMENT	DEPT. NAME	MANAGER
	X P.	FRED

EMPLOYEE	NAME	SALARY
	FRED	MAX

Again the user is formulating the query in the same way in which he would do it manually. He would look up the manager of each department, then look up his salary, and find the maximum salary. He could ask the machine to display the maximum salary by typing P. MAX in the salary column.

The user is not completely free of mnemonics because of the aforementioned functions. However, a beginner does need them. To avoid the need to remember mnemonics, the functions could be on specially labeled keys.

USE OF A CONDITION BOX

In addition to displaying one or more table skeletons, as described above, the user can display another two-dimensional object, called a CONDITION BOX:

CONDITIONS

The user can display a condition box any time he wants. He uses it to display conditions that are difficult to express in the tables. For example, the query "Display all employees earning more than 2000 who work in either the TIN BENDING or MILLING departments" could be expressed as follows:

EMPLOYEE	NAME	SALARY	DEPARTMENT
P.	S	D	

CONDITIONS
D = (MILLING/TIN BENDING
S = > 2000

Multiple conditions relating to one query can be listed in this way.

INSERTIONS AND DELETIONS   The QUERY-BY-EXAMPLE user can insert new entries into the tables, or delete entries (with appropriate security constraints). Insertions and deletions are done in the same style as query operations except that "I." is used instead of "P." for insertions, and "D." is used for deletions. To insert a new employee record the user calls up the EMPLOYEE skeleton and fills it in:

EMPLOYEE	EMPLOYEE #	NAME	SALARY	MANAGER	DEPARTMENT
I.	27511	BONTEMPO C	8000	MORTON A	SYSTEMS

Similarly, an employee record can be deleted:

EMPLOYEE	EMPLOYEE #	NAME	SALARY	MANAGER	DEPARTMENT
D.	27511	BONTEMPO C	8000	MORTON A	SYSTEMS

All employees in the SYSTEMS department may be deleted as follows:

EMPLOYEE	EMPLOYEE #	NAME	SALARY	MANAGER	DEPARTMENT
D.					SYSTEMS

Similarly, the user can create a new table or add a new field to an existing table. The language permits him to create, from existing tables, a new table which is either a *snapshot* or a *view*. A snapshot merely contains the values of the data as they were at the time of creation. A view is a table that will be dynamically updated to reflect changes in the base tables.

Psychologists Thomas and Gould [8] studied the behavior of subjects using QUERY-BY-EXAMPLE. They concluded that the advantages of this type of dialogue were:

- A tabular form of representation is helpful.
- The absence of keywords is helpful.
- The user has an explicit representation of the data to work with.
- The dialogue is easy for a naive beginner to learn.
- The language is "behaviorally extendable."

ON-LINE ENGLISH   It is sometimes commented that the ultimate in user-friendly dialogue would be to make the computer communicate in the user's own language. Many attempts have been made to program computers to understand English. Unfortunately, our own language is far more ambiguous than we realize. A computer can look up the words in a dictionary but still cannot resolve the ambiguities. A highly restricted version of this communication problem is the use of English to make data-base queries.

The user of a data-base system may type a query in free-form English. The software scans this input to see what words it can recognize. A record or field name in the data-base dictionary may have multiple *aliases* which the user may employ to refer to it. One such system is Cullinane's ON-LINE ENGLISH [15], which itself has had many names. It was originally called ROBOT [16]. Cullinane called it INTELLECT, then IQS, and then ON-LINE ENGLISH.

ON-LINE ENGLISH queries a retrieve-only file which is created from an operational file or data base (as in Fig. 9.4, except that the user language cannot update the file). A system administrator specifies how this file is created and builds its dictionary. He can add more aliases to the dictionary if the users type in words that are not interpretable.

A typical query against a personal file might be:

> **USER**: WHAT ARE THE NAMES OF ACCOUNTANTS IN NEW YORK.
>
> **TERMINAL**: PRINT NAME OF ALL EMPLOYEES WITH
> CITY = NEW YORK
> AND JOB = ACCOUNTANT

The system rephrases the query so that the user can determine whether it has been interpreted correctly. It print the number of records that must be retrieved to meet the request and then prints the answer.

> **TERMINAL**: THE NUMBER RECORDS TO RETRIEVE IS 15
> JONES H.A.
> KENDAL C.B.
> :
> :
> :

The user may key in another question which relates to the same query.

> **USER**: WHICH ONES EARN MORE THAN 20,000
>
> **TERMINAL**: PRINT NAME OF ALL EMPLOYEES WITH
> CITY = NEW YORK
> AND JOB = ACCOUNTANT
> AND SALARY > 20,000
>
> THE NUMBER OF RECORDS TO RETRIEVE IS 5
> JONES H.A.
> POTTER J.B.
> :
> :
> :

A vocabulary that a particular ON-LINE ENGLISH system can use is called its *lexicon*. The lexicon contains two classes of words: those provided with the software and those entered by the administrator for this particular system. The former are called *root* words. They are words such as WHAT, WHEN, IN, COUNT, STATISTICS, ALL, HOW MANY, EVERYTHING, and so on. Every installation can use these words. The second class are words unique to a particular application, such as EMPLOYEE, TITLE, SALARY, and so on. Synonyms for these can be entered, such as WORKER, PERSON, JOB, PAY, and so on.

If the software does not understand a word, it will say so:

USER: WHAT ARE THE NAMES OF ACCOUNTANTS IN POUGHKEEPSIE

TERMINAL: I'M NOT FAMILIAR WITH THE WORD "POUGHKEEPSIE"
IF IT'S A WORD YOU EXPECT TO FIND IN THE DATABASE HIT THE
RETURN KEY.
OTHERWISE EITHER FIX ITS SPELLING OR ENTER A SYNONYM FOR
IT.

USER: presses the return key.

TERMINAL: WHAT FIELD SHOULD IT APPEAR IN?

USER: CITY

TERMINAL: PRINT THE NAMES OF ALL EMPLOYEES WITH
CITY = POUGHKEEPSIE
AND JOB = ACCOUNTANT . . . .

The user may wish to see what fields are available in a given record. He could type:

USER: WHAT FIELDS ARE IN THE CITY FILE?

TERMINAL:

FIELDS IN THE FILE CITY

FIELD NAME	SEARCHABLE	SORTABLE	FORMAT	LENGTH
NAME	FAST	YES	ALPHABETIC	30
STATE	FAST	NO	ALPHABETIC	15
POPULATION	SLOW	YES	NUMERIC	7
:				
:				

This indicates that some fields are searchable FAST. This means that these fields have a search index. SLOW means that they do not have a search index and that to find records of a given value would require a time-consuming scan of the file.

The user can sort the data on certain fields and not others.

The user can request statistics and the printing of bar graphs.

The software for ON-LINE ENGLISH and other free English query languages (LADDER, RENDEZVOUS [4]) is complex because so many types of input wording must be interpreted.

Natural English input is attractive and fascinating to users who have not used a terminal before. It encourages them to begin. Unfortunately, it also encourages them to key in questions that the computer cannot answer. In some cases these seem to the user to be highly relevant questions. This problem is referred to as *semantic overshoot*.

Furthermore, natural English dialogue does not impose a structure on the data as do the tabular forms of dialogue, such as QUERY-BY-EXAMPLE or Univac's MAPPER. This structure is often valuable for manipulating data or generating reports. Learning more structured dialogues sometimes helps users to compose complex queries which they may not have thought of otherwise. Learning the semantics of more artificial dialogues assists users to clarify their thinking about manipulating the data. Seeing the menus of a viewdata-like dialogue helps the user to find his way through a complex mass of data. These dialogue structures help the user to navigate, tell him what is available, and prod him into taking useful action.

The user community needs both structured dialogues and natural English dialogues. *It may be desirable in the future to have end-user systems that combine the two.*

REFERENCES

1. Manuals and information on the MARK IV File Management System are available from Informatics, Inc., MARK IV Systems Company, 21050 Vanowen St., Canoga Park, CA 91303.

2. GIS manuals are available from IBM Corp., 1133 Westchester Ave., White Plains, NY 10604.

3. *User's Guide to DATATRIEVE-11,* DEC Manual No. AA–C742A–TC, Digital Equipment Corporation, Maynard, MA, 1978.

4. E.F. Codd, "How About Recently?" (English dialogue with RENDEZ-VOUS Version I), in B. Schneiderman, *Databases: Improving Usability and Responsiveness,* Academic Press, New York, 1978.

5. D.D. Chamberlin et al., "SEQUEL 2: A Unified Approach to Data Definition, Manipulation and Control," *IBM Journal of Research and Development,* Vol. 20, pp 560–575, 1976.

6. G.D. Held, M.R. Stonebraker, and E. Wong, "INGRES: A Relational Data Base System," *Proceedings,* National Computer Conf., Vol. 44, 1975.

7. M.M. Zloof, "Query-by-Example: A Data Base Language," *IBM Systems Journal,* No. 4, 1977.

8. J.C. Thomas and J.D. Gould, "A Psychological Study of Query-by-Example," *Proceedings,* National Computer Conf., Vol. 44, pp 439–445, 1975.

9. M.M. Zloof, *Query-by-Example: A Data-Base Management Language,* IBM Research Report available from the author, IBM Thomas J. Watson Research Center, Yorktown Heights, NY.

10. N. McDonald and M. Stonebraker "CUPID: The Friendly Query Language," *Proceedings,* ACM Pacific Conf., San Francisco, 1975.

11. M.E. Senko, "DIAM II and FORAL LP: Making Pointed Queries with Light Pen," *Proceedings,* IFIP Congress 1977, North–Holland, Amsterdam, 1977.

12. Relational data bases are explained simply in the author's *Computer Data Base Organization,* 2nd ed. Prentice-Hall, Inc., Englewood Cliffs, NJ, 1977.

13. This example is taken from an IBM slide presentation on GIS/VS, No. GV 20–0480, Nov. 1973.

14. D. Greenblatt and J. Waxman "A Study of Three Database Query Languages," in B. Schneiderman, *Databases: Improving Usability and Responsiveness,* Academic Press, New York, 1978.

15. Manuals on IQS (also called INTELLECT and ON-LINE ENGLISH) are available from Cullinane Corporation, 400 Blue Hill Drive, Westwood, MA 02090.

16. L.R. Harris, "User-Oriented Data Base Query with the ROBOT Natural Language Query System," *International Journal of Man–Machine Studies,* Vol. 9, 1977.

10 APPLICATION GENERATORS FOR END USERS

PRODUCTIVITY
AND THE END-USER
REQUIREMENT As we have stressed, spectacular increases in application development productivity have been achieved in some corporations with the use of application generators. Most of these generators are appropriate for use by skilled professionals, however, rather than by end users. Some application generators have been sold as being "end-user tools" and then rejected because they are too difficult for end users.

Internal installations within IBM achieved a quoted *27 times improvement in productivity* by replacing COBOL with ADF (Chapter 16), but they described the type of person who accomplished this as "ADF acrobats."

End users are unlikely to become "acrobats" in the use of any complex language. Some of the best query languages and report generators are now very easy for end users to learn and use. The same good human factoring is possible and highly desirable with the application generators. A major class of application generator is, in fact, a natural extension of query languages and report generators, as indicated in Fig. 8.3.

Some data-base query languages provide the capability to update a data base as well as query it and to create relations. We illustrated *updating* with QUERY-BY-EXAMPLE in Chapter 9. Relations can also be *created* with QUERY-BY-EXAMPLE by filling in a blank skeleton.

Although QUERY-BY-EXAMPLE was designed to be a data-base query language, many of its users are in fact using it for application development. This has been clear from their presentations at GUIDE and SHARE conferences.

At IBM's T.J. Watson Research Center there are many users defining and running their own applications. They include secretaries with mail logs, correspondence, travel expense, and capital equipment applications and administrative staff with personnel records, office space control, purchase requisitions, education bookings, and so on. In addition, technical staff are using it with applications such as experiment tracking, satellite phone, system analysis, and sputtering and reactive ion etch rate recording [1]. These users create their own files or data bases, update their data, manipulate the data, and have listings printed. This saves them much paperwork.

Although QUERY-BY-EXAMPLE is easy to use, it lacks (at the time of writing) many of the features that an application generator ought to have. Many extensions to it have been proposed and demonstrated [2–4].

Other products combine data-base (and file) query and update capability with a much richer set of functions for generating reports, graphics, calculations, and application logic. They include Sperry Univac's MAPPER (Chapter 11), various extensions to APL (Chapter 13), a host of minicomputer products such as ADMINS 11, and other products listed in Box 2.1. Most of these products are not as easy to use as QUERY-BY-EXAMPLE. What is needed is a user interface, simple and seductive, to attract the vast hoards of end users who stay away from terminals, and powerful facilities for those who progress beyond the beginners' subset.

Some case histories show application generators being adopted by end users, sweeping through an organization, and having a major effect on its productivity (Chapter 11). These case histories show the possibilities, but in most organizations the potential of today's software has not been realized either by end users or DP executives. There is a cultural barrier to end-user application generation that must be overcome. That requires software with excellent human factoring and a change in both perception and techniques of DP management. Some of the best case histories are those in which the end users have done it themselves in isolation from, and often in defiance of, DP management. Much better would be a situation where DP provides the leadership.

CODASYL
END-USER
FACILITIES

CODASYL (Conference On DAta SYstems Languages), the organization that created COBOL, has formed a committee to develop facilities that enable noncomputer personnel to make use of computers [5]. Its membership is drawn from a wide cross section of the computing community, manufacturers, computer users, and other interested organizations.

The charter of this committee is given in Box 10.1.

The CODASYL committee has specified three categories of end users who use computers:

1. *Indirect.* These are end users who use computers through other people. Examples are customers, airline passengers, and so on.

2. *Intermediate.* People who specify the business information requirements that DP provides (e.g., marketing, manufacturing, education, accounting, etc.).

3. *Direct.* End users who come into direct contact with computers to accomplish their work. These people have access to terminals and include engineers, scientists, and accountants.

BOX 10.1   From the charter of the CODASYL committee on end-user facilities

Scope

To develop specifications for facilities which will allow non-computer personnel to interact with a computer and its resident data in a manner *natural* to such users. Such specifications should be candidates for potential standardization.

Program of Work

1. The committee should complete the specification of a forms-oriented End-User Facility (EUF) as described in the End-User Facility Task Group (EUFTG) Progress Report [5]. Emphasis should be given to the early availability of the specification of a viable product which lends itself to possible future enhancements.

2. The initial version of the forms-oriented EUF should address itself to user interaction with a data base definable by the CODASYL Data Definition Language and consideration should be given to future extensions to interfaces with data bases or files definable through other means.

3. The committee should organize the work so that its specifications can be published in an EUF Journal of Development, maintenance of which will be the responsibility of the Committee.

4. The committee should consider future work toward specifications of end-user facilities aimed at other classes of end users other than those addressed by the forms-oriented approach. Such consideration should, however, be given a low priority until such time as an initial specification of the forms-oriented approach has been produced.

5. Messages produced by the EUF should be accessible by COBOL communications-oriented facilities.

Source: Ref. [5].

Each class is dependent on the computer to accomplish its work, but none is trained in programming or computer operation.

FORMS-ORIENTED APPROACH   The committee believes that the primary approach should be through the use of forms. They say that this is the most natural interface to use, as the majority of end users already complete many different types of forms, such as purchase order forms, memorandums, expense forms, time sheets, tax forms, and application forms. This is also true in personal life, where we all have to deal with a multitude of forms of different types. Users are familiar with manipulating forms, preparing summaries, distributing forms, discarding copies, and amending or improving forms.

The use of forms for end-user application generators seems questionable. Forms *have* been used for some data-base query facilities, but this method of operation has not established itself as superior to well-designed on-line dialogues. On the contrary the data-base languages which have had most success with end user have been *interactive* and not forms-oriented. Some forms-oriented software has had extensive use by systems analysts but has been rejected by end users as being too difficult in some corporations.

DIALOGUE PROGRAM GENERATORS   Many end users employ terminal dialogues which have been preprogrammed for them, often in languages such as COBOL or PL/1. Such dialogues are time consuming to program and debug, especially because they must deal with any keying mistake that users can make. Many such dialogues for end users could be generated by *end users* from a description of the dialogue if suitable compilers existed. We would then have a *dialogue program generator,* a type of application generator.

In the field of computer-assisted instruction there has been much emphasis on the generation of dialogue programs from course-writing languages [6]. This was considered important because courses should be written by teachers, not programmers. Teachers cannot program and programmers cannot teach. The same is true with other types of end users. Commercial dialogues can be generated by similar techniques, although greater precision is usually needed in the handling of input. If end users everywhere have their own intelligent machines it is vital that they should be able to create their own terminal applications with some flexible easy-to-use technique.

To illustrate how simple the programming of dialogue can be made, we will discuss a language written at the San Francisco Medical Center of the University of California [7]. The language was used successfully by third-grade students (average age: 8) to produce dialogue programs for each other's use. An improved version of this language, called PILOT (Programmed Inquiry, Learning Or Teaching), now available on the Apple computer, uses a number of simple instruction codes, including the following:

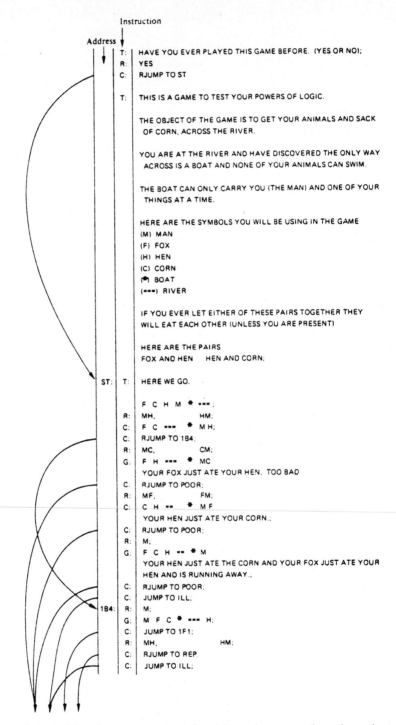

Instruction

Address

	T:	HAVE YOU EVER PLAYED THIS GAME BEFORE. (YES OR NO);
	R:	YES
	C:	RJUMP TO ST
	T:	THIS IS A GAME TO TEST YOUR POWERS OF LOGIC.
		THE OBJECT OF THE GAME IS TO GET YOUR ANIMALS AND SACK OF CORN, ACROSS THE RIVER.
		YOU ARE AT THE RIVER AND HAVE DISCOVERED THE ONLY WAY ACROSS IS A BOAT AND NONE OF YOUR ANIMALS CAN SWIM.
		THE BOAT CAN ONLY CARRY YOU (THE MAN) AND ONE OF YOUR THINGS AT A TIME.
		HERE ARE THE SYMBOLS YOU WILL BE USING IN THE GAME
		(M) MAN
		(F) FOX
		(H) HEN
		(C) CORN
		(⛵) BOAT
		(===) RIVER
		IF YOU EVER LET EITHER OF THESE PAIRS TOGETHER THEY WILL EAT EACH OTHER (UNLESS YOU ARE PRESENT)
		HERE ARE THE PAIRS
		FOX AND HEN HEN AND CORN;
ST:	T:	HERE WE GO.
		F C H M ⛵ ===;
	R:	MH, HM;
	C:	F C === ⛵ M H;
	C:	RJUMP TO 1B4;
	R:	MC, CM;
	G:	F H === ⛵ MC
		YOUR FOX JUST ATE YOUR HEN. TOO BAD
	C:	RJUMP TO POOR;
	R:	MF, FM;
	C:	C H == ⛵ M F
		YOUR HEN JUST ATE YOUR CORN.,
	C:	RJUMP TO POOR;
	R:	M;
	G:	F C H == ⛵ M
		YOUR HEN JUST ATE THE CORN AND YOUR FOX JUST ATE YOUR HEN AND IS RUNNING AWAY.,
	C:	RJUMP TO POOR;
	C:	JUMP TO ILL;
1B4:	R:	M;
	G:	M F C ⛵ === H;
	C:	JUMP TO 1F1;
	R:	MH, HM;
	C:	RJUMP TO REP.
	C:	JUMP TO ILL;

Figure 10.1 The programming of a dialogue by a seventh-grade student using the PILOT language, now available on the Apple computer. (Reproduced with permission from Reference [7].)

T:　　Type the following.

R:　　Recognize the following item in the response.

R2:　　Recognize either of the following two items in the response (R3 provides for three items, and so on).

G:　　Good. If the response is recognized, type the following.

B:　　Bad. If the response is not one that can be recognized, type the following.

C:　　Control, such as transfer to another point in the programming.

Figure 10.1 illustrates the use of these instructions. It shows the work of a 12-year-old student in building a program to represent the puzzle of the fox, the hen, and the bag of corn that must be transported across a river. Other students used the same language to create computer dialogues of their own invention. The results covered a very wide range of different types of dialogues.

In the examples, "RJUMP" means *transfer when a response is recognized.* The language also contains conditional branching facilities.

The machine must recognize what the user types in. Sometimes the response can be one of a small group of precise replies. This is the case with the dialogue in Fig. 10.1. In other cases, approximate replies, numbers within a certain range, misspelled words, and so on must be acknowledged.

In the world of cheap computers, networks, and data bases, we need end-user dialogue generators which, as in the illustration above, are child's play.

DIALOGUES FOR GENERATING DIALOGUES　　　An attractive way of generating a dialogue is to *use* a dialogue employing the same terminal. The designer uses the terminal to specify the dialogue he wants to create, then to test and adjust the dialogue.

If the process is intended for end users without programming skills the rules of Box 8.3 should apply. Dialogue generators can be designed for persons with no programming skills.

Suppose that a dialogue is to be created in which the user will fill in a panel on the screen. The dialogue for creating this dialogue might proceed as follows. The designer begins by being presented with a matrix on the screen, such as that at the top of page 154.

The designer can refer to a row on the screen by typing its number. He can refer to a column by typing its letter. Any block on the matrix may become a field. The designer can refer to a field in the matrix by typing its two-dimensional address (e.g., 1B, 4C, 6F, etc.). He can refer to a group of fields by typing 3B to 3E or 2A to 12A, and so on.

When he types an area of the matrix the terminal asks him how that

	A	B	C	D....	Z
1					
2					
3					
4					
:					
40					

PLEASE TYPE AN AREA OF THIS MATRIX

area is to be used, thus:

DESIGNER: 1

TERMINAL: ROW 1

PLEASE INDICATE WHAT TYPE OF FIELD IS REQUIRED:
1. INPUT VARIABLE
2. COMPUTED VARIABLE
3. TEXT
4. FIELD HEADING
5. BLANK

DESIGNER: 3

TERMINAL: TYPE THE FULL CONTENTS OF THIS FIELD INCLUDING BLANKS

DESIGNER: FACTORY WORK ORDER

TERMINAL:

	A	B	C	D....	Z
1	FACTORY WORK ORDER				
2					
3					
4					
:					
40					

PLEASE TYPE AN AREA OF THIS MATRIX

The designer indicates similarly that row 2 will be blank. He then selects field 3A and indicates that it will be the heading "APPROXIMATE DATE DUE"; the areas can be made to be of any length. He selects field 3B and indicates that this will be an input variable. The terminal asks for its format.

TERMINAL: TYPE THE FORMAT OF INPUT VARIABLE 3B

DESIGNER: 12/31/99

This indicates a numeric field in three parts with the maximum values as shown.

The terminal displays the result so far:

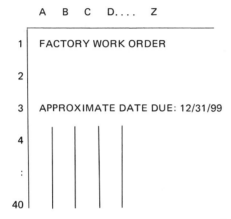

Row 4 is blank. Row 5 is indicated to be a set of headings:

PLEASE TYPE AN AREA OF THIS MATRIX

The designer indicates that fields 6A to 13A will contain an input variable.

TERMINAL: TYPE THE FORMAT OF INPUT VARIABLE 6A TO 13A

DESIGNER: 9999

The terminal again displays the result so far:

A   B   C   D....   Z

1	FACTORY WORK ORDER							
2								
3	APPROXIMATE DATE DUE: 12/31/99							
4								
5	QTY	CATEGORY	SIZE	MATERIAL	DESCRIPTION	UNIT PR.	LABOR CH.	TOTAL
6	9999							
7	9999							
8	9999							
9	9999							
10	9999							
11	9999							
12	9999							
13	9999							

The designer continues until all the fields of the panel have been specified. Where fields are computed variables, the designer specifies how they are computed:

TERMINAL: 14H
                HOW IS THIS FIELD COMPUTED?

DESIGNER: 14H=6H+7H+8H+9H+10H+11H+12H+13H

The designer builds up the screen a step at a time, making adjustments as he wishes. When it is complete the system can present users with a blank panel to fill in. The designer will specify any checks for completeness or accuracy that should be applied.

STANDARD   When one studies the dialogues that have been
DIALOGUES   implemented [8] one can be impressed by the
                      number of interactive ways there are of achieving
the same end result. In spite of the diversity of alternative dialogue structures, many of the different end-user results can be achieved with a small group of *standardized* dialogues.

There are two giant advantages in standardizing dialogue structures rather than allowing a proliferation of different forms of dialogue to be written for different applications. First, application-independent software (or microcode or hardware) can be produced. The task of creating and debugging customized dialogues for each application is very time consuming and expensive. Application-independent dialogues can be built into the software or facilities for distributed intelligence. It could be provided not only by computer manufacturers and software houses, but also possibly by telecommunications companies as a feature of "intelligent networks" such as AT&T's ACS.

Second, standard dialogue structures provide *familiarity* for end users. Users become familiar with a certain method of obtaining information or achieving results. This familiarity is important in helping many users to overcome their fear of computers. Your use of the *telephone* and the various sounds it makes is standardized, and this is essential for the public using it. Similar standardization is desirable in computer dialogues for mass users.

Among the possibilities for standardized dialogues are the following:

1. Menu Selection Dialogues

The user receives a list of items on a screen and selects one of them. This results in another list being displayed, from which he selects one item; and so on. If the response times are fast, he can quickly narrow down his choice to one in millions.

Such a system can display frames of information. Some are frames of data; some are menu frames which enable the user to find other frames. Each frame has a unique number which the user can record and hence obtain that frame directly without any preamble. Having found a frame, the user can read the next or previous frame in a sequence. Some frames contain pointers to other frames. Some contain YES or NO, or other questions, which cause the user to select another frame implicitly.

This is the basis of the European *viewdata (videotex)* systems such as Britain's *Prestel,* which can provide an information service and computer applications on the home television screen [9]. Experience with large numbers of people providing information for viewdata has shown that an amazing range of computer applications can fit into this standard dialogue structure. Some very complex decision-making processes can be split into a tree structure in which each node of the tree is a relatively simple decision which can be represented on one menu screen. For example, medical prediagnosis interviews have been constructed in this fashion. The patient entering a clinic answers a set of questions presented by a terminal. The choice of next question' is determined by the patient's answers to the previous ones. The dialogue contains a variety of cross checks about the conclusion that is being reached.

For repetitive use in commercial situations such a dialogue needs fast response times (ideally less than a second) and the ability to make shortcuts, and hence requires distributed intelligence.

People who have never touched a terminal before find viewdata very easy to use. Its use of color and block graphics can make it very appealing. Some computer vendors are making it a standard end-user facility.

2. Data Entry Dialogues

Data entry dialogues have been designed which can handle a variety of different types of data entry. Some such packages are parameter driven, so that features in the package can be utilized or omitted through the selection of parameters.

The user may fill in screen formats, respond to prompts, or respond to menus or other screens. The data entered may be checked for valid character type, permissible values, range, and so on, and preestablished messages returned to the operator when entries are invalid. Groups of entries may be totaled on various fields or columns and further checks applied (e.g., that percentages add to 100, that a balance is zero, or that a hash total has a certain value). Audit controls can be applied to the data. Given such software the designer creates the formats and messages, but does not write any programs.

3. Data Output Facilities

Data output software has been designed to generate reports and screen displays, fill in preprinted stationery, edit the output, and perform calculations. Report generators are in widespread use.

4. Data-Base Dialogues

As discussed in Chapter 9, there are a variety of languages designed to extract information from a data base, search the data base, create listings, and screen displays or reports.

5. Text Entry and Editing

Advanced text-handling systems provide the ability to enter text, modify it, edit it, have its spelling checked, right-justify it, and fit it into appropriate page sizes, retrieve stored portions of text and edit them into new text, change type fonts, index and abstract it, and so on. Such facilities may become a standard dialogue on future word-processing machines.

6. Graphics Dialogues

A picture is worth a thousand words. The use of graphics on computer screens is a much more effective way of conveying information for some applications than lists of figures or tables. Packages exist which will automatically plot curves from data or create a variety of types of charts, and in some cases allow the user to interact with the charts. The user may adjust the display to obtain it in a form that is most meaningful to him, and may be able to change certain variables and observe the effect that such a change has on the results.

Very effective graphics software is available for certain specific applications.

7. Applications Used by the General Public

There are many applications which members of the general public could carry out for themselves, such as obtaining banking and travel agent services; obtaining bookings for theaters, restaurants, ballgames, rented cars, and hotels; obtaining insurance; and so on. The magnetic-stripe bank card with the third (writable) stripe could form the basis for some of these applications. So could viewdata (videotex) television sets. In some countries it has been proposed that computer terminal services for the public should be made available in public libraries.

Standardization of techniques that are easy to use, such as viewdata and QUERY-BY-EXAMPLE, will increase the familiarity of computer interaction and remove much of the fear that end users have.

REFERENCES

1. S.P. de Jong, "The System for Business Automation (SBA): A Unified Application Development System," Research Report RC 7955 (No. 34539), IBM Research Division, Yorktown, NY, 1979.

2. S.P. de Jong, and M.M. Zloof, "Application Design within the System for Business Automation (SBA)." *Proceedings,* 12th Design Automation Conf., Boston, June 1975, pp. 69–76.

3. S.P. de Jong, and M.M. Zloof, "Communications within the System for Business Automation (SBA)," Research Report RC 6788, IBM T.J. Watson Research Center, Yorktown Heights, NY, October 1977.

4. M.M. Zloof, and S.P. de Jong, "The System for Business Automation (SBA): Programming Language," *Communications of the ACM,* Vol. 20, No. 6, pp. 267–280, June 1976.

5. CODASYL End-User Facilities Committee Status Report, North-Holland Publishing Company, Information and Management 2 (1979), 137–163.

6. For example, IBM's COURSEWRITER Language, IBM Manual No. Y26 1580, IBM Corp., White Plains, NY, 1979.

7. J.A. Starkweather, "A Common Language for a Variety of Conversational Programming Needs," in *Computer Assisted Instruction, A Book of Readings.* R.C. Atkinson and H.A. Wilson, eds., Academic Press, New York, 1969.

8. See video training courses by James Martin on the design of terminal dialogue in Deltak's *Advanced Technology Library,* Deltak, Oak Brook, IL 60521.

9. James Martin, *Viewdata and the Information Society,* Prentice-Hall, Inc., Englewood Cliffs, NJ, 1982.

11 END-USER-DRIVEN COMPUTING

When DP professionals admit, reluctantly, that end users can create their own applications (most do not admit anything of the sort!) they usually think of simplistic applications only, such as making data-base queries of a rather artificial textbook nature:

LIST ALL EMPLOYEES WITH JOB = ACCOUNTANT,
SALARY ≤ 20,000 AND YEAR-OF-HIRE > 1975.

This chapter describes a case study of *complex* applications for production control in a factory that makes particularly intricate products. All the applications were created by the end users without any help from the DP department. This experience is described, at least by its enthusiasts, as the predominant computer success story in recent years in that factory.

WHITE-COLLAR PRODUCTIVITY

The need to improve the productivity of white-collar workers is generally recognized and much talked about. Almost two-thirds of the United States work force are white-collar workers. For the last decade their overall productivity has improved little.

National productivity *as a whole* cannot improve much unless there is a change in the productivity of the growing white-collar segment.

Many studies have been done on the productivity of white-collar workers. A general conclusion is that technology alone is not enough. It is *people* who improve productivity—their work attitudes, their attention to time and efficiency, and above all, their motivation [1,2].

Motivation is a complex subject. People need to be motivated by their work itself. They need an atmosphere that values achievement. Most people respond well when challenged to make improvements, but in much white-collar work this challenge is missing.

Various corporations have improved employee motivation by allowing them to *participate in the design of their jobs.* Employee participation has been used to redesign offices, improve form design, and modify work flow as described in this chapter. Regardless of computers this has been effective in improving the work methods, improving employee morale, and improving productivity.

The term "paper*less* office" is sometimes used. It is rather similar to the terms "horse*less* carriage" or "wire*less* telegraphy." For the first twenty years of the horseless carriage it was a vehicle shaped as though it might be pulled by a horse. It took twenty years to discover that a good shape for a motorcar was quite different. It took twenty years to discover that the main application of wireless technology was broadcasting, which had a quite different topology from wireless telegraphy. Similarly in some organizations it will take twenty years to discover that the flow of work in the *paperless* office should be quite different from the flow of work designed for paper.

Much administrative invention is needed to create efficient operations in the paperless office environment. Employee participation in this process of invention is vital. The sweeping changes that are needed will often become a very small price to pay at a time—a rapid succession of very small improvements coming from many employees. Many such employees will find that their jobs are more challenging when they learn to use computers as described in this chapter.

MANUFACTURING   The story begins in the late 1970s. The dispatchers,
CASE STUDY   foremen, expediters, and other staff who make the
                factory operate did almost everything with pencil-and-paper methods, aided by a few huge computer listings. They asked DP for on-line production control applications and DP said that would take a few years. There were, however, big expensive problems on the shop floor that needed computer control.

The manufacturing department assumed responsibility for bringing in a machine with which they hoped they could create production control functions independently of the DP department. A rental (not purchase) UNIVAC computer was selected because of demonstrations of this system being employed by end users for manufacturing control within Sperry Univac, using a software system called MAPPER.

The DP department was somewhat aggravated. The MAPPER enthusiast we interviewed described their reaction:

> We're going to give them enough rope to hang themselves. The machine will be out of the door in 30 days!

Initially, there were four end users. This grew to several hundred. The system was a spectacular success and the culture of using MAPPER spread to many other applications. At the time of this study no programmers or DP professionals were involved. The applications had been created by shop floor personnel and later as the culture spread, by end users in other areas.

WORK IN PROGRESS

In the beginning the concern was entirely with work in progress.

The shop floor area supervisors used to spend about 4 hours a week creating their work-in-progress reports. There were nine supervisors, so the labor saved in automating this would pay for a small system. All the supervisors were badly pressed for time and could put the saved time to good use.

It took 2 days to create a MAPPER work-in-progress reporting facility in which the status of jobs was entered into screens. As soon as work-in-progress reporting was computerized, it revealed what was known but rarely admitted: control on the shop floor was very loose. With pencil-and-paper reporting, inaccuracies crept in, and much fell through the cracks.

> The supervisors would say things like: "I saw Joe working on that so I don't need to write that that's in my area." But then Joe got sick on Wednesday and didn't come back. The report went from area 1 to area 2. The guy in area 2 didn't pick up Joe's job. The guy in area 1 couldn't put it back on his report. His report was gone. So the computer never knew about it. All this stuff kind of got lost by the wayside.

The introduction of terminals soon brought the realization that much tighter control was possible. Initially, it caused some painful adjustments.

> The area supervisors went crazy. They said: "Look at this. That says $12 million in my area. I've only got $9 million." Stuff got put on the side. They forgot about it. They never claimed it. If a guy *thought* he was going to have something done, he'd not put it in the work-in-progress report.

With MAPPER everything became real-time—no pencil-and-paper reports at the end of the week. The *expediter* in the factory is a general problem solver. He finds out why orders are late, reshuffles the scheduling of jobs, is notified of jobs that are held up due to missing parts, and tries to locate such parts. The expediter can be greatly helped in doing this by having better information.

> He'll say: "That machine is one day late. How come?" Well that machine is late because that subassembly is late. Why is that subassembly late? Because the PC card is late. Why is that PC card late? Because this bracket isn't there.

MAPPER permitted the supervisors and expeditors to create the information reporting that they needed. A supervisor could build files and create data entry screens with which shop floor workers could enter data into these files. The files could be manipulated in a diversity of ways. The supervisors and expediters could search for information in them and could generate any form of reports that they needed. This began to appear to be the tool they needed for gaining control of the highly complex operations that constitute the movement of work through the factory. To do so would greatly improve the shop floor productivity.

An order was scheduled to hit the floor on day X. Sixty-eight percent of the time the components weren't there. They never tracked an order as being overdue until the due date came. They missed *their own internal* projection dates most of the time.

A step at a time the reporting procedures were created to deal with this situation. The users tended to think of the software as a replacement for their filing cabinets, paperwork, and reports. However, unlike these, it could coordinate information from many different areas.

MAPPER

MAPPER is a Sperry Univac software system running on Series 1100 computers. It stands for "MAintaining, Preparing, and Processing Executive Reports." Its processing capability has steadily grown over the years and it is now capable of doing many of the functions normally found in commercial data processing. The applications in most of its installations, however, are created by end users.

MAPPER is an on-line system. Its users create files, reports, and processing procedures at display terminals. Reports can also be printed. Hundreds of users can employ it at the same time on a large system and can transmit reports to one another's terminals.

Users learn to use it, typically, in a 2-day class. Its simple functions are easy to use and these are used most of the time. However it has *many* functions and variations of functions, and learning to use all of them takes some time. Most users never learn all the functions. Other enthusiastic users enjoy their newfound skill and experiment with all the functions they can. Some become expert on MAPPER's intricacies, but this expertise is not needed to obtain results.

Calculations and logic can be expressed in simple FORTRAN-like statements. These enable MAPPER to do complex processing if required.

DATA BASE

MAPPER employs a collection of shared tables or files of data—a simple form of relational data base. There can be many different files. They are arranged into groups of eight, which users are encouraged to think of as filing cabinets. Each filing cabinet has eight drawers and each drawer contains a file of reports. Every report in a drawer has the same format and can be displayed on a terminal screen. These reports can be created, stored, updated, searched, transmitted, analyzed, and manipulated by the end users.

The filing cabinet (for reasons known only to Univac) is called a *mode*. The drawers are called a *type*. Each report in the drawer is referred to with a *report identification number* (RID). The on-line storage of MAPPER can contain many filing cabinets. The eight drawers in a cabinet are labeled B through I. The cabinet also contains a drawer, type A, containing nonformatted data. Each drawer can contain a small or large number of reports and each report can contain a small or large number of lines of data, many thousands if necessary.

To control security each terminal is identified and each user is identified when he signs on with a password. When he signs on, a user is placed into a given mode (filing cabinet). Each mode has two numbers. Even numbers are for read/write capability and odd numbers are for read-only access.

A report is often too large to display on a screen at one time. The user can scroll it left and right or up and down. The user can also indicate the first line of the report to be displayed. It might, for example, be the 105th line of a 180-line report. The report can be displayed in any of six formats. Some of these formats may condense it by omitting some of its fields. The user can define and change the formats.

The user can sort the reports by any field, or by up to five fields. He may sort it so that the most important information is at the top. For example, he may sort it by *estimated date of completion minus scheduled delivery date* so that items in the greatest danger of being late are at the top of the report.

Each report contains a standard line that shows the date and time of the last update, the last person to update the report, the date of origin of the report and its report identification number.

DATA ENTRY

In many cases a user creates a skeleton format of a report which is designed for data entry. The same user, or other users, perhaps keyboard operators, will enter data into the skeleton. Various checks can be applied to the data entry.

SEARCHING

The filing cabinet drawers can be searched in a variety of ways:

- A *single report* can be searched for specified lines of data, *all reports* in a drawer can be searched, or certain selected reports can be searched.

- A single field type or multiple field types can be the basis of the search.

- The search can be for fields of a given value and fields of a range of values.
- The search can be for arithmetic combinations of fields, for example all lines with

(forecast completion date – scheduled delivery date) > 0.

- Data can be searched on the basis of a mask with multiple fields or partial fields.
- Data can be searched using a previously stored procedure.

MATCHING DATA   Data in one filing cabinet drawer can be *matched* against data in another drawer. For example, two report types might contain the field *product number.* MAPPER might be instructed to create a report in which data about the product from both of these drawers is combined into a single new report. This is essentially like a JOIN operation in relational data-base parlance. Given the search and match capabilities a user can browse in the filing cabinets to extract information in a wide variety of different ways.

REPORT FORMATTING   The user can format reports in many different ways. He can select field types to be displayed. He can display totals, subtotals, or averages. The fields can be combined with arithmetical expressions. The report can be sorted on any field, grouped into ranges of values, summarized, and so on.

Stored together with each report type (i.e., for each drawer of the filing cabinet) are the six formats in which the report can appear. The report can be displayed or printed, or transmitted to a distant station.

REPORT PROCESSING FUNCTIONS   A variety of functions are available to the terminal users in employing MAPPER. These are listed in Fig. 11.1. A variety of computing operations are possible with functions such as *ARITHMETIC* and *TOTALIZE.* In addition, the user can employ the *RUN* function. This enables an experienced user to build a processing routine which can be stored and executed when needed. An inexperienced user often employs routines that have been created by a skilled user. This greatly increases the versatility of MAPPER. Figure 11.2 lists functions usable in the *RUN* mode. It includes *IF* and *GO TO* functions. The user of a *RUN* function may invoke the name of the routine and insert appropriate parameters.

INTERFACE TO OTHER SYSTEMS   MAPPER is normally used as an interactive system, but it can interface to other, batch systems. It may retrieve a batch file for processing in MAPPER, or pass data from MAPPER to batch systems.

- Display Report
- Add Report
- Delete Report
- Duplicate Report
- Add Line
- Delete Line
- Duplicate Line
- Search Report
- Search Update Report
- Find (positional search)
- Sort Report
- Print Reports
- Index Reports
- Search List
- Totalize (data compute)
- Replace Report
- Punch (card output)
- Arithmetic (equation solver)
- Match Reports
- Match Update Reports
- Reformat Reports
- Remote Auxiliary Device Output (print, cassette, diskette)
- Historical Data/Batch File Access
- Batch Start
- Batch File Retrieve
- Append Report
- Message Switching (station to station)
- Locate (character string)
- Change (character string)
- Date Analyzer
- Demand Processing
- Remote System Run (via data link)
- Run (functions in Fig. 11.2)

Figure 11.1 Basic functions that **MAPPER** users normally employ interactively. (Reproduced by permission of Sperry Univac [3].)

The DP department in this case study used large IBM computers. After MAPPER had been in use for some time data began to be interchanged between the DP IBM systems and the end users' MAPPER system.

For greater efficiency or versatility MAPPER can also link to batch runs in its host UNIVAC 1100, written with conventional programming. It could connect to a conventional data base in host computer. If a complex bill-of-materials explosion is done, for example, this *could* be done in MAPPER, but is probably better done with conventional programming or, better, via an application package. If the users want to sort a file of more than 5000 items, for efficiency this may be done as a batch-sort operation. A screen asks the user what is to be sorted. The user fills in the blanks on the screen. The data are then batch-sorted and returned to MAPPER and placed in the requisite storage area. The batch run sends a message to the user saying that the sort is done.

- Display
- Arithmetic (equation solver)
- Search (field or fields)
- Search Update (reports)
- Search List
- Search List Update
- Read Line
- Write Line
- Read Continuous
- Index
- Match (reports)
- Match Update
- Add To (append)
- Add On (append)
- Date (analyzer)
- Locate (character string)
- Message Switching
- IF (qualification)
- CHG (variable change)
- GO TO (branching)
- Rename (result save)
- OUT (to display)
- Wait (stall)
- Tape Cassette
- Totalize (data compute)
- Sort
- Replace Report
- Delete Report
- Print (high speed)
- Batch Start
- Find (positional search)
- Auxiliary print
- Reform (form change)
- Add Report
- Duplicate Report
- RUN (start another Run Function)
- Remote Run (start a Run in a remote MAPPER via data link)
- Patch Port (MAPPER as remote processor)
- Variable (memory cells)
- LOG (run logging)
- SUB (subtotaling function)
- Line Add, Delete, Duplicate

Figure 11.2 Functions usable when MAPPER is operating in its RUN mode. (Reproduced by permission of Sperry Univac [3].)

TRAINING AND HELP

The end users typically take a 2-day training course in order to employ MAPPER. This proved to be ample. Once they are experienced with its basic functions, the users may wish to extend their skills with it. This can be accomplished with the HELP function. MAPPER is designed to be largely self-instructional. End users are encouraged to *experiment* with functions they have not used and with the many variations of each function.

The enthusiastic end users in this case study enjoyed experimenting with it and took a pride in being able to accomplish new operations. Peer-group pressure developed among the MAPPER enthusiasts to learn how to put the system through its paces.

MESSAGE SWITCHING

Users can transmit data from their station to other users' stations. They can transmit either a screen of data or an entire report. Often they transmit messages which they key into their terminal rather than data stored in the files.

A message is addressed to a specific terminal. If it is a printer, the message will be printed. If it is a screen unit, a beeper will sound on that unit so that the user can display the message. If he is in the middle of report processing, he can make the message wait until he is ready to display it.

Automatically appended to messages which are sent are the date and time the message was sent, the station sent from, and the sign-on name of the sending user.

USAGE COORDINATOR

The data in the filing cabinets are created and shared by many users. It is necessary to have a *coordinator* who controls this. He should know what types of data are in what filing cabinets and should make the data consistent as far as possible. He also controls the security procedures governing how the data are used.

The *coordinator's* job is broadly equivalent to that of a data-base administrator, but it is much simpler. A data-base administrator is a highly trained professional concerned with elaborate data structures and machine performance. The MAPPER coordinator in this case study was an end user who was given one more course than the other users. It was a part-time job. The system is designed to help the coordinator keep track of its files and users.

In many other installations also the coordinator is an end user, thereby maintaining the separation of the MAPPER environment and the DP organization. An important aspect of the software is the set of tools which it provides to the coordinator for managing how the installation is used and preventing its getting out of control.

TRIAL-AND-ERROR EVOLUTION

In the case study, as in most user-driven systems, the end users had only a vague idea in the beginning what they would be likely to create with MAPPER. The perception of what was needed grew in a trial-and-error fashion. New administrative procedures were created around the systems capability. New end users and managers steadily joined the club of people who used MAPPER to enhance their work.

The same results could not have been achieved with formal systems analysis, requirements specification, requirements freeze, and coding (the life cycle of Fig. 4.1). Nor could they have been achieved with prepackaged application software, although application software combined with MAPPER could have been powerful.

Initially, the users and management did not grasp all the ramifications of the system. How could they? They started with work-in-progress reporting and it just grew. They added one thing after another, usually reacting to current pressures and problems. It expanded to a system that became very broad in scope.

SPEEDING UP ORDERS

A vital company objective was that the time from the receipt of an order to the shipment of that order should be as short as possible.

The process of assembling products is complex because they have many components. Often assembly is held up because the necessary components or subassemblies are not yet available.

The expediter is an important individual in resolving such holdups and trying to make the flow of work through the factory as speedy as possible. MAPPER came into use for tracking the orders through the factory. It was used to control the physical inventory of products, subassemblies, and components. This stock was held in different locations. An expediter could determine what locations held stock.

Electronic components had to be fitted onto frames. Sometimes partially completed frames would sit idle because not all the components necessary to finish them existed in the stock available to the assembling department. The frames that were assembled *incomplete* were tracked on MAPPER. The expediters used MAPPER to allocate stock to those frames that were the most urgent in terms of customer demand or holding up other products. Soon these shortages were filled automatically by the system wherever possible. MAPPER produced "expedite" lists for total gross shortages. Expediters or managers could sort these by different parameters and prioritize them by customer or by scheduled delivery date.

Rather than partially complete a number of frames that must sit idle because of shortages, the system ensured that frames which could not be completed were generally not started. This lowered the capital tied up in work in progress. The production schedules could make exceptions for urgent orders or for changing requirements. The shortages that were created from frames which were assembled incomplete were calculated by MAPPER.

An employee whose work is held up because he needs parts has a run called *Wish List.* He indicates how many he needs of what parts. MAPPER first checks the *stockroom.* If the parts are there, it sends a message back giving the shelf location.

If they are not in the stockroom, it looks at *systems test* and then works its way back until it gets to the *staging area*. It then looks for the *components* of the part in the stockroom. If they are not there, it sends a message to *purchasing*. It may send a message to *fabrication* because it knows what *they* have.

WHAT-IF QUESTIONS

Eventually, the production schedules used MAPPER to experiment with "what if" questions. They could determine what shortages would be created *if* certain sales orders were filled. They could determine the effects of speeding up certain urgent orders. These end users invented for themselves a simulation capability that enabled them to achieve what they perceived to be the optimum scheduling of work under the rapidly changing and turbulent pressures of the factory.

As the control capability tightened, the number of "behind schedule" conditions was reduced. It was reduced to zero much of the time.

ENGINEERING CHANGES

Many engineering change orders went out to the shop floor each week. These were originally on memos, some of which went astray. The engineering changes became handled via MAPPER. MAPPER indicates whether the engineering change applied to *all* parts of a class, to just a specific order, to five parts in an order, or whatever.

Engineering change orders often caused delays.

> Sometimes the thing would sit around for weeks. Somebody would eventually notice and say: "You shop-floor people have had this for weeks. What's the problem?" They would say that engineering was holding it up. Who in engineering? Who put a hold on it? They would track engineering and nobody would know. "That thing was scrapped and I told Jim Smith 3 months ago that I didn't have the thing any more." But this never got into the system.

Steadily, the on-line reporting procedures were created to prevent such delays. Delays were automatically highlighted on the expediters' screens. For an engineering change the name and telephone number of the responsible engineer was eventually captured on the MAPPER reports so that the engineer could be contacted immediately if there were questions. The reports were steadily modified to deal with the problems that arose.

SPREAD BEYOND MANUFACTURING

Some of the end users who succeeded with MAPPER became very excited about it. It opened up new horizons for them. They had never dreamed before that they could instruct a powerful computer system. Their imaginations worked overtime. Some of them adopted a missionary role and tried to get converts in other departments.

Many departments other than manufacturing began to use the system. A dominant concern of the organization is providing the customers with the best possible service. This service includes the rapid resolution of any customer complaints. Complaints are of many different types and are handled by many different departments. A section of the customer services department coordinates this and must know at all times what department is handling each complaint. It must know how long each complaint has been in a department to ensure that none gets lost or unreasonably delayed.

The marketing department used to produce a month-end report listing all complaints and their status. This report took 4 working days to complete. Now, instead, all complaints are entered into MAPPER. The complaints are given a status code. Every time the status of a complaint is changed this is recorded by whatever department is handling the complaint. Before using MAPPER these status changes were keypunched once a week.

The customer services department thus created a tool for tracking the handling of complaints in a much better fashion. They made many refinements to this tool. The status of a complaint can be found immediately if a customer telephones. The overall handling of complaints has been improved and speeded up. Each complaint has a *complaint number,* but often this is not known. The complaints can therefore also be accessed by *customer name, date received, date closed,* or *unsatisfactory condition report number.* The complaints can be sorted by *complaint number, date received, department currently handling the complaint,* or *type of product.* This sorting capability helps the customer services department to review and improve the overall handling of complaints. Any department, product, or customer with an excess of complaints can be spotted immediately.

If they sort the complaints by date received, they can see the oldest ones and exert pressure on any that are taking too long. They can see which departments need to improve their turnaround time and can summarize complaints by department. The flexibility of reviewing the complaints in different ways enables the customer services department to achieve the best handling of complaints even though this is done by many different departments.

Like most of the other uses of MAPPER, machine time is not really significant in this process. About 100 status changes to complaints are entered per day. Much more significant is the flexibility and power given to the customer services department in dealing with customers.

OTHER APPLICATIONS

MAPPER created a culture of its own among end users. A newsletter was created for MAPPER users and steadily, more personnel began to employ it. The following lists some of the MAPPER applications 3 years after its introduction. All of these applications were created by end users, without help from DP, to solve their own problems.

Monitoring the use of test equipment

Materials management

Shipping

International marketing

International contract reports

Diagnostic reports

Work-load analysis

Inventory reports

Breakdown reports

Analysis of breakdowns by type and cause

Engineering changes

Inventory costs

Production information

Customer delivery reports

Problem investigation analysis

Shop floor analysis for expediters

Subassembly tracking

Reports on department capacity of production

Production scheduling

Machine monitoring reports

Expediting systems

Shop floor dispatching and control

Component shortage reports

Vendor analysis

Purchase order reports

Work-in-progress tracking

Performance analysis

Open order reports

Customer complaint reports and analysis

Where-used reports

Lead-time analysis

Identification of slow-moving stock

Tool control

Personnel resource control

Test equipment control

Machine load log

Quality reports and analysis

Contract sales orders

Changes in orders

Master parts stock status

Labor reports

Customer information

Budgets

Period cost counts

Product-line planning

Prototype development support

Capital expenditure tracking

Order entry

Order picking, packing, and shipping

Invoice preparation

Pricing information

Reports to aid forecasting

Salesmen commission payments

Overtime analysis

Customers' returned goods analysis

Transport cost reports

Engineering change order control

Printed wiring card assembly dispatching

THE DP DEPARTMENT'S ATTITUDE

The DP department remained aloof and sceptical for some time. They said: "You can't do that. Users aren't smart enough to do that." However, the MAPPER usage and hardware steadily grew from its small beginning. It became clear that the data being created and filed with MAPPER was important to other DP areas.

For a long time *we* were MAPPER users and *they* were DP professionals. So they thought we didn't know what we are doing. Now it's changed. Now data passes on-line between MAPPER and the IBM system, back and forth.

MAPPER usage spread to the *stockrooms,* to *purchasing,* to *marketing,* and to other areas.

We had a paper report from DP. It didn't contain what my manager wanted, so he said get that information. Well, it was hundreds of pages, so I said which ones shall I work on first? He said work on the ones with the most bucks. Now if that had been on MAPPER, I would have sorted it by descending dollar value, matched the items against my open order file, found out the open orders, found out the due dates, and sorted it to find the ones that are due first. It would take me minutes instead of weeks.

After 3 years of MAPPER use its success was clear to DP. DP wanted to take it over so that they also could create applications faster. It is generally desirable that the coordinator's role with MAPPER should be linked to the corporate data administration function. As with all end-user data processing the data formats ought to be made to conform to a strategic data plan *if* the data are likely to be exchanged between separate systems.

However, for DP to take over the MAPPER operations completely would be very wrong. *The great strength that the end users brought to the installation was their knowledge of their job and ability to adjust the procedures a small step at a time as the needs were perceived.*

MORAL   The moral of this case study is that *we have grossly underestimated end users.* Three years after the first introduction of MAPPER, this was a *very* impressive computer installation. Without DP help it had done much more than most installations to raise factory productivity, improve customer service, and generally increase the corporate profitability.

This has also been true in other MAPPER installations. The Santa Fe railroad has a MAPPER installation with 2000 terminals serving about 50 rail yards. There are plans to expand this service to 170 rail yards. The system has 4000 *types* of reports and a *total* of 200,000 reports, some with hundreds of lines. An average of 2½ million transactions are processed each day [4]. The principal applications relate to control of the car inventory, way-billing, and the control of vans which are piggybacked on the railroad cars. Labor productivity improved after installing the MAPPER system. More freight could be carried with a given number of employees. In 1978 the labor hours increased only 2.5% but the ton-miles earning revenue increased 12.8%. In a four-year period the freight carried doubled, but because of the user-created applications there was no increase in clerical administrative personnel. A stockbroker research report concluded that "based on a cost of $8 per manhour, the potential exists for a saving of $72 million in operating costs, or about $1.50 per share" [5]. The Sante Fe applications were designed by nonprogrammer end users. There was no involvement by their DP organization, which operated large IBM machines [4].

Some end users are amazingly bright people. They need the right tools and encouragement. Many end users want to create their own facilities but have not been given the tools to do it. The majority have not yet glimpsed at the possibilities. In showing the facilities described earlier to one typical end user, the comment was made: "If I had something like that I could save 40 to 60 hours a month." This realization needs to spread among white-collar workers everywhere (and some blue-collar ones).

When writing this book I talked to software and system architects in the computer and software industry. All of them understood the need for improving the productivity of application creation, but almost all of them thought that this must come via DP experts. Highly influential software architects talked about end users as though they were idiots and told one story after another to reinforce this view. There are certainly top executives who will never cross the cultural threshold into using their own terminal. There are certainly bigoted users who describe computer staff members as "little tin Hitlers." But there is also a world of intelligent users with problems to solve if only they had the right encouragement and software.

Much computing *ought* to be developed by end users as in this case study. For such end users to develop their own computing, the following facilities are needed.

- An interactive system with screen terminals.
- Application generation software which is data-base and report-oriented, preferably with graphics capability.
- This software needs to be elegantly human-factored and easy to use. The human factoring of MAPPER could be improved substantially.
- A complete absence of DP jargon. There is no need for difficult words or acronyms.
- Software that end users can learn to use well in 2 days.
- Good instruction, encouragement, and sympathy.
- Self-teaching software in which the HELP function is skillfully written. Computer-aided teaching at the terminal should guide and test the user, and encourage him to experiment.
- A management approach that seeks out the early adapters and motivates them to encourage their less adventurous colleagues.
- Linkage to a data-base facility with modern techniques of data-base administration.
- Tools built into the software for managing and controlling its use.
- Encouragement and cooperation from DP, not competition with and isolation from DP.
- DP information center management as described in Chapter 19, linking the user-driven activities to the other corporate computing, data-base, and network resources.
- General management that motivates the end users to invent and acquire the facilities they need.

- A feeling of employee participation in the redesign of their work, and coupled to this an understanding by all such employees of the need for productivity. An understanding by management of the pyschological factors affecting productivity is needed.

REFERENCES

1. *The Challenge of Increased Productivity,* EDP Analyzer, Vol 19, No. 4, April 1981, Canning Publications Inc., Vista, CA.

2. R.C. Beaird. *Industrial Democracy and Participation Management in Labor Issues of the 1980s,* Corporate Planning Division A.T.&T., Basking Ridge, NJ, 1980.

3. Sperry Univac Series 1100 *MAPPER 1100 User Reference Guides* UP9193, 94, and 95, Sperry Univac, New York, 1980.

4. Information from L. Schlueter, Sperry Univac, to whom the author is grateful.

5. "Research Report on Santa Fe Industries, Inc.," from L.F. Rothschild, Unterberg, Towbin, New York, 1979.

12 PROGRAMMING BY END USERS

THE NEED FOR PROGRAMMING   In the case study described in Chapter 11 the end users did not *program* (in the normal sense of the word). Much can be achieved without programming. However, some end users require applications too complex to create without programming but which nevertheless have the characteristics of user-driven computing:

- They must be created quickly.
- When created they must be modified frequently, substantially, and quickly.
- The user can specify his requirements only vaguely; a trial-and-modification approach to development is needed.
- The traditional DP development cycle is too slow and inflexible.
- Such programs are sometimes used only once.

Among the most important such programs are those that help senior management with current major decisions, such as: Should they take over another company? Should they rent or lease equipment? Should they raise prices? Should they change the sales force incentive plan?

An important aspect of managing a business is the answering of "what if" questions. The better these are answered, the greater the potential profit. They tend to have the following characteristics:

- A key decision is pending.
- Time is short.
- There are many interrelated factors.
- The parameters of the decision may change as the solutions are explored.
- A high degree of flexibility is essential.

The programs for these decisions can often employ an existing data base. The programs need an excellent report or graphics generation capability. But unlike the applications in Chapter 11, much computation may be needed.

Sometimes such programs are written by a programmer and an end user who understands the problem, working together. Sometimes highly skilled users, professionals or executives, learn to program for themselves.

Not many end users write programs. Among those that do are actuaries, designers of various types, production planners, financial and budget planners, financial analysts, various types of researchers, and senior management staff. It is valuable for certain types of staff with professional or intellectual jobs to be able to make computers work for them directly so that they can change their programs as often as they want. They build up a library of their own personal routines, which can greatly enhance their effectiveness.

The hardware for personal computing is improving rapidly, with desktop computers and distributed processing dropping in cost and computer networks becoming more widespread. Some end users have computers or terminals at home as well as in their offices.

Instead of being wholly dependent on a DP department which may be overworked, unresponsive, and possibly aloof, end users can program their own requirements, keep their own files, and manipulate data obtained from distant data bases. This is desirable because only the end users truly understand the subtleties of their own applications, especially if they are complex.

END-USER PROGRAMMING LANGUAGES　　　　To encourage end-user programming, languages are needed of a higher level than COBOL, PL/1, and FORTRAN. They require the properties listed in Box 12.1.

The attempt to produce languages for interactive use has followed two lines of attack. The first was to adapt existing languages for terminal use. The second was to think afresh and design new languages for the new environment. The advantages of the former approach were that the terminal language would be familiar to existing programmers and that a program written at the terminal could be stored for batch or job-shop operation. The advantages of the second approach were that the terminal could be made easier to use and the language could be easier to learn. The language could be made more concise and more powerful for terminal operation. Many future developments are possible in the second approach, which could employ revolutionary new language features requiring special keyboards or light pens and graphics and powerful nonprocedural forms of coding.

Several such languages are being employed by end users. The author's choice would be APL or NOMAD. I would *not* choose BASIC. NOMAD [1] seems to be a good choice where the applications are strongly data-base and report-oriented. APL [2] seems a good choice where there is much computation, logic, or matrix manipulation.

Using either NOMAD or APL it is *very* easy for beginners who have never programmed to take the first steps and to achieve something of value relatively painlessly. Both languages enable a user to learn a simple subset and continue to expand his knowledge of the language as he requires. Both link to data bases. Both can be used to write programs of great complexity when needed. Both enable results to be obtained much faster than with COBOL and PL/1.

BOX 12.1   Programming languages for end users to use need to have the following properties

1. They are interactive, designed for terminal use.

2. It is very easy to write beginners' programs. More difficult features can be learned a step at a time.

3. They can use existing or specially created data bases (preferably relational data bases) and high-level data-base manipulation commands.

4. Default options exist so that a program takes intelligent actions when not instructed to do otherwise. For example, it creates reports in a reasonable format if the user does not specify any specific format.

5. High-level nonprocedural routines are available for most operations: that is, the user tells the system *what* to do rather than *how* to do it.

6. Easy-to-use graphics capabilities exist with which attractive charts can be created and manipulated (in color where possible).

7. On-line instruction and HELP facilities are always available to users.

8. There are good on-line debugging aids, and debugging can proceed incrementally.

APL and NOMAD are languages more closely attuned to the way people think than is COBOL or FORTRAN. COBOL and FORTRAN force people to understand the computer; APL and NOMAD force the computer to understand people.

CONCISENESS   Programming languages vary greatly in their power and conciseness. This is illustrated in Fig. 12.1, which shows a simple operation programmed in five languages. Studies of programming costs in the United States reveal costs of about $10 per line of code. The costs of obtaining results with NOMAD or APL will be a fraction of COBOL costs and much less than BASIC, even if their cost per line is the same as COBOL and PL/1 (because each line of code gives more results). In fact, the fourth-generation languages typically give a substantially lower cost per line.

With a concise language such as APL, a large complex application can be programmed with fewer people. If there are fewer people, there will be fewer communication problems. Fairly complex applications are programmed by *one* person in APL (which really solves communication problems), whereas if done in COBOL, a substantial team would be needed.

NOMAD   A language designed specifically to operate with a data-base system can be made more concise than an independent language. The user does not have to define the data. NOMAD [1] is designed for time-sharing use employing a relational data base. NOMAD contains particularly powerful commands which enable a knowledgeable user to obtain results quickly.

For example, a statement such as

LIST CUSTNAME ADDRESS ZIP LASTDATE ACCOUNTTOTAL

contains the LIST command and the names of five fields. NOMAD creates a listing of these, appropriately formatted. It puts headings at the tops of the columns, these headings being specified in the data-base data descriptions. It formats the date field with slashes between the month, day, and year. It automatically skips to new pages and puts numbers on the pages. It can calculate ACCOUNTTOTAL as instructed in logic associated with the data base.

If the user then said LIST AVERAGE (ACCOUNTTOTAL), it would calculate the average of the previous ACCOUNTTOTAL values.

If the user had said LIST BY CUSTNAME . . ., the listing would have been sorted into CUSTNAME sequence.

An end user can initially learn to use NOMAD as a data-base query facility, next learn some of its report formatting capabilities and then can progress to learning to use it as a full programming language. He can use DO groups (like PL/1), IF-THEN and ELSE statements, and (for nonstructured enthusiasts) GO TO statements.

APL is discussed in Chapter 13. NOMAD is discussed in Chapter 14.

PROGRAMMING
FOR SENIOR
MANAGEMENT   Computerized assistance to senior management to help them make vital decisions is one of the most important areas of user-driven computing. Sometimes senior managers learn to handle a language

```
000100 IDENTIFICATION DIVISION.
000200 PROGRAM-ID.              CALCULATE-MEAN.
000300 AUTHOR.                  PAUL GIBBONS.
000400 INSTALLATION.            BERMUDA ELECTRIC LIGHT COMPANY.
000500 DATE-WRITTEN.            JANUARY 1981.
000600*
000700 ENVIRONMENT DIVISION.
000800 CONFIGURATION SECTION.
000900 SOURCE-COMPUTER.         NCR-IRX.
001000 OBJECT-COMPUTER.         NCR-IRX.
001100 INPUT-OUTPUT SECTION.
001200 FILE-CONTROL.
001300     SELECT DATAFILE      ASSIGN TO DISC.
001400     SELECT PRNTFILE      ASSIGN TO PRINTER.
001500*
001600 DATA DIVISION.
001700 FILE SECTION.
001800 FD  DATAFILE
001900     BLOCK CONTAINS 20 RECORDS
002000     RECORD CONTAINS 15 CHARACTERS
002100     LABEL RECORDS ARE STANDARD.
002200 01  DATAREC.
002300     05  NUM              PIC 9(13)V99.
002400 FD  PRNTFILE
002500     BLOCK CONTAINS 1 RECORDS
002600     RECORD CONTAINS 132 CHARACTERS
002700     LABEL RECORDS ARE OMITTED.
002800 01  PRNTREC.
002900     05  FILLER           PIC X(10).
003000     05  PRNT-MEAN        PIC Z(12)9.99.
003100     05  FILLER           PIC X(106).
003200 WORKING-STORAGE SECTION.
003300 01  TOTAL                PIC 9(15)V99    VALUE ZERO.
003400 01  N                    PIC 9(13)       VALUE ZERO.
003500 01  MEAN                 PIC 9(13)V99.
003600 01  EOF                  PIC X.
003700     88  END-OF-FILE                      VALUE "Y".
003800*
003900 PROCEDURE DIVISION.
004000 MAIN-LINE.
004100     OPEN INPUT DATAFILE.
004200     OPEN OUTPUT PRNTFILE.
004300     MOVE "N" TO EOF.
004400     PERFORM READ-FILE
004500         UNTIL END-OF-FILE.
004600     DIVIDE TOTAL BY N
004700         GIVING MEAN.
004800     MOVE MEAN TO PRNT-MEAN.
004900     WRITE PRNTREC
005000         AFTER ADVANCING 2 LINES.
005100     CLOSE DATAFILE PRNTFILE.
005200     STOP RUN.
005300 READ-FILE.
005400     READ DATAFILE
005500         AT END MOVE "Y" TO EOF.
005600     IF NOT END-OF-FILE
005700         ADD 1 TO N
005800         ADD NUM TO TOTAL.
```

Figure 12.1 The same result programmed in five languages, showing the conciseness of APL and NOMAD. These five programs each read a set of numbers, calculate their mean, and print the result [3].

FORTRAN

```
      DIMENSION X (100)
      READ (5,10) N, (X(I),I=1,N)
   10 FORMAT (I5, (E15.2))
      S=0.0
      DO 9 I=1,N
    9 S=S+X(I)
      A=S/N
      WRITE (6,20)A
   20 FORMAT (E15.2)
      END
```

BASIC

```
   10 DIM X (100)
   20 LET S=0
   30 READ N
   40 FOR I=1 TO N
   50 READ X (I)
   60 LET S=S+(I)
   70 NEXT I
   80 LET A=S/N
   90 PRINT A
  100 DATA
      - - - - -
      - - - - -
  XXX END
```

NOMAD

```
   READ DIGITS  LIST AVG (DIGITS)
```

APL

$$+/X \div \rho X \leftarrow \square$$

Figure 12.1 (Continued)

like APL themselves; sometimes programmers are trained to assist them. These programmers are different from the typical DP programmer in that they acquire a thorough understanding of the application. Their skills are often closer to those of systems analysts than to those of coders.

Robert C. Fisk, the vice-president of finance at STSC, Inc., employed APL for the following applications:

1. Pricing decisions

2. Lease versus buy decisions

3. Acquisition analyses

4. Incentive plan design

5. Capital funding decisions

6. Investment scenario analysis

He discusses them in Ref. [4], from which the following extract is reproduced by kind permission of the publisher.

1. Pricing Decisions

Pricing has always been a challenging discipline, but given the inflation we've had to deal with in the late 1970s, pricing has never been such a delicate issue. The costs of running a business are constantly increasing. Effective pricing management, in addition to the management of productivity, is key in maintaining satisfactory profit margins and the financial viability of an ongoing business.

Like other key business decisions, pricing decisions are complex because they depend on several factors, such as:

- *Product mix.* How will a change in price for one product affect sales for related products?
- *Existing contractual commitments.* How will a change in price affect total company revenues if some contracts (e.g., government contracts) limit price increases?
- *Product demand.* Will a price increase negatively impact demand for our product?
- *Competitive pricing.* Will a price increase result in a significant competitive disadvantage?
- *Product cost.* What does it cost to create, sell, and service the product?
- *Product value.* Should the market price be independent of product cost?

All of these factors require making assumptions. The objective is to maximize revenue and profit. What happens to total company revenue if the price for product X is increased by 8 percent? If the product is new, when will the break-even point occur? What will margins be if we undercut competitive pricing by 10 percent?

2. Lease Versus Buy Analyses

Financial officers are frequently faced with lease versus buy decisions. Consequently, this type of application system will probably be used over and over again once it is written.

For example, you're buying a piece of equipment and you want to know the least costly alternative—owning or leasing. The choice depends on many factors:

- The equipment's economic life to you
- Its economic life in the marketplace (i.e., the expected value of the equipment in the marketplace when your company no longer has use for it)
- Your ability to use the investment tax credit and accelerated depreciation
- Who pays other ongoing costs (e.g., maintenance, insurance, and personal property taxes)
- Purchase options available during the lease term
- The cost of funds to your company
- The ratio of the purchase price to the pure lease price
- Your company's required investment hurdle

Each alternative—buying or leasing—has its own projected cash flow. For example, the buy alternative may have cash flowing out of the corporation to repay debt and to pay for maintenance. It also results in cash flowing into the corporation from tax savings and from the sale of the equipment at some future date. A comparison of the present value of the cash flows of each alternative will indicate which alternative is best. If the expected market value of the equipment is difficult to predict, you can assign probabilities to alternative market values, run the model for each alternative, and then graph the results.

3. Acquisition Analyses

Like a lease versus buy decision, the decision to acquire another company at a given price is binary—should we or shouldn't we?

The answer, to a significant extent, is derived from an analysis of the consolidation of projected financial results for both companies. If the marriage of two companies results in cost savings due to the elimination of redundant activities, this should be factored into the analysis.

If the projected financial results of the marriage are superior to the projected results of the acquiring company alone, then it makes sense (financially, at least) for the acquisition to be pursued. Ultimately, an improvement in earnings per share must result if the acquisition is to be considered successful.

4. Incentive Plan Design

If your environment is dynamic (like STSC's is), incentive plan models will probably have a limited life. You'll create an incentive model for one year and then throw it away when the basic incentive algorithm becomes obsolete.

The objective here, of course, is to optimize the cost of your incentive plan, realising that you don't know *exactly* what the financial results will be—for the company as a whole or for its various performance centers and cost centers. The controlling assumption is that the size of incentive payments is related directly to performance. You wish to fairly and competitively reward individual performance; however, total compensation should not exceed an established percentage of revenue.

Frequently, under such constraints, creating an incentive plan is a trial-and-error process. Alternative incentive algorithms must be tested under varying assumptions. What if some performance centers exceed plan, while others fall below plan? What if the total company exceeds plan or falls behind plan? How will each of these scenarios affect the cost and the incentive value of our plan? The more you play the "what if" game, the closer you will get to the optimum incentive plan.

Occasionally, it may be necessary to create and throw away several incentive plan models in one year. *APL* offers the power and the flexibility to do this and still meet targeted completion dates.

5. Capital Funding Decisions

Capital funding decisions encompass some very familiar and basic decisions on how to run a business. Should we go public? Should we fund our growth with bank debt, or with a private placement of debt, or should we sell additional stock?

Of all business decisions, this is certainly one of the most complex. More debt probably means a weaker corporate balance sheet and possible restraints in the way the business is run. But, it can also mean a higher return to existing stockholders if the corporate return on investment (ROI) exceeds the cost of borrowed capital. On the other hand, more equity in the business means a stronger balance sheet and probably more flexibility in the way the business is run. But, it can also mean a lower return for existing stockholders if the new capital is put to work at a lower ROI than that which the corporation has been enjoying.

The number and combinations of "what if" possibilities here are enormous:

- What if interest rates rise? Fall? By how much?
- What if the stock market rises? Falls?
- What if our company grows 15%? 20%? 25%?

- What if additional capital is $2 million? $10 million? $100 million?
- What if our margins increase? Decrease?

The decision is made by calculating the impact of the most likely set of values for these factors on earnings per share. The alternative that results in the highest projected earnings per share is probably the best choice.

6. Investment Scenario Analysis

Typically, the financial planning process includes at least the following three elements.

- Goals in key results areas (e.g., earnings per share and return on equity).
- A limited number of financial resources. This includes any or all of the following:
  (a) Cash flow demand internally
  (b) Some limited capacity to borrow additional capital
  (c) The ability to sell stock to bring in equity capital
- A list of alternative investment opportunities (e.g., new products, cost-saving programs, training, and new equipment). The return from each alternative may or may not vary directly with the amount of investment in that alternative.

The problem then is to decide how much money, if any, to allocate to each investment alternative. This usually involves an iterative process using a number of "what if" questions. What if investment in product A is increased at the expense of product B? What if all funds are invested in opportunities D and E and all others are dropped? What will the result be on the corporate balance sheet, on the company's revenue growth rate, and on earnings per share in each case?

These applications are typical of user-driven computing for senior management. Management of a tightly controlled corporation today ought to use computer models for setting and maintaining the corporate direction. They should be indispensible to top management. But *much* greater speed and flexibility is needed than with the traditional DP development cycle. Programmer-analysts of a high skill level should work directly with senior management. They must use languages of high productivity which access corporate data bases. They should be able to quickly generate reports and preferably be able to generate color graphics displays and charts for management to study, which can be manipulated instantly to explore "what-if" questions.

APL has been used in many other areas which need user-driven computing. It is discussed in Chapter 13.

REFERENCES

1. D.D. McCracken, *A Guide to NOMAD for Applications Development*, National CSS, Inc., Wilton, CT, 1980. The most readable book on NOMAD.

2. L. Gilman and A.J. Rose, *APL, an Interactive Approach*, 2nd ed., Wiley-Interscience, New York, 1978. Possibly the best book on APL.

3. The COBOL version of Fig. 12.1 was programmed by Paul Gibbons, Bermuda Electric Light Company, Bermuda. The FORTRAN and BASIC versions are from the University of Colorado *Computing Newsletter*, March 1971. The NOMAD version was provided by Richard Murch.

4. R.C. Fisk, *"What If: The Making of a Vice President of Finance,"* in *APL in Practice*, A.J. Rose and B.A. Schick, eds., John Wiley & Sons, Inc., New York, 1980.

13 THE WORLD OF APL

INTRODUCTION   The computer world is divided into people who are wildly enthusiastic about APL and people who do not like it. There are not many in the middle. Mathematicians praise its capability to manipulate matrices. Skilled programmers find it gives scope to their ingenuity, and play games to see how many operations they can carry out in one line of code. Others find it an efficient language for handling on-line files in relational form. Users of FORTRAN and similar languages have criticized its syntax. Jean Sammet, in her massive work on programming languages [1], says: "I cannot become enthusiastic about a language which has this notational complexity." From our point of view, it is an easy way to enable an end user who has never programmed, to start using a computer, and experience seems to show that he will normally join the ranks of the enthusiasts. Often, his enthusiasm will rival that of a religious convert.

Some organizations and some end-user departments become filled with APL enthusiasts. A good part of IBM's internal data processing is done with APL, some of it by bright end users. Although APL was initially used as a mathematical language, it is now used more for data processing [2, 3].

EASY TO BEGIN   Part of the appeal of APL is that a *child* can *begin* to use it. A simple subset can be learned that converts a terminal into a simple but exceedingly powerful desk calculator.

CALCULATOR OPERATIONS   A user can learn APL's basic calculator operations in 5 minutes or so. It could not be more straightforward. Thus:

USER: 3 + 7   RETURN   (Pressing the RETURN key indicates the
                                end of the statement)

COMPUTER: 10   (The result)

USER: 5 × 7.43   RETURN   (*Note:* The multiplication sign is different
                                from the letter X)

COMPUTER: 37.15

USER: 23 + 14 – 8   RETURN

COMPUTER: 29

USER: 4 ÷ 7   RETURN

COMPUTER: 0.5714285714

USER: 5 × ¯7.43   RETURN

COMPUTER: ¯37.15   (The signs for negative numbers are
                               raised as shown)

USER: 6 ÷ 0   RETURN

COMPUTER: DOMAIN ERROR

Floating-point numbers can be entered.

USER: 1.46E5   RETURN

COMPUTER: 146000

USER: 1.46E5 × 2   RETURN

COMPUTER: 292000

Exponentiation can be used and employs the symbol "*":

USER: 4 * 2   RETURN

COMPUTER: 16

USER: 4 * 5   RETURN

COMPUTER: 625

USER: 4.3216E4*2.134*.679E¯1 * 1.211   RETURN

COMPUTER: 59278.64236

The handling of multiple arithmetic statements proceeds from right to
left, and in this we find the first possible source of confusion because the

rule is different from both conventional arithmetic and other programming languages. Thus:

USER: 6 + 7 × 2 RETURN

COMPUTER: 20

USER: 7 × 2 + 6 RETURN

COMPUTER: 56

Brackets are used to define which operation is done first:

USER: (7 × 2) + 6 RETURN

COMPUTER: 20

Variables may be named and set to a value by means of a left-pointing arrow. Their value is printed simply by typing the symbol. Thus:

```
USER:   PI ← 3.14159      RETURN
        R ← 4.18          RETURN
        A ← PI × R * 2    RETURN
        A                 RETURN
```

COMPUTER: 54.89111712

```
USER:   C ← PI × R × 2  RETURN
        C               RETURN
```

COMPUTER: 26.2636924

VECTORS AND MATRICES

APL does not operate only on single numbers, like a cheap pocket calculator; it can also operate on strings of numbers or tables of data. (A single number is called a *scalar;* a string of numbers is called a *vector;* a table is called a *matrix.* Each number in a vector or matrix is called an *element.*)

The user may enter a vector thus:

USER: 1 17 1281 3 58 RETURN

The user could assign a variable name to a vector, thus:

USER: X ← 26 79 45 12 4 105 67 23 9 17 RETURN

When the machine is told to add two vectors, it adds each of their elements in turn:

```
USER:   X ← 26  79  45  12  4  105  67  23  9  17        RETURN
        Y ← 356  678  123  34  549  801  412  89  71  90  RETURN
        X + Y                                             RETURN
```

COMPUTER: 382 757 168 46 553 906 479 112 80 107

```
USER:   Z ← X + 12  RETURN
        Z           RETURN
```

COMPUTER: 38 91 57 24 16 117 79 35 21 29

The values of X remain the same and the user could print them:

```
USER:  X                                    RETURN
```

COMPUTER: 26 79 45 12 4 105 67 23 9 17 RETURN

The user cannot manipulate two vectors which have different numbers of elements:

```
USER:  1  6  8  9  +  2  3  8  RETURN
```

COMPUTER: LENGTH ERROR

```
        1  6  8  9  +
        2  3  8
```

The user can create a matrix by expressing the numbers of rows and columns that he wants. This is done with the function ρ (the Greek letter "rho," pronounced "row").

If he wants a matrix of 12 columns (one for each month of the year, say) and three rows, he enters

```
USER:  3  12 ρ  RETURN
```

The first entry is the number of rows. The second is the number of columns.

The user could fill in the matrix with the same instruction:

```
USER:  4  2ρ  1  8  6  9  27  4  41  8  RETURN
```

```
COMPUTER:   1  8
            6  9
           27  4
           41  8
```

The user could give the matrix a name:

USER: FRED ← 5 3 ρ RETURN

COMPUTER: FRED

```
26  79   45
12   4  105
67  23    9
17  26   79
45  12    4
```

Here the machine has created a matrix called FRED with five rows of
three columns and has filled it with the values of the vector X (above). X
has fewer elements than FRED, so the machine repeated the elements until
the matrix was filled.

The user can refer to individual elements of a vector or matrix. The
element in row 2, column 3, of FRED is addressed as FRED [2,3] .

This element can be changed as follows:

USER: FRED [2,3] ← 6 RETURN

COMPUTER: FRED

```
26  79  45
12   4   6
67  23   9
17  26  79
45  12   4
```

As with vectors, all the elements of a matrix can be multiplied or otherwise manipulated at once. This ability to manipulate vectors and matrices is
one of the powerful features of APL.

With the command PLOT the user can have a chart of the matrix
plotted.

The illustrations above were for two-dimensional matrices (tables).
Multidimensional matrices can be used. A three-dimensional matrix might
be used to show how a business table changes when assumptions are varied.

Some APL-based software allows a variety of types of charts to be
drawn of APL matrices. Some of this graphics software is easy to use but can
create spectacular charts, in color if a color terminal is used.

REDUCTION

One of APL's most useful functions is the *reduction* function (/), which reduces an array of values
to a single element.

+ / Y means the sum of the element values in vector Y.

Thus, if a businessperson has a vector called SALES which gives the sales for each month of a year, the total sales can be calculated with + / SALES.

The number of items in a vector can be found with the ρ function. If the SALES vector had 12 elements, then ρ SALES is 12. This enables an average to be calculated, as follows:

$$+ / \text{SALES} \div \rho \text{ SALES}$$

This is the basis of the expression $+ / X \div \rho X$ in Fig. 12.1. The equivalent COBOL expression is vast. (Averages are likely to be calculated frequently; therefore, a language could have an AVERAGE function, as shown in the NOMAD version of this in Fig. 12.1.)

Many different operators can be placed in front of the reduction function.

Γ / SALES means the element in SALES with the maximum value.

L / SALES means the minimum value in SALES.

USER: A ← 12 14 16 18 20 RETURN
+/A   RETURN

COMPUTER: 80

USER: Γ/A   RETURN

COMPUTER: 20

USER: L/A   RETURN

COMPUTER: 12

The operation proceeds in a right-to-left fashion. Thus –/A calculates $(((20 - 18) - 16) - 14) - 12 = {}^-40$.

USER: –/A   RETURN

COMPUTER: ⁻40

USER: ×/A   RETURN

COMPUTER: 967680

USER: */A   RETURN

COMPUTER: DOMAIN ERROR
*/A
^

[The result of (((12 14) 16) 18) 20 is too large.]

□ is the symbol for input and output. □← means "Print the value of what follows," and A ← □ means "Request input, and set A to the resulting value after the input is evaluated." Thus:

USER: A ← □   RETURN

COMPUTER: □ :

    USER: 23　42　56　78　12　RETURN

    USER: □ ← A   RETURN

COMPUTER: 23　42　56　78　12

An input request can reside in another expression. Thus:

    USER: +/A ← □   RETURN

COMPUTER: □ :

    USER: 12　14　16　18　20　22　24　26　28　30　RETURN

COMPUTER: 210

The mean of a set of values can be calculated as follows:

    USER: +/A ÷ ρ A ← □   RETURN

COMPUTER: □ :

    USER: 10　12　14　16　18　20　22　24　RETURN

COMPUTER: 17

The standard deviation of N values,
can also be computed with one statement.

    USER: +(+/((A−(+/A) ÷ ρ A) *2) ÷ ρ A ← □) *.5　RETURN

COMPUTER: □ :

    USER: 10　12　14　16　18　20　22　24

COMPUTER: 4.582575695

Skilled APL users often like to type a lengthy statement such as this. It is a challenge to do an entire calculation in one statement. However, for the average user to attempt this would be asking for trouble; he is likely to make errors. A parenthesis omitted, for example, would give the wrong result. In all human–machine dialogues it is better to break the input into units sufficiently small that the user is unlikely to make a mistake. The following would be a better way for most people to calculate the standard deviation:

USER: M ÷ (+/A) ÷ ρ A   RETURN
          B ← (A–M) *2   RETURN
          C ← +/B   RETURN
          D ← (C ÷ ρ A) *.5 RETURN
          A ← ☐   RETURN

COMPUTER: ☐ :

USER: 10 12 14 16 18 20 22 24 RETURN
        D   RETURN

COMPUTER: 4.582575695

The calculation could be put into the form of a named routine, so that it could be easily repeated. The operator ∇ is used to name, and also to end, a subroutine. Thus:

COMPUTER	USER	
↓	↓	
	∇ SD	RETURN
(1)	A ← ☐	RETURN
(2)	M ← (+/A) ÷ ρ A	RETURN
(3)	B ← (A–M) *2	RETURN
(4)	C ← +/B	RETURN
(5)	D ← (C ÷ ρ A)*0.5	RETURN
(6)	'MEAN ='; M	RETURN
(7)	'STANDARD DEVIATION =';D	RETURN
	∇	

The user can then use the program simply by typing its name, SD:

USER: SD

COMPUTER: ☐ :

USER: 10 12 14 16 18 20 22 24

COMPUTER: MEAN = 17
              STANDARD DEVIATION = 4.582575695

USER: SD

COMPUTER: ☐ :

USER: 1.2E5 3.27E4 3057 1.111E5 3.7E4 9.31E3

COMPUTER: MEAN = 52194.5
              STANDARD DEVIATION = 46425.4355

The user has now written a simple program as he might do on a programmable pocket calculator.

Many end users fall into the writing of simple programs almost without realizing that they are programming, as a step-at-a-time enhancement of the calculator function.

Skilled end users such as engineers, researchers, and financial analysts often build their own personal collection of subroutines. Their power in using these steadily grows as time goes by.

REPORT GENERATION AND QUERY FUNCTIONS

By using the calculator functions, end users can begin to use APL without learning to program. They can also enter the APL world without programming by using its extensions for data-base query and report generation.

APL has been extended by a variety of organizations to create data-base query and update facilities, report generators, graphics generators, and application generators. Some of these are designed for end users with no programming skills, and meet our criterion that end users can learn to employ them usefully in 2 days of training. The advantage of linking these end-user facilities to APL is that powerful processing routines can be created and added to them by staff members (or users) who can program in APL.

These APL-related facilities have been created by IBM, by user organizations, and by software and time-sharing organizations. In particular, STSC markets APL*PLUS [4], which includes a variety of such facilities. IBM markets an inquiry facility called APL Data Interface (APLDI II) [5] and a report generator called A Departmental Reporting System (ADRS II) [6].

APL DATA INTERFACE

The APL Data Interface is designed for end users who manipulate large amounts of data, but who cannot necessarily program with APL. It is used by business planners, analysts, production controllers, researchers, auditors, actuaries, and the like. Its input can originate from most IBM file and data-base systems. Information in multiple separate files can be linked together through common data.

End users are guided through the proper procedures by "prompt" messages at the terminal. Functions are provided for end users to select information and manipulate it in standard ways (i.e., summarize, cross-tabulate, count, sort, accumulate statistics, etc.). Information can be selected using logical expressions (and, or, less than, equal to, etc.) or using computed values.

The end users can manipulate the information on a screen. The following commands are available for scrolling and manipulating files and can be employed with the *program function* keys of a terminal:

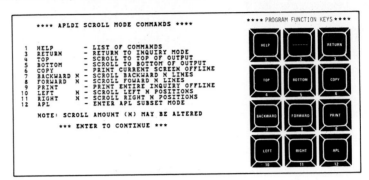

The user can specify a sort field. He can build an index into a file on any given field, which can be used to speed up the query process.

ADRS   ADRS is an APL-based system with which end users can enter data, update files, query files, and generate reports and simple graphic charts. It employs simple English-like commands, of which Box 13.1 gives examples. The user can display a file of data on the screen and scroll through it with SCROLL MODE commands such as those above. He can sort the file, temporarily delete columns, create subtotals and totals, or have the file printed in a variety of ways.

He can enter data with the INPUT command. He can make rapid changes to data by rapidly scanning a row or column with the FASTROW or FASTCOL commands, and changing one or more fields. With the SETUP command he can initialize columns for the storage of data, and then proceed to enter data into the columns created. With CALCULATE he can use the calculator features of APL to calculate and store results without saving the calculation statements.

The user can accomplish much with the first six commands of Box 13.1. These are about as simple to learn as the operation of a pocket calculator.

BOX 13.1   Typical commands used in ADRS, an APL-based report generator.

ENTER	TO ACCOMPLISH
SETUP	Initialize columns for storage of data.
INPUT or FASTCOL	Store records in the data base.

(Continued)

BOX 13.1 *(Continued)*

or FASTROW	
LIST	Print an informal report as a proof list of the raw data.
CALCULATE	Calculate and store results without saving the calculation statements.
PROGRAM and COMPUTE	Write and store a program; compute and store the results.
SETREPORTS	Formal report headers, footnotes, titles; print options such as subtotals and overflow for regular reports; preprocessing. Patterned output.
REPORTS	Print one or more reports.
SORT	Rearrange the records in the data base based on record content.
SELECT	Select particular records to print in subsequent reports based on record content.
PLOT	Print point graphs and histograms of selected data.
SETUP	Add, delete columns; change column headers; make columns wider or narrower; change decimal point settings within columns.
ERASEROWS	Erase one or more rows from the data base selected by record content.
ROWID	Change an existing row identifier; print a numbered list of ROWIDs to help in calculations down the page and in writing print patterns; insert ROWIDs in the file for jobs that do not require sorting.
SETPAGE	Change page length, page width, and top and bottom margins from initial settings of 66, 130, 5, 5. Set page numbering and date stamp.
SETSPACE	Set line spacing (single, double, triple spacing, etc.)
SEPARATORS	Change the "entry" separator from a comma to another character.
RESTART	Set the restart switch on—the next print operation will request a starting ROWID or page no. and set the switch off again.
PRINTER	Set the output destination to the terminal, disc, or high-speed printer.

BOX 13.1 *(Continued)*

HOLDPAGE	Stop report printing at the end of each page to allow cut-form entry.
ADDLOCK	Prevents adding new rows to the data base. Invoking the command again turns it off.
IDLOCK	Prevents changes to rows currently in the data base. Next use removes the lock.
JOBNAME	Assign a name to a group of columns for input, fastrow, plot, or ship.
SETCON	Initialize consolidation options.
CONSOL	Execute the consolidation.
READER	Receive remote operator data files for consolidation.
SHIP	Remote operator command to indicate file ready for consolidation.
DATACHECK	Restore file after damage by interrupted input/edit command.
RESUME	Continue an interrupted function.
SUMMARY	Summarize files with compound ROWIDs before consolidation.
RESTORE	Restore summarized files to original condition for updating (after consolidation).
SETDEC	Alter decimal settings for specific rows and columns.
KEEP	Optional, but should be used at the end of a work session (instead of "save"). Erases all programs (except user-written) and prompts you to save the workspace, thereby reducing storage requirements in the library. You will be prompted to copy the programs from the master workspace at the next "load" operation.

The generation of reports can range from simple listings to highly complex structures. The report generation features include the following:

- Describing and saving report formats.
- Modification of existing reports.
- Embedding text within the body of a report.
- Left/right justification.

- Automatic centering of descriptive text, such as data names over columns or groups of columns in a report.

- Vertical and horizontal spacing under user control.

- Automatic date, time, and pagination.

- Top and bottom margin control.

- Switching of column definitions within a report. This is useful for tiered reporting structures.

Figure 13.1 gives an example of a report produced with ADRS [6]. ADRS enables its user to create various types of printed charts, such as bar charts and point graphs. Figure 13.2 gives an example.

```
Corp. Std. Report                 CORPORATE EXPENSE REPORT                                    JUNE
     No. 202                            BY REGION                                             1979


 *********    ******************************   ****************   ******************   *******
 *CATEGORY*   *           EXPENSES         *   *    BUDGET    *   *   PRIOR YEAR   *   * P/C *
 *********    ******************************   ****************   ******************   *******
                                                        Percent            Percent    Percent
                                                        Y-T-D      Prior    Actual       of
                                                        Actual     Year     Versus     Total
               Prior      JUNE      Y-T-D     Y-T-D     Versus     Y-T-D    Prior      Y-T-D
    Item       Expense    Expense   Expense   Budget    Budget    Expense   Year       Expense
 ----------    -------    --------  -------   -------   ------    -------   -------    -------
EASTERN REGION - NEW YORK   MGR: R. JONES
Travel          1,300      300.00    1,600     2,000       80      1,000     160          14
Equipment       2,310      270.00    2,580     3,000       86      1,500     172          22
Services          628      105.00      733       500      147  A     444     165           6
Utilities         352       30.00      382       250      153  A     200     191           3
Special           160       22.00      182       200       91        288      63           2
Rental            648       75.00      723       600      121  A     900      80           6
                -------    --------  -------   -------   ------    -------   -------    -------
TOTAL EAST      5,398      802.00    6,200     6,550       95      4,332     143          53

CENTRAL REGION -  CHICAGO    MGR: T. SMITH
Travel            872       50.00      922     1,000       92        900     102           8
Utilities         360       92.00      452       400      113  A     300     151           4
Rental            455       59.00      514       600       86      1,000      51           4
                -------    --------  -------   -------   ------    -------   -------    -------
TOTAL CENTRAL   1,687      201.00    1,888     2,000       94      2,200      86          16

WESTERN REGION - LOS ANGELES  MGR: L. WHITE
Travel          1,480      180.00    1,660     2,000       83      1,500     111          14
Equipment         300     (150.00)     150     1,500       10      1,000      15           1
Special         1,600      240.00    1,840     1,000      184  A    N/A      N/A          16
                -------    --------  -------   -------   ------    -------   -------    -------
TOTAL WEST      3,380      270.00    3,650     4,500       81      2,500     146          31
                =======    ========  =======   =======   ======    =======   =======    =======
GRAND TOTAL    10,465    1,273.00   11,738    13,050       90      9,032     130         100
                =======    ========  =======   =======   ======    =======   =======    =======




NOTE: "A" indicates expense items exceeding                          PRINTED:
      year-to-date budget.                                           JULY 10, 1979 - 2:48 PM
                                        (1)
```

Report Example

Figure 13.1 Example of a report produced from ADRS. Note that data are specified in rows and columns; totaling and subtotaling is provided, together with heading and footnotes. Text is also provided across several columns.

```
                          EASTERN REGION
            1979 - MONTHLY CUMULATIVE EXPENSE COMPARISON
                          (Six Expense Items)

7000:----+----+----+----+----+----+----+----+----+----+----+----+
     :    :    :    :    :    :    :    :    :    : B  : B  : B
     :    :    :    :    :    :    :    :    :    : B  : B  : B
6000:----+----+----+----+----+----+----+----+----+:-B--+-B--+-B--+
     :    :    :    :    :    :    :    :    : B  : B  : B  : B
     :    :    :    :    :    :    :    :    : B  : B  : B  : B
5000:----+----+----+----+----+----+----+----+:-B--+-B--+-B--+-B--+
     :    :    :    :    :    :    :    : B  : B  : B  : B  : B
     :    :    :    :    :    :    :    : B  : B  : B  : B  : B
4000:----+----+----+----+----+----+----+:-B--+-B--+-B--+-B--+-B--+
     :    :    :    :    :    :    : B  : B  : B  : B  : AB : AB
     :    :    :    :    :    :    : B  : B  : B  : B  : AB : AB
3000:----+----+----+----+----+----:-B--+-B--+-B--+-AB-+-AB-+-AB-+
     :    :    :    :    :    : B  : B  : B  : AB : AB : AB : ABC
     :    :    :    :    :    : B  : B  : AB : AB : AB : AB : ABC
2000:----+----+----+----+----:-B--+-AB-+-AB-+-AB-+AB--+AB--+*AB-+
     :    :    : B  : AB :ABC F:ABC F:ABC :ABC :ABC F:ABCD F:ABCD F
     :  :B : AB :ABC F:ABCD F:ABCD F:ABCD F:ABCD F:ABCDEF:ABCDEF:ABCDEF
1000:-+AB-+-AB-+-ABC-+ABCDEF+ABCDEF+ABCDEF+ABCDEF+ABCDEF+ABCDEF--F
   : B   F:ABCDEF:ABCDEF:
  0:ABCDEF+ABCDEF+ABCDEF
    1     2     3     4     5     6     7     8     9    10    11    12

                    MONTHS    JANUARY - DECEMBER

Expense Item
 A) Travel           D) Utilities
 B) Equipment        E) Special
 C) Services         F) Rental

Column Description
 1) Y-T-D January     7) Y-T-D July
 2) Y-T-D February    8) Y-T-D August
 3) Y-T-D March       9) Y-T-D September
 4) Y-T-D April      10) Y-T-D October
 5) Y-T-D May        11) Y-T-D November
 6) Y-T-D June       12) Y-T-D December
```

Figure 13.2 Example of a bar chart from ADRS. The user can specify text for vertical and horizontal axes as required.

Files can be searched with a variety of selection criteria. The ROWID, row identifier, can be used or other fields can be used for searching with logical operators such as =, ≠, <, >, ≤, and ≥. The command ANALYZE permits operations involving multiple files.

Security is provided via sign-on codes and passwords. Specified rows or columns in the data can be individually protected.

These facilities are broadly similar to other query systems and report generators—perhaps not quite as well human-factored as the best. The APL connection, however, gives skilled users much more power. APL programs can be written and stored away, and can be called on to analyze the data or perform complex computations.

APL DIALOGUES FOR NONPROGRAMMERS

Like an interactive program in any other language, an APL program can be written so that it interrogates its user. The user need have no knowledge of APL or programming. A typical interrogation dialogue is as follows:

USER: RENTAL

COMPUTER: SKIP MOST OF INPUT?

USER: N

COMPUTER: TAX BRACKET AS A DECIMAL
        ☐ :

USER: .52

COMPUTER: TAX ON PROPERTY (PER YEAR)
        ☐ :

USER: 1012

COMPUTER: MANAGEMENT RATE AS A DECIMAL
        ☐ :

USER: .1

COMPUTER: UTILITIES (PER YEAR)
        ☐ :

USER: 280 + 70 + 80

COMPUTER: UPKEEP (PER YEAR)
        ☐ :

USER: 400

COMPUTER: INSURANCE (PER YEAR)
        ☐ :

USER: 700

COMPUTER: BASIS OF PROPERTY
        ☐ :

USER: 35000

COMPUTER: INTEREST ON LOAN AS A DECIMAL
        ☐ :

USER: .08

COMPUTER: LENGTH OF LOAN (YEARS)
        ☐ :

USER: 20

COMPUTER: PERSONAL USE AS A DECIMAL
        ☐ :

USER: .5

COMPUTER: LENGTH OF DEPRECIATION (YEARS)
        ☐ :

USER: 25

COMPUTER: MAXIMUM RENT (PER YEAR)
        ☐ :

USER: 6 × 200

COMPUTER: AMOUNT OF LOAN
        ☐ :

USER: 25000

COMPUTER: SKIP MONTHLY CALCULATION?

USER: N

Here is the section of code in the program "RENTAL" with which this dialogue was written:

```
(8)   'TAX BRACKET AS A DECIMAL'
(9)   BRK ← ☐
(10)  'TAX ON PROPERTY (PER YEAR)'
(11)  TAX ← ☐
(12)  'MANAGEMENT RATE AS A DECIMAL'
(13)  MGT ← ☐
(14)  'UTILITIES (PER YEAR)'
(15)  UTL ← ☐
(16)  'UPKEEP (PER YEAR)'
(17)  UPK ← ☐
(18)  'INSURANCE (PER YEAR)'
```

```
(19)  INS ← ☐
(20)  'BASIS OF PROPERTY'
(21)  BAS ← ☐
(22)  'INTEREST ON LOAN AS A DECIMAL'
(23)  INT ← ☐
(24)  'LENGTH OF LOAN (YEARS)'
(25)  YRS ← ☐
(26)  'PERSONAL USE AS A DECIMAL'
(27)  PERS ← ☐
(28)  R3: 'LENGTH OF DEPRECIATION (YEARS)'
(29)  DPR ← ☐
(30)  'MAXIMUM RENT (PER YEAR)'
(31)  RENT ← ☐
(32)  'AMOUNT OF LOAN'
(33)  BAL ← LON ← ☐
(34)  'SKIP MONTHLY CALCULATION?'
(35)  → 2+(126)X1'Y'=(,☐)(1)
```

The instructions for computing rental income then followed.

This is typical of the dialogues that users write in APL. A user can then either fill in the values as the program requests, or modify portions of the program when it seems desirable. Some end users have written elaborate programs in APL, such as cash flow models, shop floor scheduling aids, and programs for establishing plans and budgets. APL manipulates matrices with ease, and this capability has been used for handling files and small relational data bases. In some cases records are extracted from a large traditional data base and transmitted to a separate machine for end-user manipulation with APL.

REFERENCES

1. J.E. Sammet, *Programming Languages, History and Fundamentals,* Prentice-Hall, Inc., Englewood Cliffs, NJ, 1969.

2. A.J. Rose and B.A. Schick, eds., *APL in Practice,* John Wiley & Sons, Inc., New York, 1980.

3. L. Gilman and A.J. Rose, *APL, An Interactive Approach,* 2nd ed, Wiley-Interscience, New York, 1978. (Possibly the best book on APL.)

4. APL*PLUS is available from STSC Inc., 7316 Wisconsin Avenue, Bethesda, MD 20014.

5. *APL Data Interface II, Program Description/Operations Manual,* IBM Publication No. SH20-6147, IBM, White Plains, NY, 1980.

6. *A Departmental Reporting System II, User Guide,* IBM Publication No. SH20-2165-0, IBM, White Plains, NY, 1980.

14 NOMAD

Whereas APL was originally designed for complex computation, NOMAD was designed for storing and manipulating data in a data base.

Like some other fourth-generation languages NOMAD has its own database management. It combines the facilities of a data-base management system, a report and graphics generator, and a very high-level programming language. It combines the features of a procedural and nonprocedural language. Beginners who have never programmed find it very easy to achieve results of value by using the nonprocedural statements.

A basic subset of the syntax of NOMAD is particularly easy for non-programmers to understand. This may be perceived by glancing at Fig. 12.1. It is possible to write statements in APL which are difficult for another person to understand. The statement in Fig. 12.1 takes some thought, for example. This can make it difficult to *maintain* or modify programs in APL unless the author has followed structuring rules designed for ease of mainte-nance. (The author could find almost no APL writers who *do* follow such rules.) Conversely it is generally easy to understand and modify what another person has written in NOMAD.

NOMAD is available from National CSS [1]. Some users employ it with time sharing. Some run it on their own computers. The current version is called NOMAD 2. We will simply write "NOMAD" to refer to the latest version.

CONVERSATIONAL AND PROCEDURAL MODES   The NOMAD language contains both procedural and nonprocedural statements. The user operates in two modes: *conversational* and *procedural.* Users usually learn the conversational mode first. This contains nonprocedural commands. These are executed interactively, one at a time, as they are issued.

206

The nonprocedural commands can also be executed in the procedural mode along with procedural statements which extend the range of their logic.

A typical example of a nonprocedural command is LIST, illustrated in Fig. 14.1.

A one-time command can generate a report. As we commented earlier, NOMAD automatically generates page numbers and column headings, and does not have to be told how to format the report.

The user can generate a wide variety of reports or charts of the data, can update the data, add new fields, change the data-base structure, generate

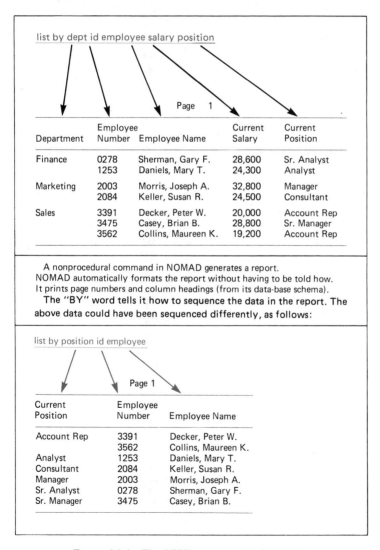

Figure 14.1　The LIST command in NOMAD.

statistics, perform calculations on the data, and change the data in generic ways to ask "What if?" questions.

Although valuable uses of NOMAD are accomplished with a small number of easy-to-use commands like the LIST command in Fig. 14.1, the full language is comprehensive and can accomplish almost anything that could be done in COBOL. Most end users employ only a small easy-to-use subset of the language. They can be taught to achieve powerful results in a few hours.

STORED PROCEDURES

Routines which will be used again can be stored by NOMAD. The user can call and execute the routine with a single statement naming the routine, for example:

TRIAL-BALANCE

Such routines can consist of procedural or nonprocedural statements, or both. With nonprocedural statements the user might build up an elaborate report which he wants to have printed periodically, or wants other users to have access to. The routine might include the performing of calculations, or the posing of "What if?" questions.

With the procedural code a user or analyst might create a program or subroutine that users employ.

Users often store a lengthy procedural command, such as a LIST command, in order to save time by not having to key it in again.

NOMAD'S DATA BASE

The heart of NOMAD is its data base. NOMAD can store data in relational form [2] and can also store in hierarchical form by means of pointers embedded in the records, which are followed automatically when operations which refer to the hierarchical structure are used. Sometimes hierarchical and relational structures are combined.

Like other data-base management systems it can access data sequentially or randomly. It has features for security, privacy, integrity, and for checking the accuracy of data. It has concurrency controls and locks for when multiple users have simultaneous, shared access to the data. It protects the data from system failures, and uses automatic audit trails.

Security and integrity features are particularly important on a data base which can be accessed with powerful end-user languages.

RELATIONAL STRUCTURES   In a relational data base, each record is stored individually with no pointer linkage to other records. Sometimes requests for data require data in more than one type of record to be combined. This *joining* of the files (relations) is done when the data are requested or updated.

Any model of data [3] can be represented in a relational form. The advantage of doing this is flexibility. Any record can access without going through a parent record. Different files of records can be *joined* if they contain a common field to assemble information from more than one file. This is done in a dynamic fashion and can meet unanticipated requests for information in a fully flexible way.

HIERARCHICAL STRUCTURES   Some records are never retrieved without also retrieving a parent record. For example, an account master record may have several transaction records associated with it. The transaction records are never retrieved without also retrieving the master record.

NOMAD allows this type of data to be stored in a hierarchical form.

The upper record of a hierarchy is called a *master* and the lower records are called *segments* (Fig. 14.2). The relationship between the master and its segments is automatically maintained by NOMAD by means of pointers embedded in each record. Pointers in the master record give the internal addresses of the dependent segments; these segments are usually stored close to the master. Pointers in each segment give the internal address of the corresponding master.

NOMAD supports multiple-level hierarchical structures.

The advantage of the hierarchical structuring is efficiency, when following the hierarchical paths. The advantage of the relational structuring is flexibility, but this would sacrifice some performance when hierarchical paths need to be followed repetitively. NOMAD supports hybrid data bases which contain both relational and hierarchical structures.

SETTING UP THE DATA BASE   The structures of data are defined to NOMAD in a schema such as that illustrated in Fig. 14.3.

The schema may contain column headings, alternate names for fields (aliases), details of integrity checks that are applied to the data, security controls, details of how a derived field should be computed, and details of access methods.

A user may build his own files. He may do this in a simple fashion, avoiding some of the complexities shown in Fig. 14.3, as follows:

```
MASTER EMPLOYEE INSERT = KEY (ID);
  ITEM ID A4 HEADING 'EMPLOYEE: NUMBER';
```

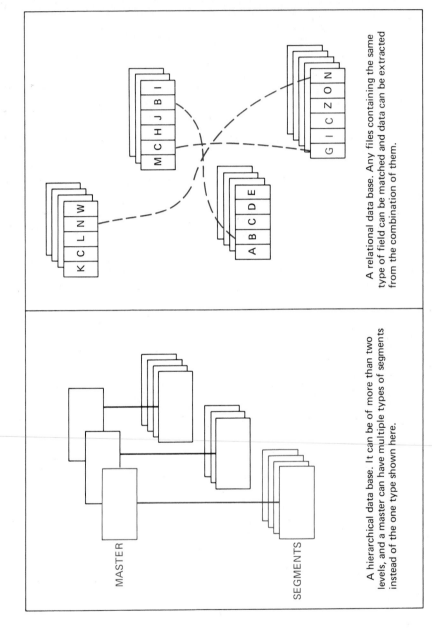

A hierarchical data base. It can be of more than two levels, and a master can have multiple types of segments instead of the one type shown here.

A relational data base. Any files containing the same type of field can be matched and data can be extracted from the combination of them.

MASTER

SEGMENTS

Figure 14.2   NOMAD handles hierarchical or relational data bases, or both together.

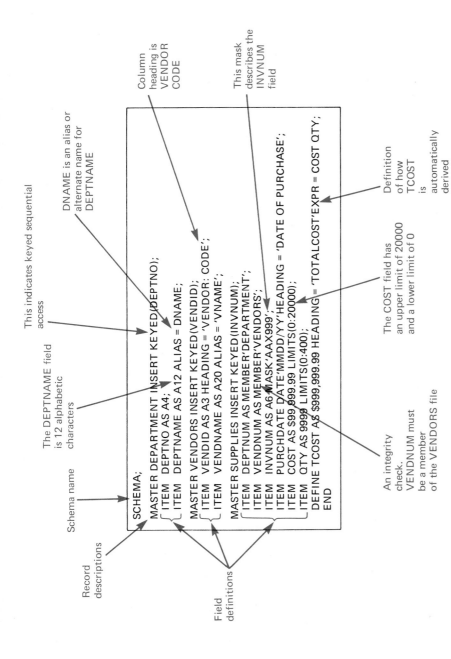

Figure 14.3 A NOMAD data-base description. The description can also contain details of passwords for security purposes.

```
ITEM EMPLOYEE A20 HEADING 'EMPLOYEE: NAME';
ITEM DEPT. A12 HEADING 'DEPARTMENT';
ITEM SALARY $99,999 HEADING 'CURRENT: SALARY';
ITEM POSITION A12 HEADING 'CURRENT: POSITION';
```

This data description is for the data shown in Fig. 14.1. The phrase INSERT = KEY (ID) indicates that ID is the primary key and new records are inserted using this key.

It is wasteful to store DEPT or POSITION as twelve alphanumeric characters (as A12 implies). Department or position could each be stored as a one-character code and NOMAD could look up the meaning of the code. The person who defines the file could write:

```
DEFINE DEPARTMENT A30 EXPR (DEPT DECODE (1 = 'FINANCE',
    2 = 'MARKETING', 3 = 'SALES', . . . .))
```

TYPES OF DATA-BASE ACCESS

NOMAD supports the following types of data-base access:

- KEYED—key sequential access can be used in specifying multiple item keys. Data can be logically ordered by the key items in ascending or descending sequence.

- BTREE—Balanced Tree Indexing is a technique with extremely efficient random-ising of records is possible for very large files. NOMAD places these records automatically; this access method is well suited for large applications which must support intensive activity on-line, such as queries.

- TABLE LOOK-UP—NOMAD has a number of table look-up techniques that allow data from different masters, segments, or even different data bases to be combined to form a logical file.

- COMBINING DATA BASES—NOMAD supports the technique of combining two or more separate data bases. One command, the DBADD allows users to temporarily extract information from different data bases.

- EXTERNAL FILES—Any fixed length sequential data file can be accessed by NOMAD and can be included in the internal design of any system. NOMAD will recognize it as a data base. This has many benefits where there is a mixture of files and data bases in an installation.

INTEGRITY CONTROLS

NOMAD's data integrity features include the following:

- LIMITS—Each item may be assigned an upper and lower range of values, or it must be a member of a set of values, for example, "M" or "F" for SEX.

- MASK—The system may verify that alphanumeric data items conform to a specified character pattern. An item PARTNO, for example, may be required to be of the form

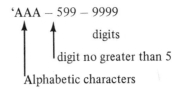

'AAA – 599 – 9999

digits

digit no greater than 5

Alphabetic characters

- MEMBER—Consistency between data groups can be ensured. For example, a value of SUPPLIER field is entered into a PART record and the system automatically checks the SUPPLIER file to ensure that it is a valid supplier.

- SAVE AND RESTORE—When updating a data base a transaction may impact different records. The old data is not destroyed until the new data is correctly and completely in place.

SECURITY FEATURES

Data-base security features include the following:

- PASSWORDS—A password, controlled by the data-base administrator, may be required from the user before he is granted access to the data.

- READ ACCESS RESTRICTIONS—Logic may reside within the data-base description which controls data retrieval based on information content. For example, an employee may be able to examine personnel records only for employees with a job classification code lower than his own.

- UPDATE ACCESS RESTRICTIONS—Similar to READ ACCESS RESTRICTIONS, logic within the data-base description may control conditions until the data can be updated.

- ENCIPHER—A user may store data in enciphered form using the United States National Bureau of Standards cryptography algorithm. To decipher this data a key must be provided by the user. This key is not stored anywhere in the data base itself.

ADDING NEW DATA

A user can easily add new records to a data base. Suppose, for example, that a report has been printed as follows:

list empno name address birth sex dependents

EMPLOYEE NUMBER	EMPLOYEE NAME	ADDRESS	BIRTH DATE	SEX	DEPEN-DENTS
42	FLYNN, HENRY	4 OAK TRAIL, HOBOKEN N.J.	01/24/33	M	3
48	STEIN, HARRY	3 MARSHALL CT., WESTPORT CT.	01/10/47	M	1
104	DISCALA, ANN	2 CENTER ST., NORWALK CT.	06/01/40	F	2
341	SHERWOOD, LESLIE	5 TRADER LANE, STAMFORD CT.	08/04/43	F	1
1328	RAND, PAUL	MULBERRY LANE, SCARSDALE NY	03/20/29	M	2

The user can employ the PROMPT command to add a new employee to the data base and types:

PROMPT EMPLOYEE

The system then asks the user for the value of each field, in turn:

```
EMPNO=>234
NAME=>smith, kim
ADDRESS=>119 danbury rd., wilton pa.
BIRTH=>02/21/45
SEX=>f
DEPENDANTS=>0
```

NOMAD prints the record for verification before adding it to the data base:

```
EMPNO=234   NAME=SMITH, KIM   ADDRESS=119 DANBURY RD., WILTON PA.
   BIRTH=02/21/45   SEX=F   DEPENDANTS=0
```

The user may now repeat the LIST command and see the new data in place:

list empno name address birth sex dependents

EMPLOYEE NUMBER	EMPLOYEE NAME	ADDRESS	BIRTH DATE	S E X	DEPEN-DENTS
42	FLYNN, HENRY	4 OAK TRAIL, HOBOKEN N.J.	01/23/33	M	3
48	STEIN, HARRY	3 MARSHALL CT., WESTPORT CT.	01/10/47	M	1
104	DISCALA, ANN	2 CENTER ST., NORWALK CT.	06/01/40	F	2
341	SHERWOOD, LESLIE	5 TRADER LANE, STAMFORD CT.	08/04/43	F	1
1328	RAND, PAUL	MULBERRY LANE, SCARSDALE NY	03/20/29	M	2
234	SMITH, KIM	119 DANBURY RD., WILTON PA.	02/21/45	F	0

CHANGING A SET OF VALUES

As on other relational data-base systems, an entire column, or collection of fields of one type, can be changed with one command.

A user could increase the salary of every employee in the data base by 7% with the following command:

CHANGE SALARY = SALARY * 1.07 WITHIN DATA BASE

The salary of everybody in the accounting department could be changed as follows:

```
SELECT DEPT = 'ACCOUNTING'
CHANGE SALARY = SALARY * 1.07 WITHIN DATA BASE
SELECT CLEAR
```

LOADING OTHER FILES INTO NOMAD

Often NOMAD data bases are loaded from other files, or from other data bases, to create a separate system in which NOMAD's decision support capabilities can be employed. NOMAD has a powerful LOAD command which accomplishes this. Sometimes fields need to be converted when the NOMAD data base is loaded so that they match other existing data.

Often the DP organization converts and loads data which the end users then employ.

FAST DATA ENTRY

To accomplish fast interactive data entry into NOMAD for routine operations, data-entry screens may be specially designed. NOMAD provides a flexible easy-to-use screen design capability. With this it is possible to build dialogues for repetitive activities, or to display data differently from the standard NOMAD formats. Some analysts build menu-driven data entry applications.

NOMAD'S LIST COMMAND

The LIST command, illustrated in Fig. 14.1, is highly versatile, as well as easy-to-use.

It can be used for simple data-base queries. For example, "list all customers of 303x computers in Connecticut":

```
LIST BY ORGNAME WHERE STATE = 'CONNECTICUT'
AND MODEL BETWEEN ('3031', '3033').
```

NOMAD can list average values of a field, standard deviations, maximums, minimums, median values, variances, a count of values, etc. Thus departmental costs may be examined as follows:

list by deptname cost avg (cost) median (cost) variance —
(cost) stddev (cost)

DEPT. NAME	COST	AVG COST	MEDIAN COST	VARIANCE COST	STD DEV COST
FINANCE	600.00 450.00 250.00	433.33	450.00	30833.333333	175.594229
MARKETING	150.00 600.00 300.00	350.00	300.00	52500.000000	229.128785
SALES	400.00 600.00	500.00	500.00	20000.000000	141.421356

It can take a sum of a set of values of a field. In the following illustration the budget cost and actual cost items on each project are summed:

list by project sum (bud-cost) sum (act-cost)

PROJECT NUMBER	SUM BUD-COST	SUM ACT-COST
10	3,380.96	4,094.59
20	3,494.03	3,226.15
30	4,964.52	4,950.30
40	4,351.28	4,891.43
50	5,514.11	5,579.93
100	705.88	2,578.07
200	4,257.39	4,784.27
300	4,714.52	4,703.91
400	1,487.13	1,499.31
500	4,055.18	4,569.18

Project number 100 has an actual cost much higher than budget cost, so the user may take a detailed look at project 100:

select project = 100

list by taskno sum (phrs) sum (ahrs) —
sum (bud-cost) sum (act-cost) total all

TASK NUMBER	SUM PLANNED HOURS	SUM ACTUAL HOURS	SUM BUD-COST	SUM ACT-COST
1	1.50	6.86	45.00	205.80
2	1.20	2.94	36.00	88.20
3	2.60	9.28	69.25	236.93
4	1.50	6.82	30.00	136.40
5	6.25	26.64	141.25	616.08
6	7.50	29.92	145.00	589.28
7	8.75	24.92	239.38	705.38
========	=========	=======	=========	========
	29.30	107.38	705.88	2,578.07

Row totals, column totals, and subtotals for individual variables can be requested simply:

This requests a total for each row.

This requests a total for the entire report.

list by prodname skip 2 across months sum (sales)
(rowtot)(total)

PROD NAME	JAN SUM $SALES PER MONTH	FEB SUM $SALES PER MONTH	MAR SUM $SALES PER MONTH	APR SUM $SALES PER MONTH	MAY SUM $SALES PER MONTH	JUN SUM $SALES PER MONTH	TOTAL SUM $SALES PER MONTH
BLIVETS	$651.38	$556.91	$470.10	$497.56	$576.14	$316.16	$3,068.25
JARVERS	$400.68	$208.59	$442.18	$161.11	$282.21	$444.48	$1,939.25
LINKERS	$168.23	$204.12	$278.08	$253.55	$193.95	$243.36	$1,341.29
WIDGETS	$534.90	$473.40	$581.20	$1,327.45	$688.53	$885.77	$4,491.25
	$1,755.19	$1,443.02	$1,771.56	$2,239.67	$1,740.83	$1,889.77	$10,840.04

list by month salesman quota sales:

overquota subtotal bonus subtotal total

QUOTA SUMMARY REPORT
ACTUAL FIGURES IN HUNDREDS OF DOLLARS

MONTHS	SALESMAN	QUOTA	SUM $SALES PER MONTH	DOLLARS OVER QUOTA	OVER QUOTA BONUS DOLLARS
JAN	CRANDALL PRUDENCE	$910	$919.62	$9.62	$0.58
FEB	FOSTER LAFAYETTE	$250	$278.32	$28.32	$1.70
	HOOKER THOMAS	$450	$455.18	$5.18	$0.31
	PORTER SARAH	$75	$81.20	$6.20	$0.37
*				$39.70	$2.38
MAR	CRANDALL PRUDENCE	$600	$610.44	$10.44	$0.63
	HOOKER THOMAS	$650	$698.54	$48.54	$2.91
	WELLES GIDEON	$90	$93.14	$3.14	$0.19
*				$62.12	$3.73
				$111.44	$6.69

"WHAT IF?" CALCULATIONS

Businesspersons often want to explore a situation by asking "What if?" questions. What if the interest rate goes to 19%? What if sales are down by 5%? This can be easy to do with NOMAD.

Consider the above report showing sales and salespersons' quota bonuses. The salespersons earn a 6% bonus on all dollars of sales over their quota.

Sales executives might ask the hypothetical question, "What would be the effect on paid bonus dollars of a 1% increase in sales over this period?" To answer the question they key:

CHANGE SALES = SALES * 1.01 WITHIN DATA BASE

They run the report again with a modified title:

change sales = sales * 1.01 within database

title 'quota summary report' fold 'projection of 1% increase —
   in all sales' fold 'fisures in hundreds of dollars'

quota2

QUOTA SUMMARY REPORT
PROJECTION OF 1% INCREASE IN ALL SALES
FIGURES IN HUNDREDS OF DOLLARS

MONTHS	SALESMAN	QUOTA	SUM $SALES PER MONTH	DOLLARS OVER QUOTA	OVER QUOTA BONUS DOLLARS
JAN	CRANDALL PRUDENCE	$910	$928.82	$18.82	$1.13
	PORTER SARAH	$100	$100.11	$0.11	$0.01
*				$18.93	$1.14
FEB	FOSTER LAFAYETTE	$250	$281.10	$31.10	$1.87
	HOOKER THOMAS	$450	$459.72	$9.72	$0.58
	PORTER SARAH	$75	$82.01	$7.01	$0.42
*				$47.83	$2.87
MAR	CRANDALL PRUDENCE	$600	$616.54	$16.54	$0.99
	HOOKER THOMAS	$650	$705.53	$55.53	$3.33
	WELLES GIDEON	$90	$94.07	$4.07	$0.24
				$76.14	$4.56
				$142.90	$8.57

The right-hand column gives the answer. They could then explore a 2% increase in sales and so on.

An attractive feature of NOMAD is that "What if?" questions can be answered without altering the original values in the data base. The users type SAVE OFF, meaning that the feature of NOMAD which SAVES any data base changes if *off.* They can then make any "What if?" changes they want without affecting the data base. At the end of the session NOMAD prompts the users to ask whether they want to save the changes.

TEXTUAL REPORTS Textual reports can be stored in NOMAD and variables inserted into them from the data base. The following is an example:

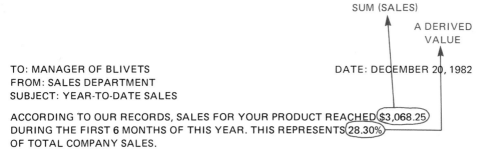

SUM (SALES)

A DERIVED VALUE

TO: MANAGER OF BLIVETS   DATE: DECEMBER 20, 1982
FROM: SALES DEPARTMENT
SUBJECT: YEAR-TO-DATE SALES

ACCORDING TO OUR RECORDS, SALES FOR YOUR PRODUCT REACHED $3,068.25
DURING THE FIRST 6 MONTHS OF THIS YEAR. THIS REPRESENTS 28.30%
OF TOTAL COMPANY SALES.

IF THESE FIGURES DO NOT AGREE WITH YOUR RECORDS, PLEASE CONTACT US
IMMEDIATELY SO THAT WE CAN RESOLVE ANY DISCREPANCIES.

THANK YOU IN ADVANCE FOR YOUR COOPERATION.

DAVID S. JUSTICE
SALES DEPARTMENT MANAGER

Text can be stored in the NOMAD data base with long variable-length alphanumeric strings and special format control characters which specify the output format.

RELATIONAL   It is often necessary to extract data from multiple
OPERATORS   files and combine them to produce one report.
                        NOMAD, like other relational data-base systems,
provides a range of relational operators for *joining* data from one or more
data bases. The relationships between the data need not be predefined. Two
data bases are combined on the basis of a common field type which is part
of both.

The relational operations include:

EXTRACT   all data from the first data base, along with matching data from
                the second data base.

SUBSET   only data from each data base that match.

REJECT   only data from the first data base that does not have a match
                  in the second data base.

MERGE   all the data from the first data base and all the data from the
                  second data base regardless of matches.

EXTRACT ALL   all data from the first data base along with all matching data
                  from the second data base.

SUBSET ALL   only data from each data base that matches, including all data
                  that matches from the second data base.

As an illustration, a corporation purchased a tape of IBM computer installations from a market research firm. It converted it to a NOMAD data base. It could then create a wide diversity of reports from it.

The tape contained a code of which the first four digits was a Standard Industry Code (SIC), which identified the industry of the company. Another previously existing data base contained details of companies and also had a table of SIC codes. Reports needed to be generated in which these codes were matched (a relational join).

Matching is done as follows:

LIST BY SIC ORGNAME MODEL
EXTRACT MATCH
FROM INDUSTRY SICCODE
ITYPE STATE

This results in a report with SIC, ORGNAME, and MODEL from the original file and ITYPE and STATE from those records in the INDUSTRY file which have the same values of SICCODE.

The field which is the basis of the matching has a different name in the different file. These different names of equivalent fields have to be equated. SICCODE is the first field after the MATCH [FROM INDUSTRY] clause, so it is matched to SIC.

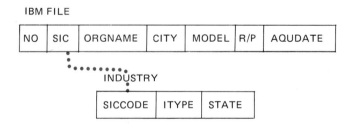

IBM FILE

| NO | SIC | ORGNAME | CITY | MODEL | R/P | AQUDATE |

INDUSTRY

| SICCODE | ITYPE | STATE |

GRAPHICS   Graphics charts can be created by NOMAD in an
                          easy-to-use, nonprocedural fashion.

The PLOT command procedures graphics reports with similar syntax to the LIST command. Thus the user could say:

LIST BY PRODUCT ACROSS MONTH SUM (SALES-AMOUNT) or
PLOT BY PRODUCT ACROSS MONTH SUM (SALES-AMOUNT)

Figure 14.4 shows the result of this plot command.

The item following the word ACROSS is treated as the independent variable. The statement identifies the dependent variables to be plotted. The dependent variables must be numeric. The independent variables need not be.

The PLOT command may state what type of plot is needed. The options include a LINE, SCATTER, BAR, and PIE chart. If this is not stated, NOMAD selects an appropriate chart type.

In the command

PLOT ACROSS PRODUCT SUM (SALES)

PRODUCT is not a numeric variable; therefore, NOMAD selects a bar chart with a separate bar for each product showing the sum of its sales.

Plots can be designed for a printer, plotter, or screen terminal. The NOMAD command may state NEW PLOT or NEW COLOR to indicate a new plot or new color for each BY item in the command. Specific colors, patterns, or textures (of pie or bar charts) can be requested.

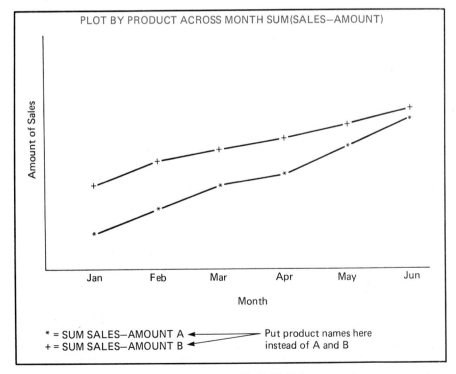

Figure 14.4   Use of the NOMAD PLOT command.

Pie charts can have exploded portions. Bar charts can have clustered bars, stacked bars, or hidden bars. Different fonts and character sizes can be specified on a plotting machine.

NOMAD will select its own scales for the axes but the user will often want to state or change the range of values on the scales. Users will often want to make adjustments to their plot to improve its usefulness or attractiveness.

ARRAYS

Various types of arrays can be declared and used in NOMAD. NOMAD commands can then apply to all the items in the array.

NOMAD handles fixed-length or variable-length arrays, and one-dimensional or multidimensional arrays. A time series is treated as a special type of array with various functions designed for handling it.

When any type of array is printed with a PRINT command, the subscripts of the array are printed above each item. Thus SALES may be declared as a one-dimensional, fixed-length array with four values:

ITEM SALES (4)

When it is printed it appears as follows:

PRINT SALES

	1	2	3	4
	---	---	---	---
SALES =	1400	1475	1580	1522

If a variable length array is declared the user does not have to be concerned with how many elements the array should have. It can be expanded to fit the needs.

In a time series an array could have an index value which is a calendar date. The user declares a starting date, SDATE, and a periodicity for the series. Thus

ITEM REVENUE AS $99,999,999.99 ARRAY

SDATE 01/01/81' MONTHLY

The word ARRAY would instruct NOMAD to create a *variable length* array. The index value would be the first date of each month starting January 1981.

The additional declaration index as DATE 'MONTH-YEAR' would cause NOMAD to print the month above each value instead of an index number:

PRINT REVENUE

JAN-81	FEB-81	MAR-81	APR-81
--------	--------	--------	--------

REVENUE =	1,061,954.98	1,097,934.41	1,242,416.38	1,426,781.45

MAY-81	JUN-81	JUL-81	AUG-81
--------	--------	--------	--------
1,379,612.72	1,213,031.68	1,202,307.07	1,376,957.58

SEP-81	OCT-81	NOV-81	DEC-81
--------	--------	--------	--------
1,277,874.59	1,555,188.39	1,446,681.18	1,381,566.52

JAN-82	FEB-82	MAR-82	APR-82
--------	--------	--------	--------
1,665,312.35	1,691,233.42	1,558,731.09	1,459,320.78

MAY-82	JUN-82	JUL-82	AUG-82
--------	--------	--------	--------
1,527,075.48	1,690,121.34	2,039,385.02	1,869,282.31

SEP-82	OCT-82	NOV-82	DEC-82
--------	--------	--------	--------
1,779,502.66	1,927,270.67	1,554,418.03	1,796,187.57

JAN-83

2,351,962.65

All the variables in an array can be manipulated with one command referring to the array by name. The entire array may be printed or plotted, on select portions of it. Individual items in an array can be modified or used by referring to them with their subscript, e.g., SALES (3).

PROCEDURAL STATEMENTS

The procedural portion of the NOMAD language contains statements which can express logic rather like a conventional programming language, but often with fewer statements. It contains operators which perform arithmetic, comparison, logic operations, if tests, table look-up, and concatenation.

The code can contain IF statements such as:

```
IF (ALL (ITEM-QUANTITY GT 6)) THEN PRINT 'YES';
```

It can contain DO groups, like PL/1:

```
IF CODE GT 8 THEN DO;
  PRINT 'INVALID CODE';
  ERRORCOUNT = ERRORCOUNT + 1;
END;
```

It can contain GO TO statements, although a user may be trained to avoid using these.

It can contain ON statements such as:

```
ON ERROR DO;
  IF CODE LE 5 THEN RETURN;
  PRINT CODE 'WAS LESS THAN 5';
  PRINT 'PROCESSING CONTINUING';
END;
```

It can contain nested IF statements, ELSE statements, nested DO groups, and so on:

```
IF logical-expression 1
   THEN IF logical-expression 2 _____
      THEN command 1;
      ELSE;
   ELSE command 2;
```

Commands/or DO-groups can be dependent on a FOR statement. They may execute *for* variables on certain values, or *for* certain positioning instances in a data base:

```
FOR ITEM-QUANTITY = 1 TO 500 STEP 2 DO;
  PRINT ITEM-QUANTITY;
END;
```

NOMAD can also execute string manipulations, trigonometrical calculations, and statistical functions.

Many end users do not employ the more complex procedural statements. They use the simpler nonprocedural code and sometimes do elaborate calculations on data from the data base—for example, building financial models. The procedural statements, however, greatly extend the range of applications which NOMAD is used for. Often systems analysts working with users do the procedural coding.

STATISTICS   NOMAD contains built-in software for statistical
                                        calculations. The LIST, PLOT, and other commands can refer to averages, medians, variances, or standard deviations. In addition, NOMAD performs the following types of statistical calculation and reporting:

- multiple regression
- polynomial regression
- stepwise regression

- T-test
- chi-square
- basic statistics
- simple linear regression

Results can be returned not only in report format but also as a data base.

HOW IS NOMAD BEING USED?

How is NOMAD being used in practice? Box 14.1 summarizes some comments on this. It divides the use into those of single users and those involving multiple departments. Single users can do their own thing without too much interference with any other use of computers. Multidepartment users need data administration controls and more planning. Administrative and control users may also need data administration because their applications relate to other DP applications. They often require the services of an Information Center, as described in Chapter 19.

NOMAD has extremely valuable uses in planning. Its user-friendliness has caused many managers and staff who never expected to program a computer to adopt at least its nonprocedural syntax and create their own uses.

Administrative staff can save themselves time by having their own electronic filing cabinets and being able to manipulate data. Users entering and keeping their own data often take much more care with its accuracy.

Executives use NOMAD to keep an eye on critical figures, schedules, or results. Sometimes they have data bases and applications created for them which allow them to do daily checking. They can investigate poor figures in an *ad hoc* fashion.

Auditors can capture data, for example, from each branch of a bank, and apply their tests to it without programmers or other bank staff knowing what they are looking for. This can reduce the chances of undetected fraud.

In one large bank the bankers used NOMAD to analyze financial portfolios. They need to detect changes in market trends and compute the effects of possible actions. In the area of certificates of deposit (CDs) NOMAD is used to:

- identify all CDs bought and sold by clients
- prepare accounting and management reports which show the type of purchases, values, interest rates, and maturity dates for each CD
- physically print the CD for the purchase.

A utility company which provides gas to 2.7 million customers uses

BOX 14.1 Examples of how languages like NOMAD are being used

	PLANNING	ADMINISTRATION AND CONTROL
SINGLE USER	Managers and high-level staff do ad hoc planning, build financial models, explore "what if?" questions, etc. Users often set up their own data and create their own	Administrative and clerical staff keep their own electronic filing cabinets. Managers monitor the status of departmental data. Canned, repetitive applications are often used, sometimes set up by an Information Center.
MULTIPLE DEPARTMENTS	The language is used for prototyping so that applications that will be used by multiple departments can be checked out by these departments before full coding. Executives explore "what if?" questions on multidepartmental data. The language is used for overall financial planning with organization-wide data, often with ad hoc use of preestablished data bases.	Executives monitor data from multiple areas. Organizationwide financial control mechanisms are employed. The language is used for project management, production control, and expediting status reporting, and many cross-departmental applications. End users invent modifications to work flow, and better administrative mechanisms. Auditors capture data and conduct examinations. Cross-departmental applications need good data administration. Applications are sometimes set up by an Information Center.

NOMAD in its instrument division. This division is responsible for the maintenance and repair of over 1,000 different types of electronic instruments of the company's four plants and 6,000 miles of gas lines.

Effective maintenance requires fully accurate and current information to be kept on all instruments. Details such as the frequency of repairs, how long the repairs take, cost of repairs, and often management statistics, are kept. NOMAD is used to process and report this information. In addition, it is used for inventory of spare parts, ordering procedure for parts, and indicating from whom the parts should be ordered. Employing NOMAD, the users have reduced the cost of repairs. The company is working towards a fully integrated forecasting and budgeting system.

In many companies users have compressed hundreds of pages of batch reports into summaries and charts which highlight important information. This condensing of data can be modified interactively by the on-line users.

When applications which will be used by multiple departments are needed, NOMAD is sometimes used as a prototyping tool. Future users of the application can check it out and add to it. Users are often not sure what output they want from a system. NOMAD can give them a prototype to experiment with and decide what is valuable. In one large publishing company the marketing vice president and sales manager used NOMAD to create the types of reports they thought would be useful for the sales department staff. The staff checked these out and made many requests for improvements. The sales manager successively refined the reports at a terminal. Some of the changes required additional data, which were extracted from available DP files.

One of the most valuable aspects of end users employing languages like NOMAD is that they can change their own administrative procedures. They can lessen their paperwork, improve the information flow, and improve the way information is used. To some extent they can redesign their own job. Many find this exciting and so productivity is improved not only by the more efficient use of computing but also by the improvement of morale and job attitudes of white-collar workers. Psychological factors effect productivity as much as good uses of technology.

REFERENCES

1. *NOMAD 2 Reference Manual,* National CSS, Wilton, CT, 1981.

2. Relational data bases are described in Chapter 9 of James Martin, *Principles of Data-Base Management,* Prentice-Hall, Inc., Englewood Cliffs, NJ, 1976.

3. Models of data are described in James Martin, *Managing the Data-Base Environment,* SAVANT, 2 New St., Carnforth, Lancs, UK, 1981.

Video tapes are available on this subject and are part of the James Martin Advanced Technology Library, Deltak Inc., 1220 Kensington Road, Oak Brook, IL 60521.

15 HOW DO WE CROSS THE BARRIER TO END-USER APPLICATION CREATION?

A CULTURAL BARRIER
Many end users are intelligent enough to create applications and have need for computing which is more adaptable to their rapidly changing requirements. On the other hand, most end users have a major cultural barrier to overcome. They are usually frightened of terminals and regard the *creation* of computer applications as a mystique entirely beyond their reach.

Nevertheless, the best case histories of end users doing *their own* application creation are *very* impressive. The contrast between this form of DP development and the classical development cycle is extreme. Both types of development have their place, but the entire computer world needs to move strongly toward user-driven applications and creation of these applications by the end users themselves where appropriate.

Most organizations, however, have a huge hurdle to get over in establishing the spread of end-user computing. How can this hurdle be crossed?

To enable non-DP-skilled end users to create applications the software needs to be human-factored very well. It must be user-friendly and non-threatening. *We have stressed that such software exists now.* It is being put to excellent use in a few organizations, as described in Chapter 11, for example.

Certain highly skilled end users learn to program. Again they need faster results than they would obtain from DP and the ability to change their programs quickly and experiment. Excellent experience has been achieved with NOMAD, APL, RAMIS, FOCUS, and other such languages. *Again the software exists* and is being put to good use, but planners, research staff, financial analysts, and particularly the staff surrounding senior management ought to be using it *far more*.

If the software exists now, why is it not in more widespread use?

Overcoming this cultural barrier is something that each organization has to confront on its own rather than waiting for any overall change in the computer industry. The information center approach described in Chapter 19 is valuable. In many of the most interesting case studies an innovative end user or end-user department has taken the initiative and changed the way computers are used.

TWO IMAGES   The reader should create in his mind two vividly contrasting images of the use of computers in a corporation. In the *first image* all application creation is done by a hard-pressed DP group using COBOL, with formal systems analysis and requirements specification. There is an application backlog of years. The results when eventually produced are of limited value for user-driven applications. Whether structured programming and structured analysis is used makes little difference to the contrast of these two images.

The *second image* is one in which end users create applications. The shop floor supervisors, expeditors, and the purchasing, marketing, and personnel departments all create computerized reporting and control procedures with a data-base-oriented application generator. This increases the productivity and efficiency of these departments, decreases the capital tied up in inventory, work in progress, and machine tools, and improves customer service. The financial staff, budget controllers, planners, and engineers create the programs they need in APL or FOCUS. DP creates the heavy-duty applications plans the data bases and networks and helps the end users employ computers to run their departments better. End users of many types throughout the corporation are inventing how they use computers to improve their own productivity and are constantly adjusting their own applications.

The second image is what much data processing *ought* to be like. It needs an infrastructure and support facilities created by DP. It needs substantial coordination in data-base planning. Within this controlled framework end users create the applications they need. These controls are vital for all applications other than those which are purely personal and not shared or maintained by other people.

The DP representative to the users becomes a consultant, helper, and instructor. For the applications programmed by DP he creates prototypes for end-user approval.

DP MANAGEMENT
ENCOURAGEMENT
OF END USERS
       How should management bring about this second form of computer usage? How can the cultural barrier be crossed?

First, DP management needs to be committed to the concept of end users creating their own applications where appropriate. (For many applications it is not appropriate.)

Many DP managers do not encourage end-user application creation, for a variety of reasons:

They do not understand the capabilities of software such as MAPPER or NOMAD.

They underestimate the capabilities of the end users.

They think that end users doing their own thing will lead to chaos.

They do not want to lose any of their empire.

In fact, DP managers could make life much easier for themselves if they encouraged end-user application creation. This would lessen the pressures on DP. It would lessen the end-user frustration. It would lessen the complaints about DP. Coupled with DP's own use of the same high-productivity tools, the new application software gives the DP manager the opportunity to be a hero in his organization instead of a whipping boy.

SOFTWARE SELECTION

Next, appropriate software and facilities need to be selected. These will differ considerably from one organization to another: data-base resources, networks, data-base query languages, information retrieval, report generators, application generators, and time sharing with end-user languages.

We referred earlier to a *technique analyst* (TA), whose job it is to know the capabilities of the types of software in Fig. 2.1. If the software is for *end-user* application development, its human factoring needs to be examined carefully.

Many end users in future organizations will be categories 3 and 4 of Fig. 8.1. These will not have programming skills like the APL users. They need software which is genuinely appropriate for such nonskilled users. As we commented earlier, much of the software sold as end-user software is not appropriate for the mass of end users. The *2-day test* should be applied to it. Can the end user for whom it is intended learn to use it well in a 2-day course, and then not forget how to use it when he does something else?

To bring terminals to as many users as possible we need to remove the *fear* of computing. It must be made to seem as simple and natural as possible. This can be achieved only if the end-user terminal dialogue is elegant, easy to use, and psychologically effective.

FEAR OF TERMINALS

A high proportion of the people who *ought* to be using computer terminals are afraid of them. They imagine that the device and its dialogue is complicated and that they will not be able to deal with it correctly. They expect that it will display things, as it has done in the past, to which they do not know how to respond. Rather than be made to seem a fool they try to avoid becoming involved with terminals. Many programmers and analysts do not anticipate this attitude. They enjoy and experiment with terminals and often fail to comprehend that other people are afraid of them.

Recently, in a branch office of a major computer manufacturer, a new and impressive terminal facility was demonstrated to me. It would have provided the salespeople with all manner of information of value to them. Unfortunately, no salespeople used it, apparently because they felt it was too complicated for them. They were frightened of appearing foolish in the office. If computer salespeople avoid the use of terminals for this reason, how much more so will the general run of potential end users?

A terminal dialogue need not be bewildering. There are always many ways of achieving equivalent results with a terminal. It is desirable to select software that is appropriate for the users in question. Dialogue techniques that are good for most potential users are quite different from those that are good for programmers and analysts. Dialogues for most end users need the properties listed in Box 8.2. Much software is sold as being end-user software when it does not have these properties.

END-USER
TRAINING

The training of end users is critical. A carefully designed course needs to be put together for them. It should be designed to motivate them strongly so that they understand the reason for changing their old comfortable habits. It should completely omit any technical jargon that is unnecessary (and most of it is unnecessary). It should translate the technical words into more pictorial images, such as describing the *modes* of Univac's MAPPER as "filing cabinets." The course should have much hands-on-training so that all students physically use the terminals and become familiar with them.

Good software for end users has HELP functions and self-training functions so that the student can query the system when necessary and continue his learning at the terminal whenever he wishes. The training course should ensure that he is comfortable obtaining further training this way.

A simple subset of the capabilities should be taught first, deliberately omitting the more complex functions or functions infrequently used. The student may have several weeks of live experience of this subset and then return to class to learn more advanced features.

It is very important to make the facility *seem* as simple as possible at first. Once the end user has crossed the threshold of using and accepting the product and is beginning to be comfortable with it, he can learn more features. In the cases we studied, time and time again the most underestimated area was education. Some DP professionals become so excited about a facility that they think the end users are bound to share their excitement, but they do not until after substantial training and hands-on experience.

When end users program (and much can be accomplished without programming), they should be taught good programming techniques, in a simple fashion. Cincom's manual on their MANTIS language, for example, contains an easy-to-read chapter on structured programming techniques.

When end-user systems have been successful for some years, they often grow large. When that happens another form of training is needed to help users understand what is available to them on the system so that they can employ it effectively. The Continental Bank in Chicago provided users with information via STAIRS (IBM's information retrieval system). In the beginning they did not provide enough information for users' needs, but that was steadily remedied. After three years the system had 90 disc drives of information, all quickly accessible by terminal users. The number of users grew to over 5000. This was too many to send to classes whenever the system was further enhanced. When this happens it becomes necessary to develop newsletters about the system or, better, use the system itself to teach the users about new facilities. A self-teaching system becomes vital.

DP LEADERSHIP   In many corporations the end-user management has introduced computer systems independently of DP because of the long backlog, because of a perception of poor DP service, or merely because they wanted to be in control of their own system. In other cases DP has encouraged and provided the facilities for end-user application creation. The latter course is usually the better, provided that the users are genuinely able to use their own inventiveness and can modify their own applications as and when they want. It is better because DP can create the data bases and networks that are needed and link the user systems into the overall corporate needs.

In many cases, unfortunately, DP are not yet believers in end-user application creation, or are not sufficiently flexible in permitting a good system choice. DP may, for example, be committed to one computer vendor when the end users want a software facility from another vendor.

In some of the best managed cases, DP personnel are the driving force. They combine conventional data processing with a well-researched understanding of the diverse facilities which this report discusses. They do thorough computerized data-base planning, provide end-user data-base languages, information retrieval systems, networks, and give the end users their own minicomputer systems where appropriate, linking them to an overall plan.

Most of the software packages that we have described can be installed quickly. MAPPER installations such as that described in Chapter 11 have typically been brought into initial operation within a week. The same is true with Microdata's Reality and other such packages. The Continental Bank STAIRS system mentioned above was made operational in 60 days. This included a linkage to the bank's large IMS data bases so that data could be extracted from these data bases and reformatted for end-user searching and retrieval with STAIRS.

When such packages can be installed quickly on a trial basis, little can be lost by trying them. They could be dropped after a few months if the end users do not find them valuable. Usually, their use gains hold and steadily grows. It will often become difficult to remove them, so a careful choice of package should be made from the start. A good package is one that will enable the usage to keep growing into more powerful forms. The users should evolve from queries or information retrieval to report generation, graphics generation, application generation, and possibly simple types of programming. Many of the packages are too limited to permit this growth.

PILOT SYSTEMS   A valuable approach is to try out pilot systems (prototypes) and see how they work. The organization should remove them fairly quickly if they prove inappropriate. There should be no stigma attached to an experiment which is tried quickly and fails. Experimentation is necessary in exploring this new frontier. The cost of the experiments should be low, and can be low with today's software.

In some cases an end-user facility has been selected and pilots are installed with it in many different areas of the organization. Some are more successful than others. Terminals connected via telephone lines or a corporate network can be installed at any location. Portable terminals can be used by executives who travel. In some cases this is done internationally.

One executive described his experience with pilots as follows:

> You could spend years doing requirements planning and trying to decide what the users really want. The best thing to do is to get on with it; get some people using the tools and see how they feel. Adapt to their feelings. Put the data that they want on-line. Help them generate the reports they want.
>
> Unlike traditional data processing you can get these tools on the air very quickly.
>
> Our approach was to keep the time horizon very short. If we could put something up in 2 weeks it was worth doing. Sometimes we completely changed it and redid it. But then in 4 weeks we had a product rather than still sitting around talking about requirements.

With user-driven computing most people are not certain what the users' needs are, or what will work well and what will not. The best way to find out is to *try something,* start people using it, determine their feelings about it, and modify it as necessary. This approach would be totally impractical with COBOL, PL/1, or the traditional approaches to DP development. With RAMIS II, MAPPER, STAIRS, FOCUS, and the like, it works well.

SELLING   Where DP personnel are in the driver's seat, they need to do considerable *selling* to encourage the end users to employ the facilities. When the *information center* concept is used, as described in Chapter 19, a function of information center representatives should be to motivate, encourage, and train the end users. In some DP organizations compensation of these representatives includes a bonus related to the number of end users who utilize the systems. One highly successful DP executive is an ex-IBM sales manager who now has his technical representatives *on a quota system,* like computer salespeople.

Some on-line applications make sense only when many users employ them. The ability to move work from one manager's work queue to another electronically can save a manager much time, but only if all the persons he communicates with in the organization use the same type of facility. Electronic mail is useless if only one person has it. On-line systems for helping supervisors and expeditors improve the flow of work through a factory needs input and reports relating to many aspects and areas of the factory. The office-of-the-future environment becomes efficient when it interconnects an entire organization rather than one office.

One successful approach is to take new DP trainees, with none of the habits of traditional DP, and give them the task of spreading the system usage. People coming right out of college are doing an excellent job with this objective and finding it exciting. Often new graduates without experience in DP learn the new languages and techniques faster than DP staff much experienced in older methods.

The system, in many cases, maintains statistics on the numbers of users and how much they use the system. In some cases a user will obtain 1% of his information electronically, in some cases 50% when the facility is mature. One executive quoted 80%. The objective should be to expand this percentage. This needs good understanding of the end users, selling, help, handholding, and the development of the right types of data bases.

MOTIVATION   The primary motivation of end users is a personal one. They ask: *"What will it do for me?"* Often, they do not perceive the effort of change to be worth it. A perception of substantial benefit is often necessary to overcome the fear of terminals.

A major personal benefit is the saving of time. Managers spend much time on paperwork that could be automated. They could automate it themselves if they had a facility such as MAPPER (Chapter 11). For *most* white-collar workers better automation could save at least 2 hours a day of their time.

The pressure of time is the reason many end users do not employ the new facilities. They are too busy to go on a training course, too busy to learn, too busy to practice. It is necessary to make them understand that the expenditure of 2 days *now* will save them 2 hours a day in the future. The investment will be paid back manyfold.

They spend a lot of effort thinking about their product, or thinking about their customers and how to do things for them. But they spend very little effort thinking about how effectively they use their time. With these tools they ought to think about how to save their own time; how to cut out the paperwork and telephoning and running about.

One DP executive who had been exceptionally successful in generating end-user motivation gave the following advice:

> Don't think about automating this or automating that. Think about productivity. Saving a professional's or an executive's time. Increasing an executive's span of control. Increasing the goods that a given resource can produce.
>
> The good professionals and executives are an extremely valuable resource. How can you buy more time for them?

In many of the most successful case histories, *top management* provides motivation. If top management understands that the electronic office is the key to productivity and makes this feeling known, much will follow. User-driven computing needs strong management encouragement. Users must be encouraged to experiment. Some applications will prove to be great, most will need modifying, some will be scrapped. The cost of those that are scrapped is much less than the cost of conventional DP development. Progress is made by trial and error, Darwinism, successive small improvements.

The computerized corporation of the future will be *highly* automated, with at least one terminal for every two employees, little paperwork, and strong participation by end-user management in developing and continuously refining the procedures. The objectives will be higher productivity, better products, better customer service. The growth of the electronic organization needs the grass-roots participation of everybody. This participation needs to fit into an organized and controlled framework. In most corporations a revolutionary change in DP methods is needed to accomplish this. Senior management needs a vision of what is now possible.

MOTIVATION SCHEMES   Once end-user involvement in computing is started it is generally desirable to spread it as fast as possible (with appropriate controls). Corporations do this in a variety of ways.

Some write a monthly column in the house magazine. Personnel everywhere are thus made aware both of the activity and management approval of it.

The corporation in the case study of Chapter 11 created a newsletter about end-user use of the software. This is published monthly. It contains many descriptions of how end users have improved corporate productivity or customer service by creating applications with MAPPER. It contains a MAPPER coordinator's column, hints for users, and summaries of what data are available via MAPPER. Users' "candid" comments are published regularly together with a photograph of the user in question. Typical comments are:

"MAPPER has saved me 20 hours a week."

"I was able to accept more responsibilities."

"It has eliminated 60% of our clerical work."

"In the last 6 months our printed wiring card returns have tripled. Without MAPPER it would have been impossible to keep up."

"I can now find an order immediately instead of going to the WIP book, which is a day out of date."

The software vendor could help to get such a newsletter started and contribute a monthly column to it.

The same corporation selects a *MAPPER person-of-the-month*. Details of this person are written up together with their achievement with MAPPER.

Some organizations give prizes to creative end users. Awards are also given for outstanding scores in on-line examinations in usage of the software. Other organizations have a prestigious club of outstanding users of the system, or users who have originated valuable applications. The club sometimes has an annual conference in Bermuda.

A particularly strong way to motivate end users is to let them know that they are more promotable if they have the skill to generate reports or applications. In some cases secretaries or administrative staff have pulled themselves up from a life of low-paid clerical work by learning how to generate computer applications.

Some organizations put games, puzzles, and competitions on the computer terminals. This encourages users to try out the terminals and overcome their fear of them. Games or not, many end users have discovered that using application generators is fascinating and fun.

In many corporations there is *no* end-user participation in creating computer applications and the DP management regard this as indicating that the end users *cannot* participate. In fact, there was no attempt to show them what is possible or to motivate them. The best case histories show that participation by a very broad cross section of end users is possible with today's software and highly beneficial. But the motivation and training of end users is critical.

EARLY ADAPTERS   In all organizations there are some persons who love the new methods and some who hate them. Some people want to experiment, want to use the machines, and will try anything new. Some stay in the office late at night to play with the terminals.

A highly effective way to introduce user-driven computing is to identify the enthusiasts—the early adapters. The early-adapter end users should be encouraged to have a terminal in their office. DP management should give these people access to data bases, information retrieval systems, electronic mail, viewdata, or anything else that may be useful. In particular, they should give facilities for generating reports and creating applications.

The information center representatives (with a bonus linked to user acceptance of their facilities) should seek out the early adapters, especially those in influential positions. The early adapters, when they have something useful working, tend to exert peer-group pressure on their colleagues. They show their associates how they are using their terminal and encourage them to do the same. The emphasis can then swing to the early-adapter-minus-one individuals, then early-adapter-minus-two. The late adapters will eventually yield to the influence of the rest.

Where possible, end-user management should make their own decisions about what is worth paying for. As far as possible, the costs and savings should be in their own budgets. There are then realistic decisions about what is economically viable.

> How did we find the early adapters? I guess if you have been in a firm for any length of time you are familiar with the different managers and know who are willing to try things. You know who will take a positive attitude and find things to improve rather than just saying it's no good. The management know who those people are. But sometimes you get surprises.

Some early adapters are particularly respected by their colleagues. In one organization a system was installed for portfolio managers—people who select stocks and bonds and who manage money. Some portfolio managers are high flyers. They have been exceptionally successful in their choice of investments. Their colleagues strongly want to achieve the same success. The DP management in this organization selected the high flyers who were also adaptable to the use of terminals. When these end users were seen to employ their terminals and talk about them enthusiastically, the other end users were anxious to copy them.

STAGES OF ACCEPTANCE

End-user attitudes to new terminal facilities often goes through four stages:

STAGE I.   They regard the devices as toys.

STAGE II.   Neutral. They think there *may* be some benefit or there may not.

STAGE III.   They cross a hurdle and perceive the facility as worthwhile.

STAGE IV.   They think it unwise *not* to be part of the activity.

Going through these stages is a step-by-step process that requires work on the part of the technical representatives and good selection of the early adapters.

The most critical stage is stage I. No professional or manager wants to spend time with something that is regarded as a toy when he has meaningful work to do. When terminals are first introduced, they should give something of clear value so that the *toy* perception does not persist.

Different people pass through the stages at different rates. The early adapters may pass immediately through the toy stage and want to try the facility. Others are much more skeptical. The very late adapters view the terminals as toys for years to come.

An individual using the new tools for the first time has to pass a point of being comfortable with them. That will take some time and needs some effort. Using the tool needs to become a habit, like using the phone. Then suddenly the user starts to perceive ways of enhancing the process. The tool becomes part of the way he thinks about his job. When a group of users reach this stage they start to discuss how the facilities could be used better. At that stage the applications can evolve rapidly, driven by the users, if the software has the capability to facilitate this fast *ad hoc* evolution.

Good DP representatives can help to get users past the comfort stage quickly.

The computers themselves ought to disappear from view. People do not think about the electricity company's generating plant or the telephone company's control office. The user should see only the terminal and the services it gives—the information retrieval; the electronic mail; the ability to create his own files, generate reports, and send the reports to other people's terminals. Most terminals should be the same so that he can sit at any terminal and use these services, or process his work queue. Some people should have such a terminal at home.

Once this is achieved, you can put computing into the hands of the business manager, like the telephone. He decides how he uses it and controls his budget for this usage.

TERMINALS AT HOME

It is important to have cheap terminals. They should be distributed around an organization in masses. Most people should have access to one and many should have them on their desk. Once users employ them, new functions can be added as the most meaningful ways are found of providing information.

Some end users have terminals at home. Some are portable terminals; some are display terminals. What the computer industry needs is a cheap portable display terminal; then executives can carry their electronic office with them.

Some users handle their electronic mail at home or process their work queue. Some prefer to develop reports or create applications in the relatively unharrassed environment of their home. Some like to work at home weekends or in the evening. A terminal at home allows a workaholic to indulge himself to the full.

In some cases married people who like to look after their children at home are extending their earning power with home terminals.

TOP MANAGEMENT   The culture of end-user application creation is not likely to spread to top management except for those rare individuals who regard the computer partially as a hobby. Increasing numbers of senior management are *using* terminals as the terminal dialogues become easier (like viewdata) and the levels of executives below senior management are promoted. The color graphics terminals can be exceptionally valuable for senior management.

Where senior management use computers directly or indirectly, they need staff close to them creating the displays, reports, and applications and modifying them as rapidly as their bosses would wish. When the staff of top management have access to large and diverse data bases and can search quickly for information and format it into reports and charts, information systems at last become valuable to senior management.

Some senior management have found financial models extremely valuable—in fact, indispensible once they are familiar with them. The models can incorporate the departmental budgets, sales quotas, market forecasts, econometric forecasts, and cash flow. They can monitor the financial progress and indicate where management and pressure is needed. They can answer *"what if"* questions and produce color charts. The primary skill of the staff who create and continually modify these programs must be an understanding of the business and the complex factors that affect it. If these staff members can write programs in APL or NOMAD, the results are likely to meet the true needs much faster than if a remote programming department is involved.

It has now become vital in running a corporation that senior management be supported by staff members who can generate the information and computations they need *quickly,* with elegant reports and graphics, and who can modify their reports and programs as fast as top management requires. Too few senior managers realize that this is possible and reasonable with today's software.

Box 15.1 lists the needs of end users to get through the barrier of their own application development.

BOX 15.1 What is needed to get end users through the barrier of doing their own application development?

- Application generation software which is well human-factored, user-friendly, and which has the properties listed in Box 8.2, can be learned in a 2-day training course.

- A well-designed training course that omits all technical jargon, motivates the users, and provides hand-on experience.

- A stage-by-stage approach in training the users. They become familiar and experienced with simple functions, such as data-base queries and information retrieval, before going on to more complex functions.

- Ideally a set of software encompassing the facilities of Fig. 8.3, with similar dialogue style and syntax. (Many such products from the same vendor are incompatible in style and syntax.)

- Use of a high-level programming language such as APL or NOMAD for the few sophisticated end users who have the need to program (e.g., financial analysts, planners, engineers, and the staff assistants to senior management).

- DP management who encourage end users to create their own applications rather than seeing this as a threat, but who understand the need for a centrally controlled infrastructure and data-base planning.

- An end-user perception that they have something to gain *personally,* i.e., as individuals. This gain may be the saving of time so that they have more time for interesting work and the capability to do better work.

- Top management belief in and encouragement of the spread of the electronic office with end-user participation. An understanding of the objectives of this higher productivity, better products, better service to customers.

- A strong desire to eliminate the long application backlog.

- The *Information Center* (or similar) concept of DP operation.

- DP Information Center representatives motivated (preferably financially) to make converts and *sell* the facilities to end users.

- Concentration on early adaptors among the end-user community. Demonstration that the early adaptors are doing something valuable. Extending the resources with peer group pressure from the early adaptors to early-adaptors-minus-one and so on.

- Patience, encouragement, help, training, and immediate attention to users' problems by Information Center representatives (who could be new college graduates).

- Relentless emphasis on improving the productivity of all critical end users, saving their time, and improving their decision making.

- Understanding that the change in end-user culture is a long haul that will take many years.

- Motivation of end users via house magazine, awards, notice boards, computer-user-of-the-month selection, bonuses, annual conferences, management-by-objectives interviews, etc.

- Widespread availability of cheap terminals.

- Senior management staff who generate quickly the charts, reports, and applications which top management needs.

REFERENCE

1. MANTIS Users' Guide, Cincom Systems Inc., Cincinnati, OH, 1981.

2. M. Janning, S. Nachmens, and S. Berild, *Introduction to Associative Data Bases and the CS4-System,* Studentlitteratur AB, Lund, Sweden, 1981.

16 APPLICATION GENERATION BY DP PROFESSIONALS

INTRODUCTION   Previous chapters have discussed application generation by end users. Many application generators are appropriate for DP professionals rather than end users. *Application development without programmers* often implies the generation of applications by systems analysts rather than by end users.

In efficient DP organizations today, much data processing *ought* to be generated by the systems analysts. The amount of space in this book given to *end-user* application creation is perhaps out of proportion but is a very desirable trend.

Most application generators are more difficult to use than software such as MAPPER or QUERY-BY-EXAMPLE, but are more versatile in the types of dialogues they can create. They are employed by systems analysts or information center staff working closely with end users. They permit the vital activity of prototyping to be carried out easily.

Application generators differ widely in how well human-factored they are. We illustrate this by contrasting IBM's two main generators, DMS (Development Management System [1] and ADF (Application Development Facility [2]). Good human factoring is important because it encourages use of the generator by the analysts who work with the end user and understand their applications, rather than by programmers.

The increase in productivity, or in application development speed, that has been achieved with application generators is spectacular. They clearly have a vitally important role in the future of data processing and will greatly change the systems analysis process. Some DP professionals are remarkably reluctant to recognize this. It took the DP profession 10 years to swing from assembly languages as the main form of programming to widespread use of COBOL and PL/1. It is dismal to reflect that it might take 10 years to swing from COBOL and PL/1 to application generators and other high-level facilities. The slowness of the swing and the reluctance to recognize what is happening will do great damage in many corporations.

IBM'S DMS   IBM's DMS, Development Management System, is a tool for generating interactive applications. Often complete applications are generated with it; sometimes it is used in conjunction with routines programmed in COBOL, PL/1, assembler language, or RPG II (Report Program Generator II).

It is not usually employed by end users. It forms an ideal tool for the systems analyst and can entirely change the systems analysis process where it is employed efficiently. Often the systems analyst creates a complete application. Sometimes he creates a demonstration or *prototype* which needs to be tuned by a DMS expert or to have programmed routines written to supplement it. In either case the systems analyst works with the end users, shows them his results, and refines the results repeatedly until users are happy with them and use them efficiently.

The systems analyst should be expected to learn DMS very thoroughly and become slick in using it. He should be able to create screens and dialogues very quickly. It is very easy to make adjustments to an application which do not involve non-DMS programs. This enables a systems analyst to keep users happy, making changes for them when this can improve the way they use the system. In some corporations the analysts make such changes in one hour. This is very different from an environment in which all changes are resisted and those that *are* made wait in a queue for programmers for months.

DMS can either use its own indexed sequential files or can operate with DL/1 data bases. Sometimes it is used in a data base environment but users also have some files of their own. It can operate on various models of IBM computers, including distributed systems employing peripheral 8100 or 4300 series machines.

DMS uses a "fill in the blanks" technique that makes it possible for on-line applications to be developed with little or no programming. Preprogrammed facilities are selected for functions such as data entry, inquiry, update, dialogue processing, and message switching.

The application creator describes data files, display screens called "panels," and the application processing either *interactively* through a terminal or *off-line* through the use of a series of forms. With the interactive facility, the user is prompted through each stage of the application definition. Specifications are validated to reduce errors. A HELP facility is provided which gives additional information and explains data to be entered.

DMS provides the ability to perform calculations and editing of data.

DMS FUNCTIONS   Figure 16.1 lists the main functions of DMS.
The standard data-base functions, such as inquiry and update, are provided. A data routine function provides the capability for directing messages or displays to another terminal in the network or to a printer. Program control allows the user to call another program or return to another program.

Data fields may be edited for validity using such techniques as table lookup, comparing one value with a field, and so on. The user has the capability to select editing where it is needed and to alter the sequence of processing as a result of any errors that are encountered. The calculation functions provided with DMS enable the user to perform arithmetic and simple logic operations.

The systems analyst can build an end-user dialogue employing multiple screen panels which are logically linked. He can capture data from a set of logically linked panels and construct from this logical file records or a database path involving up to four files or data bases. The updating or creation of the data records occurs after the last panel of the set is processed.

Users who are in distributed locations may generate and test applications at a central point. Restart and recovery functions are provided which allow the user to save data and instructions previously entered, in the event of a system failure.

Audit procedures are available in DMS. A log of all terminal errors is kept; this log is in some detail, which allows auditors to examine for inconsistencies.

Security is provided at various levels, such as password protection at the terminal level. Integrity controls are provided which allow the user to

- Data-Base Operations
  - Inquiry
  - Update
  - Amend/Insert
  - Deletion
  - Search/Browse
- Data Routing
- Program-to-Program Control
- User Processing
- Data Validation
- Calculation Functions
- Application Generation Through Forms
- Restart/Recovery
- Audit Control
- Security and Integrity

Figure 16.1 Functions of DMS.

verify the contents of records. Search requests can be accommodated which produce listings of keys or records.

In general, systems produced with DMS:

- Are easier to design
- Avoid most of the need for programming
- Are easier to test
- Are self-documenting
- Are much easier to maintain

In some cases DMS is used to *convert* existing batch applications to an on-line environment. The existing files or data bases of the batch system can be used for this.

The cost of re-creating an existing application in DMS is often less than the cost of maintaining that application for a year. Once it exists in DMS form, it is relatively cheap to maintain. DMS and other such application generators therefore offer a way out of the maintenance trap which is such a burden in many installations.

USE OF DMS

With DMS the system analyst can specify the screens that will be used in an interactive dialogue, how the user may respond in the dialogue, and how the responses are processed.

Suppose that he designs the opening menu shown below. From this the user can select one of the four applications shown.

```
                                                          MENU

                          **** MENU ****

              1  CREDIT MANAGEMENT

              2  ORDER ENTRY

              3  PURCHASING

              4  INVENTORY CONTROL


                 *** KEY A 1 2 3 OR 4 TO SELECT APPLICATION. ***
                 PRESS THE ENTER KEY.
```

PANEL DESCRIPTION FORM
To create this panel the systems analyst fills in the Panel Description Form shown below. He fills in a similar form for each panel he wishes to create.

The screen layout he enters contains all the fixed data, such as headings, titles, and so on, exactly as they will appear on the screen. To create this panel the systems analyst fills in the Panel Description Form shown on page 248.

The analyst may now define the first panel displayed if the end user selects the *credit management* application. This panel is shown below.

The end user may key "1" and fill in the CUSTOMER NO. if he wishes to inquire regarding credit status. The results are displayed in the upper half of the panel. He may change any of these data by keying "2" and entering the new data.

```
                                                          PANELA
         *** CREDIT MANAGEMENT SYSTEM ***

CHANGE                          CURRENT

         NAME:
         ADDRESS:
         CITY:
         STATE:
         ZIP CODE:
         CR STATUS:


   *** ENTER CUSTOMER NO.:

      KEY  1   TO INQUIRE CREDIT STATUS.

      KEY  2   TO CHANGE A CUSTOMER RECORD.
               ENTER DATA UNDER "CHANGE" ON LINE TO BE UPDATED.

      KEY  3   TO CLEAR AND RE-ENTER DATA.

      KEY  4   TO RETURN TO MENU.
```

SUPERVISORY COMMANDS
The systems analyst must specify how the end user may respond to a panel and specify the processing that will occur for each response. He specifies this in the Response Specification Card portion of the Panel Description Form. The four possible responses, "1," "2," "3," and "4," are entered in the form on page 249.

The code after each response is called a *Supervisor Function Code.* There are five classes of these codes: *display control, file and data base operations, data routing, program control,* and *system services.* Each code is one character, and it may be followed by a modifier character. The Supervisor Function Codes are shown in Fig. 16.2.

After the Supervisor Function Codes on the Response Specification Card shown above, the systems analyst could enter variable information, such as the name of a panel, the number of panels skipped in a PAGE FOR-

DMS/CICS/VS Panel Description Form

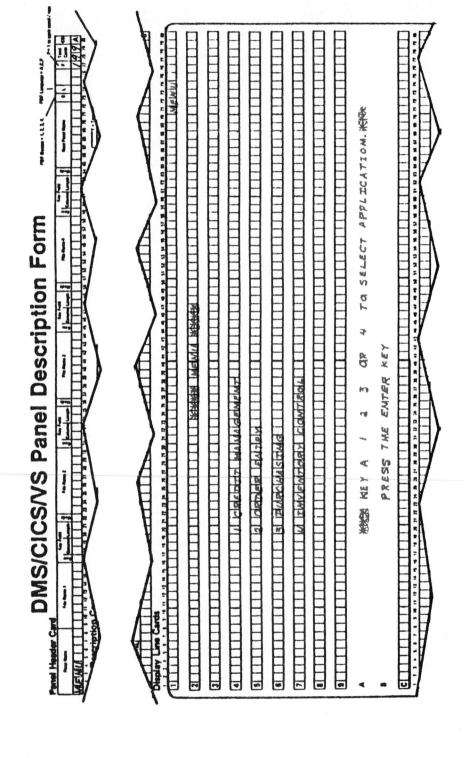

MENU

MENU MENU MENU

1 CREDIT MANAGEMENT

2 ORDER ENTRY

3 PURCHASING

4 INVENTORY CONTROL

KEY A 1 2 3 OR 4 TO SELECT APPLICATION.

PRESS THE ENTER KEY

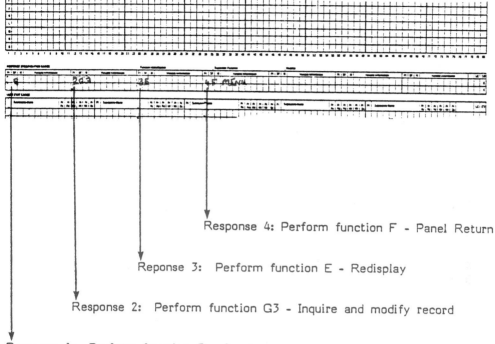

Response 4: Perform function F - Panel Return

Reponse 3: Perform function E - Redisplay

Response 2: Perform function G3 - Inquire and modify record

Response 1: Perform function G - Inquire.

WARD or PAGE BACKWARD (codes C and D in Fig. 16.2), a record or data-base identifier, and so on.

The *display control* class of functions enable the systems analyst to specify routes through the panels he designs. He can thus build a dialogue.

The *panel overlay function* produces a named display at the terminal without retaining any information from the preceding display. The *panel link function* similarly produces a named display but saves the calling panel so that it can be brought back together with any variable information that may have been entered. The *redisplay function* redisplays the current panel but in its original form without any data that the operator may have entered. The *panel return function* redisplays the starting panel of the dialogue or a named panel, and deletes all panels saved since the start of the dialogue.

The *file and data base functions* permit data retrievals, adds, deletes, updates, and searches. Sequential or random-access operations may be carried out. Single-key and multiple-key retrieval can be specified. Copies of data can be made. DMS/CICS files may be used, or DL/1 data bases.

The *data routing functions* provide the capability to send panel images from one terminal to another. Panels can be printed. Messages can be queued and stored as in a message-switching system. Either complete panels may be transmitted or data extracted from panels.

The *program control functions* allow the systems analyst to invoke programs. With the *call user program function,* a user response to a panel may call a specified program. Information from the panel will be passed to the program as specified. Sometimes a panel operation is called by a program. The *return to calling program function* extracts required information from the panel and returns control to the program.

The *system services functions* permit such operations as the use of function keys on the terminal devices, setting the time and date, and allowing users to define and code their own supervisor functions.

CALCULATION AND   DMS uses two types of commands: the *supervisory*
LOGIC COMMANDS   *commands,* shown in Fig. 16.2, and *calculation and logic commands,* listed in Fig. 16.3. With these commands calculation can be specified and the sequence of application flow can be altered according to conditions: for example, if a counter reaches zero or if the result of subtraction goes negative.

SUPERVISOR COMMANDS:

Class of Function	Function Code	Function Name
Display control	A	Panel overlay
	B	Panel link
	C	Page forward
	D	Page backward
	E	Redisplay
	F	Panel return
File and data-base operation	G	Inquiry/inquiry for update
	H	Record add
	I	Update/delete
	J	Search DMS/CICS/VS indexed files
	K	Set sequential/end sequential
	L	Cursor key select
	M	Selector-pen key select
	N	Copy
	P	End inquiry level
Data routing	Q	Data route
	R	Send/get message
	S	Send/get image
Program control	T	Call user program
	U	Return to calling program
	V	Reset/delete communication fields
	W	End transaction
System services	X	Load PF key or edit mask table
	Z	Set time, date, operator ID
	>	User supervisor function

Figure 16.2 DMS commands are of two types, *supervisor commands,* shown above, and *arithmetic and logic commands,* shown in Fig. 16.3.

Command Name	DMS Symbol/Code
Add	+
Subtract	−
Multiply	*
Divide	/
Move remainder	MVR
Move right	MOVER
Move left	MOVEL
Compare	COMP
Test display field	TEST
Set a field attribute	SET
Search a table	FIND
End of processing	EXIT
Operation complete	OPCOMP
Terminate a browse	TRMBR
Execute a new function	NEWFI
Terminate a transaction	TERM
Terminate with a dump	TERMD
Write an error message	WMSG
Redisplay	RDISP
Write no erase	WNOER
Call user subroutine	CALL
De-edit	DEDIT

Figure 16.3 DMS calculation and logic commands.

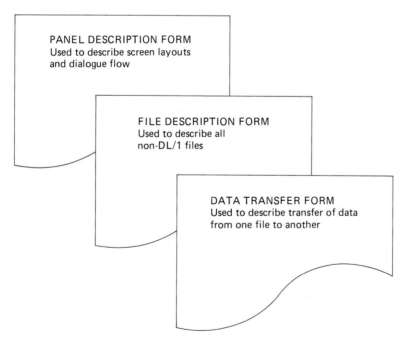

PANEL DESCRIPTION FORM
Used to describe screen layouts
and dialogue flow

FILE DESCRIPTION FORM
Used to describe all
non-DL/1 files

DATA TRANSFER FORM
Used to describe transfer of data
from one file to another

Figure 16.4 Applications are created with DMS by filling in these three forms. Many applications can be created with only the Panel Description Form if the data base they use already exists. These forms are shown in Figs. 16.5 to 16.7.

DMS/VS
DMS/CICS/VS Panel Description Form

1 — **Panel Header Card**

2 — **DL/I Description Card**

3 — **Display Description Card**

Display Description Card

4 — **Display Line Cards**

5 — **Response Specification Cards**

6 — **User Exit Cards**

7 — **Data Definition Cards**

* No. of forms per pad may vary.

1. The panel leader card contains the panel name, the file names associated with the panel, and the next panel name. The reset panel name is useful when a sequence of panels is required, for example, in a menu.

2. The DL/1 description card specifies the data bases to be accessed. With this entry the user can also, if required, specify that the panel is still in the test mode. Dumps can be provided, and trace tables are used to assist in debugging.

3. The display description card indicates specific characteristics of the panel and the features of the IBM 3270 terminal that is required, for example, the model for which the panel is intended, and the cursor position when the panel is displayed.

4. The display line cards define the static data, such as headings, titles, and narrative that is required for the screen. It is intended to be an exact image of the screen that is required.

5. The response specification cards define the processing to be undertaken from the operator's response: for example, return to main menu, display another panel, call a user program, and so on. DMS commands are shown in Figs. 16.2 and 16.3.

6. User exit cards define program exits.

7. The data definition cards define the display fields and identify the file and communication. Also, data can be entered by the operator for updating files of transmission to other terminals.

Figure 16.5 Panel Description Form.

DMS II File Description Form

Application/Project _____

Completed by _____

Sheet ____ of ____

Date ____

1 Describe fields sequentially as they appear in data record

2 In Header Card, Type (left justify) : I = ISAM, HI-ISAM Group (DISK/96 only)
   K = Key sequenced VSAM (DISK/96 only)
   B = DMS II Indexed, RG = DMS II Indexed Group, U = Use
   UG = User Suspend Group, S = Sequenced

3 In Field Description, Mode: C = character (RECODE)   P = packed decimal
   X = hexadecimal   F = fixed point binary

FILE HEADER CARD

File Name	Type	Record Length	Rec/Blk	Key Field Name	User Program Name	Index File Name	Seq. No	

FIELD DESCRIPTION CARDS

Field Name	Length	Field Name	Length	Field Name	Length	Field Name	Length	Field Name	Length	Seq. No	

GROUP FILE DESCRIPTION CARDS

Sub-Key Number	Key		Seq. No	

INDEX DESCRIPTION HEADER CARD

Index File Name	Control Break	Reference File Name	Seq. No	

NOTE: List fields sequentially as they appear in index, starting with Key field.

INDEX FIELD NAME CARDS

Key Field Name (First Card Only)	Field Data Field to be included in index	Subsequent Data Fields	Seq. No	

*No. of forms per pad may vary.

1. The file header describes the attributes of the file, such as file name; type (whether sequential, index sequential, etc.); and if indexed sequentially the key name and the program that uses the file.

2. The field description specifies the individual data fields and their relative positions within the data records.

3. The group file description is a facility to provide access to a group of files. Only a single file need be described from multiple individual files and accessed through a location index.

4. The index description header card describes details of the index associated with indexed sequential files.

5. The index field name cards are used with the index description header and detail the data fields in the index.

Figure 16.6 DMS File Description Form.

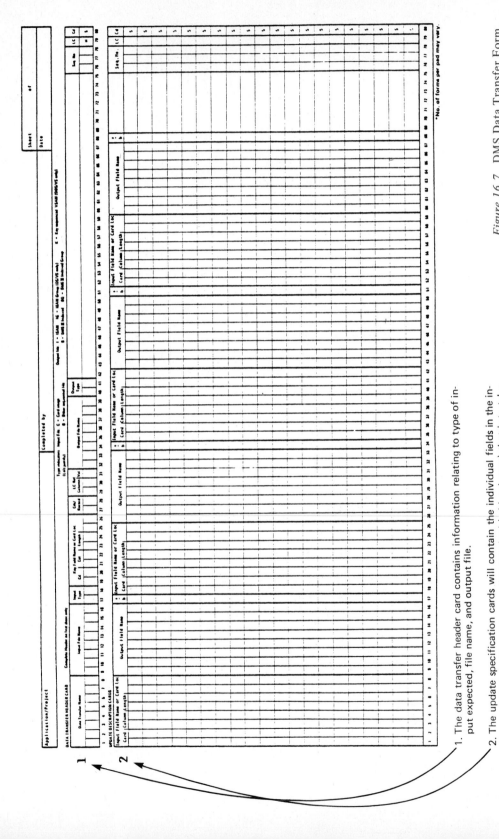

Figure 16.7 DMS Data Transfer Form.

1. The data transfer header card contains information relating to type of input expected, file name, and output file.

2. The update specification cards will contain the individual fields in the input and output files and any action required (add, subtract) that is to take place.

DMS FORMS   Some entire applications that use a previously
existing data base are created merely with a set of
Panel Description Forms. Many applications, however, require two other
forms.

DMS provides three forms for application creators to fill in (Fig. 16.4):

1. The Panel Description Form

2. The File Description Form

3. The Data Transfer Form

These forms are shown in Figs. 16.5 to 16.7.

FILE DESCRIPTION   The File Description Form describes DMS files. It
FORM   is not used if the application employs a DL/1 data
base rather than files.
Information is entered into the header card describing the file name, its
organization (key sequenced VSAM, ISAM, etc.), record size, blocking
factor, and the key field. Subsequent cards define all fields in order of
sequence.

If a file is used in multiple applications, it need be described only once
to DMS.

DATA TRANSFER   The Data Transfer Form is used to record additions
FORM   and deletions and field-by-field transfers of data
from one file to another. This form enables the
systems analyst to use data from files in *existing* applications. A utility is
provided to aid in converting the files of off-line applications to DMS files.

GENERATOR   If an application generator such as DMS is well
HUMAN   human-factored, it is reasonable to expect all the
FACTORING   systems analysts to learn and use it. Programmers
need be involved only to code exit routines for
functions that the generator cannot handle. It is highly desirable that such
a facility be used by the *systems analysts* because they work directly with
the end users and can rapidly modify their design as the end users react to
their prototype, and as they think of new features they want included.

Some application generators are powerful or versatile in what they can
create but are not well human-factored. More training and practice is needed
in coding them. The systems analysts do not learn them easily. They tend to
become tools for programmers rather than for analysts. If this causes the
analyst to once again become a middleman between the programmer and the
end user, it removes much of the value of application generation.

Often, a hybrid person is used, referred to as a programmer-analyst. The job of the analyst, however, ought to be concentrated on the applications and the end users, not on complexities of coding.

There is a marked contrast between DMS and IBM's other major application generator, ADF (Application Development Facility). Whereas DMS is easy to understand and use, ADF requires complex coding rather like JCL (Job Control Language). DMS is commonly used by systems analysts. ADF is suitable mainly for programmers and systems programmers. Programmers *do* find it easy to learn.

ADF has improved application creation productivity very much in some installations. As with DMS, it is not uncommon to find productivity improvements of 1000% over conventional use of COBOL or PL/1. As mentioned in Chapter 3, some corporations quote speeds of application creation 10 to 50 times those of conventional programming. However, these are achieved by highly skilled ADF specialists—ADF "acrobats."

A case quoted by John Deere, Inc., is typical of a person who makes himself highly skilled with ADF. A new employee, inexperienced in programming, achieved *twice* the productivity of the COBOL team on his first application, *32 times* that of the COBOL team on his second application, and *46 times* on the third [3].

Although ADF is clearly a major aid to productivity, of all the software mentioned in this book it is among the worst as to human factoring. There is no basic need for the poor human factoring. It is rather like trying to fill in your income tax return with Roman numerals. ADF is a powerful product designed by programmers for programmers. Some organizations have abandoned ADF, whereas others have built up a team with a high level of expertise and achieved impressive results. It has sometimes been abandoned because of its human factoring and sometimes because it is limited in the screen dialogues it can create, and these may be perceived as not fitting the application.

When application generators are difficult to code, they are often used by programmers rather than analysts. This is undesirable. It ought to be the analysts who are creating applications and prototypes and rapidly modifying them as the end users interact with them and make suggestions. Wherever possible, it should be the aim of the computer industry to end the analyst's role as a middleman and requirements writer.

HOW ADF WORKS   ADF is an application generator that runs under the IMS/VS data-base management system. It provides several skeletal IMS application programs and additional modules of code and data. Applications are created by directing the skeletal programs to execute application functions. This is done by means of *rules* that define aspects of the application.

Code modules perform application functions that are common to many IMS applications. These common modules are combined selectively with the skeletal IMS application programs under the direction of the rules. During the execution of ADF, the precoded modules access the *rules* to customize their behavior.

ADF is summarized in Fig. 16.8.

- Tables of parameters called "rules" specify the IMS applications desired.
- Preprogrammed modules of code can be invoked by the user for such functions as
  - Accessing the data base
  - Screen formatting
  - Data entry validation
- During execution, the modules access sets of rules to customize the result.
- Functions not supported by ADF can be programmed with conventional procedural code, or a combination of code and rules.

Figure 16.8   How ADF works: basic elements.

Figure 16.9 shows the five main groupings of modules available from ADF:

1. *Menus* that identify the user department at sign-on. *Function selection* using the function keys of the 3270 terminal. *Transaction selection* will identify the types of transactions or data that will be accessed.

2. The *key selection* prompts for keys to records or segments for retrieval from the data base.

3. The *transaction driver* is a module that controls the flow of logic to process a transaction.

4. The *screen formatter* works with IMS to format screens. The call handler allows DL/1 calls to the data base if this facility is chosen. The *auditor* has the logic to analyze the data base and the data being entered. The *message generator* informs the terminal user about conditions during processing.

5. Finally, the *interface to programmer-written modules* is provided for operations that need special processing, such as complicated calculations or audit routines.

Figure 16.10 specifies what the programmer-analyst is required to define to ADF. The screen formats require analyst definition, what data are to be displayed, and where.

The structure of the data base requires a definition indicating its contents, keys, and segments. The analyst also provides information to ADF to enable it to encode data entered in the data base and decode it when the data are retrieved. For example, a state code can be held in the data base as a two-digit code, but when displayed it can show the full name. Validation

```
┌─────────────────────────────────────────┐
│ ● Menu Modules                          │
│       Sign-on                            │
│       Function selection                 │
│       Transaction selection              │
├─────────────────────────────────────────┤
│ ● Key Selection Modules                  │
│       Prompts for key information        │
│       Builds key menus                   │
│       Accepts partial keys               │
├─────────────────────────────────────────┤
│ ● Transaction Driver                     │
│       Primary transaction logic          │
├─────────────────────────────────────────┤
│ ● Driver Contains Common Function Modules│
│       Screen formatter                   │
│       Call handler                       │
│       Auditor                            │
│       Message generator                  │
├─────────────────────────────────────────┤
│ ● Programmer-Written Modules             │
│       Special coding                     │
│       Audit routines                     │
└─────────────────────────────────────────┘
```

Figure 16.9 ADF module functions.

- ● Format and content of screens
- ● Structure and content of data base
- ● Data to encode/decode selected fields
- ● Information to validate data
- ● Format of messages and routing information
- ● Security information

Figure 16.10 The ADF Analyst-Programmer defines these functions.

criteria are also required when data are entered into the data base. The format of messages is required and, if necessary, routing information to other terminals or departments. Security information is also required from the analyst to allow ADF to decide who can retrieve, add, update, or delete transactions to the data base.

From these specifications ADF will provide:

- ● Screens for identification and sign-on of procedure users

- Screens to locate and retrieve data
- Screens that display the data for retrieval, update, and addition or deletion of segments

ADF RULES   There are two type of rules with ADF.

1. Static rules
2. Dynamic rules

Static rules are created by the ADF rule generator, which processes descriptive statements supplied by the programmer. They control the contents of terminal screens, which fields are to be displayed, and where they are positioned.

Dynamic rules can be entered into ADF from a terminal using ADF-supplied routines. The dynamic rules control such functions as sign-on profiles and the coding and encoding of selected fields. They also control the auditing and verification of data entering the system. Dynamic rules are stored in a dynamic rules data base and are accessed by ADF.

Figure 16.11 illustrates the flow of control during a typical standard ADF transaction.

1. The user enters his identification. IMS/VS dispatches the ADF *Sign-on/Option Menu Controller* to process the opening of the application. This verifies the user's authorization. The *Sign-on Profile* data base contains the authorization profiles.

2. The *Primary Menu* function formats the data for the display of the opening menu. This is displayed on the user terminal. The user selects an application and control is passed to an appropriate module.

3. The *Secondary Menu* function receives control and formats another menu display. This menu is based on the user's authority profile, the processing option selected, and the response to the primary menu.

   The user's response to the secondary menu determines which *transaction driver* is dispatched to IMS/VS control.

   Both the primary and secondary menus employ rules specified by the application analyst.

4. The *transaction driver* is composed of a number of modules which are common to all transactions. The driver loads the *input transaction rules* associated with the user's processing requirements. These were, again, specified by the application analyst.

Other functions and associated sets of rules are shown in Fig. 16.11.

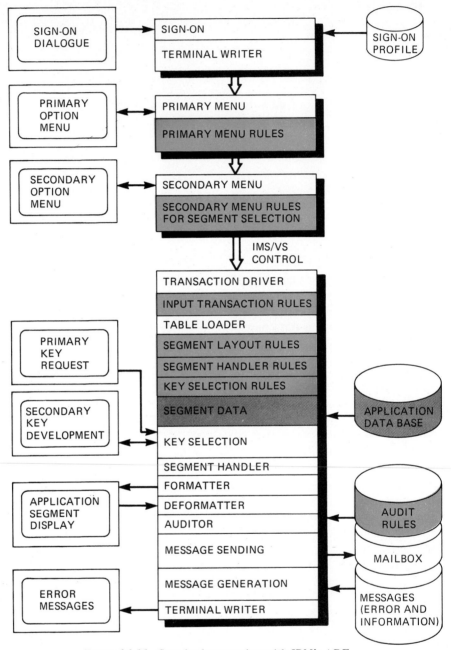

Figure 16.11   Standard processing with IBM's ADF.

CODING SAMPLE

The following is an example of the coding of ADF. It will be seen that it is more difficult than the form filling needed for DMS. Even so, it is less flexible than DMS, with which the user can create any layout for his display panels.

```
*****************************************************************************
*    APPLICATION DEFINITION INPUT STATEMENTS FOR PARTS DATA BASE
*****************************************************************************
SYSTEM   SYSID=SAMP,DBID=PA,                      RULE ID CHARS
         SOMTX=OR,                     DEFAULT SECONDARY OPTION CODE
         SIGNON=YES,                   REQUEST FOR SIGNON SCREEN
         POMENU=(A,B,C,D,F,H,I),       REQUEST FOR PRIMARY MENU
         PCBNO=1,                      PCB NUMBER FOR DATA BASE
         SDBNAME='ASSEMBLY PARTS',     DEFAULT DATA BASE NAME
         SHEADING='S A M P L E   P R O B L E M',   GENERAL HEADING
         SFORMAT=DASH,                 SCREEN FORMAT
         PGROUP=ZZ,                    PROJECT GROUP
         ASMLIST=NOLIST                GENERATE OPTIONS
*****************************************************************************
*    APPLICATION DEFINITION INPUT FOR ROOT SEGMENT
*****************************************************************************
SEGMENT  LEVEL=1,ID=PA,NAME=PARTROOT,LENGTH=50,
         SNAME='PART SEGMENT',SKSEG=18
   FIELD ID=KEY,LENGTH=17,POS=1,KEY=YES,NAME=PARTKEY,
         SNAME='PART NUMBER',DISP=YES,REL=YES
   FIELD ID=DESC,LENGTH=20,POS=27,SNAME='DESCRIPTION',DISP=YES,REL=YES
*****************************************************************************
*    APPLICATION DEFINITION INPUT FOR INVENTORY SEGMENT
*****************************************************************************
SEGMENT  ID=IV,PARENT=PA,NAME=STOKSTAT,KEYNAME=STOCKEY,LENGTH=160,
         SNAME='INVENTORY',
         SKLEFT='INVENTORY        UNIT      CURRENT ',
         SKLEFT='LOCATION         PRICE     REQMNTS ',
         SKRIGHT=' ON      TOTAL        DISBURSEMENTS ',
         SKRIGHT=' ORDER    STOCK    PLANNED  UNPLANNED'
   FIELD ID=W,LENGTH=2,POS=1,KEY=YES,TYPE=DEC,SNAME='00',DISP=NO,
         COL=1,SLENGTH=2
   FIELD ID=AREA,LENGTH=1,KEY=YES,SNAME='AREA',DISP=YES,COL=3
   FIELD ID=INVD,LENGTH=2,KEY=YES,SNAME='INV DEPT',DISP=YES,COL=4
   FIELD ID=PROJ,LENGTH=3,KEY=YES,SNAME='PROJECT',DISP=YES,COL=6
   FIELD ID=DIV,LENGTH=2,KEY=YES,SNAME='DIVISION',DISP=YES,COL=9
   FIELD ID=FILL,LENGTH=6,KEY=YES,SNAME='FILLER',DISP=NO,COL=11
   FIELD ID=PRIC,LENGTH=9,POS=21,TYPE=DEC,DEC=2,SLENGTH=9,
         SNAME='UNIT PRICE',DISP=YES
```

SUMMARY

Application generators for DP professionals are a giant step forward in achieving results from data processing. They are achieving 1000% improvement in productivity over conventional programming in which everything is coded in COBOL or PL/1. Some organizations have achieved higher gains than this. Good generators can be used for most but not all commercial DP applications, sometimes with the help of specially programmed subroutines.

The best generators are enabling maintenance changes to be made in an hour or so for most but not all changes. The application can therefore be constantly adjusted to the users' needs. They enable systems analysts to create prototypes, try them out with the users, and adjust them until the users are satisfied. Often, the prototype becomes the final application. Prototyping by analysts replaces the laborious and inadequate writing of requirement documents and program specifications. It therefore completely changes the development cycle and the job of systems analysts.

Some generators can employ existing files or data bases. They therefore provide a means of converting old applications to generator form, or converting batch applications to on-line operation. The applications then become relatively easy to maintain. For some systems this is the best way out of the maintenance trap illustrated in Fig. 6.3.

Several characteristics are needed in good application generators for DP professionals.

- They should be versatile, so that as large a range of applications can be generated as possible. Some generators are too limited in scope.

- They should be well human-factored so that all systems analysts can use them without feeling that they are being reduced to the role of a coder. Some generators look as though they are designed by programmers for programmers.

- They should be able to use existing files and/or data bases. A major form of future application creation will be: first create the data bases, then generate applications that use them with high-level data-base languages.

- They should be able to convert existing applications to generator form to make them interactive or to lessen their maintenance costs.

- They should permit most maintenance changes or changes to prototypes to be made in an hour or so.

- They should have compilers that give efficient code. Sometimes they produce better code than COBOL or PL/1 because the preprogrammed modules of code that generator selects are tightly coded in assembler language.

REFERENCES

1. *Development Management System/Customer Information Control System/Virtual Storage: General Information Manual,* IBM Manual No. GH20–2195–2, IBM, White Plains, NY, 1980.

2. *IMS Application Development Facility, General Information Manual,* IBM Manual No. GB21–9869–1, IBM, White Plains, NY, 1980.

3. D.H. Holtz, "ADF Experiences at John Deere," D303–SHARE 50, Denver, CO, March 1978.

17 THE VITAL ROLE OF DATA BASES

There is a major danger in end users creating their own applications, or in the fast, easy creation of applications by fragmented groups of systems analysts. It is the same danger that exists with the uncontrolled spread of minicomputers. The same type of data field may be created many times by different groups. These fields will have different structures. Data that ought to be coordinated will not be. Data that ought to be passed from the factory floor or the warehouse to other information systems will not be.

Overall management is needed for most data. Often, the same collection of data should be shared by multiple users, who may employ it for different purposes. This sharing and coordination of data is usually called *database* operation (Fig. 17.1).

A data base is a shared collection of interrelated data designed to meet the needs of many types of end users. It can be defined as a collection of data from which many different end-user views can be derived. The data are stored so that they are independent of the programs that use them. Adding new data and modifying and retrieving existing data are carefully controlled. Retrieving data may be carried out by multiple users in different ways with appropriate privacy controls. The data are structured so as to provide a foundation for future application development.

One system is said to contain a *collection* of data bases if they are entirely separate in structure.

REASONS FOR DATA BASE Data-base management is important for two entirely different reasons. First, it is necessary to make sure that data are used as effectively as possible. Data are an extremely valuable resource. They need accuracy,

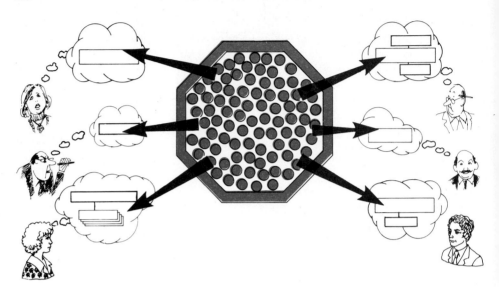

Figure 17.1   Data-base operation.

consistency, and security controls. They need to be made available to any persons or processes that ought to employ them. They can easily become a mess with multiple inconsistent copies, incompatible representations, and chaotic organization so that an executive or process cannot obtain valuable information when it is needed.

Second, a key to efficient application generation is that the data structures for an application *already exist;* they are represented in a dictionary that the software can use. The creator of the application does not need to design the data or their structuring. The data-base dictionary is the foundation of many report generators, query languages, and application generators. The term *integrated data dictionary* is used by some software vendors to describe this role. In addition to describing the data, such dictionaries may contain report headings, alternate names for data (aliases), report formats, titles for fields that can be placed in column headings, and so on. If a user asks that two fields be added together when one is binary and the other is decimal, that does not matter. The dictionary indicates their formats and they are converted to a compatible format before adding.

The data-base software can prompt users who enter data and can apply integrity checks to the data as they are being entered. These checks can be defined in the data dictionary. Appropriate audit trails can be created automatically. In some systems logic is associated with the data base (rather than with independent applications). Using this logic, events that change the data base can *trigger* actions that are taken automatically. The nature of the *trigger* and the *resulting action* are defined in software associated with the data base rather than with its users. A data base with such logic associated with it is called an *intelligent data base* [1]. (A data base with data but no associated logic might be termed a *dumb data base.* We can distinguish between dumb and intelligent data bases just as we distinguish between dumb and intelligent terminals.)

ADMINISTRATION

The coordination of data in a conventional data-base installation is done by a *data administrator* [2]. User-driven systems may employ data that have been established by a data administrator. This is an important aspect of *information center* management (Fig. 6.2).

Increasingly, *end-user software* will be used with which the users create files or data bases *independently* of the DP department and its data administration function. If the data they create are shared, it is necessary to have some form of data coordination; however, it can be much simpler than the job of a DP data administrator. The use of Univac's MAPPER, described in Chapter 11, requires a MAPPER coordinator. In the installations described in Chapter 11, the coordinator was an end user, specially trained. The coordinator catalogues the modes (filing cabinets) and types of data, attempts to remove redundancies, oversees privacy and security controls, attempts to control end users who tend to overload the system, and generally helps and advises end users. This is a straightforward job that is easy to learn. It does not have the technical complexity of the typical data administrator's job.

The MAPPER software helps the coordinator. For example, a routine called "Killer" identifies reports that have not been accessed for a long time and moves them off-line. In a typical month in the system described in Chapter 11, *Killer* might get 700 reports.

FILE SYSTEMS

It is important to distinguish between *file* systems and *data-base* systems. Much data processing uses *files* rather than data bases. A file environment has many problems.

Figure 17.2 illustrates a file environment. There are many files of records, some on tape and some on quickly accessible media such as disc. The records contain data items, shown as circles in Fig. 17.2. When a program is written for a new application or a variation of an old application, there may be a file that contains the required set of data items. Often, however, there is not, and a new file has to be created.

Suppose that a new user request needs a file with data items *A*, *F*, and *H*. These data items do not appear together in the existing files in Fig. 17.2. Other files must be sorted and merged to obtain the new file, but this will not be straightforward if the existing files do not have the required sets of keys. There may not be an *H* data item for every pair of *A* and *F* data items.

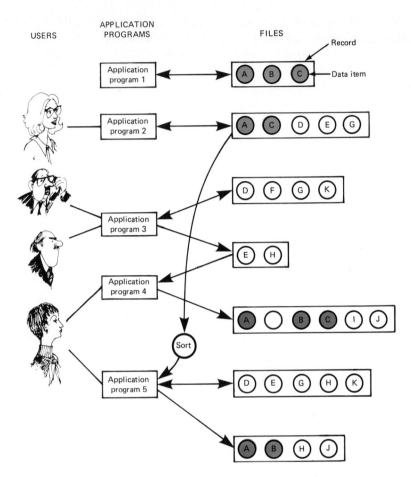

Figure 17.2 A file environment. For each new application a programmer or analyst creates a new file. A large installation has hundreds
or thousands of such files, with much redundancy of data.

PROBLEMS WITH
FILE SYSTEMS

There are three problems about the organization
of data in *files* as in Fig. 17.2. To understand them
the reader should imagine hundreds or thousands
of files rather than the seven in Fig. 17.2.

First, there is a high level of redundancy. The same type of data item is
stored in many different places. The different versions of the same data
items may be in different stages of update. In other words, they have different values. This may give the appearance of inconsistency to users. A manager obtains a report saying one thing and a terminal inquiry says something

different. With multiple copies of the same data item, it is difficult to maintain consistency or to ensure integrity of the data items.

Second, a file system is *inflexible.* Requests for information that require data items from multiple files or differently structured files cannot be answered quickly. Many ad hoc queries from a user employing a generalized query language cannot be answered. Although the data exist, information

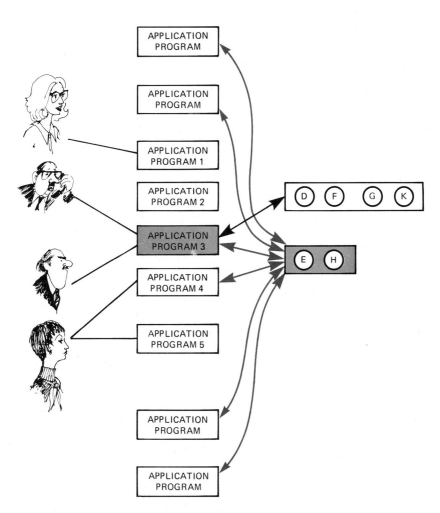

Figure 17.3 One file becomes used by multiple applications. When an application is changed (application program 3 above) and its file has to be restructured, all the programs which use that file have to be changed. A seemingly trivial change in a file environment can set off a chain reaction of other changes that have to be made.

cannot be provided that relates easily to those data. The data cannot be processed in new ways without restructuring. One sometimes hears from management a protest of the following type:

"We paid millions for that computer system and we cannot obtain the information we want from it."

Third, it can be expensive to make changes to a file system. Suppose that application program 3 in Fig. 17.2 has to be changed in such a way that its record $\boxed{\textcircled{E} \quad \textcircled{H}}$ has to be modified. Unfortunately, application program 4 uses the same record; therefore, application program 4 has to be modified. Many other application programs may also use the same record (Fig. 17.3), and all have to be changed.

A seemingly trivial change in a file environment sets off a chain reaction of other changes that have to be made. This upheaval is expensive and the programmers needed are doing other work. Sometimes the modifications are difficult to make because the applications were not adequately documented. As time goes on this problem becomes worse, because more and more programs are created. More programs have to be changed whenever a file is changed.

MAINTENANCE   Computer data in an organization are no more a static entity than are the contents of the organization's filing cabinets. The details of data stored, and the way they are used, change continuously. If a computer system attempts to impose an unchangeable file structure on an organization, it is doomed to the types of pressure that will result in most of the programming efforts being spent on modifying existing programs rather than developing new applications.

Figure 6.3 showed how programming costs have tended to change in organizations. The total programming costs in a typical organization have grown, becoming a higher proportion of the total data processing budget. However, the programming person-hours spent on new applications have fallen steadily. The reason is that the effort to maintain or modify the existing programs becomes greater and greater. It is often thought by systems analysts and data processing managers that existing programs that work well should be left alone. In reality, however, the data they create or use are needed for other applications and are almost always needed in a slightly different form. New data-item types are added. New record types are needed with data-item types from several previous records. The data must be indexed in a different way. The physical layout of data is improved. Data bases for different applications are merged, and so forth.

Two executives commented on this as follows:

End-User Executive:

For one system to make a change, it requires many other development areas to get involved in the change. We had what we thought was a *very* simple change to increase our file and we were able to change our individual system in 2 days, but the coordination with other systems took 5 months. It didn't necessarily take 5 months' worth of time on their part, but they each had their priorities and they were more concerned with doing their job than trying to take care of our problem.

DP Manager:

The frightening thing is that it's going to get even worse. We've got terrible problems today in terms of high maintenance costs, inconsistent data, inability to respond to management's needs, poor service. . . . But they're going to get much worse because government is increasing its demands; regulatory agencies are asking for more information, stricter audits, better privacy safeguards; the unions make settlements without any comprehension of their effects on DP.

One of the main objectives of a data-base system is that the data should be usable in new ways without setting off a chain reaction of difficult modifications to other programs. A program may be modified, changing in some way the data it uses, without disturbing other programs that use the same data.

The data-base management system is the entity that provides programmers or end users with the data they ask for. Like a conjurer pulling different-colored handkerchieves out of a hat, it derives its users' *make-believe* records from its store of data. It finds out what *physical* records contain the data in a given request, has a means of locating those records, and from them derives the logical records that were asked for.

DATA INDEPENDENCE

A data base is intended to make data independent of the programs that use it. The data descriptions are no longer embedded in the application programs. With a data base, either data or programs can be changed without causing the other to have to be changed. The data can be easily reorganized or their content added to. Old application programs do not have to be rewritten when changes are made to data structures, data layout, or the physical devices on which data are stored.

This independence of data is essential if data are to become a general-purpose corporate resource. In the past, data structures were devised by a programmer for his own use. He wrote a program to create a file of data. When another programmer needs the data for another purpose, it was usually not structured in the way he wanted, so he created another file. Hence the duplication in Fig. 17.2.

An old file environment is like a bowl of spaghetti. Every time you pull one piece of spaghetti, it shakes many of the others in the bowl. As time goes by it becomes steadily worse, because the number of pieces of spaghetti increases and they become more interwoven. The maintenance difficulties of file systems grow geometrically with the number of applications produced.

The intent of a data-base environment is to *insulate each program* from the effects of changes to other programs. And all programs should be insulated from the effects of reorganizing the data.

Data-base systems attempt to lower maintenance costs by separating the records the application programs use from the records that are physically stored. You might think of the user program as perceiving a *make-believe record,* a record that does not exist in physical reality. The data-base management software derives this record from the collection of data that are physically stored.

Figure 17.4 illustrates this point. When user 1 changes his record structure, his new record structure is derived from the data base by the data base management system. The change made by user 1 does not force users 2 and 3 to change *their* records.

Of course, we do not call them anything as unrespectable as "make-believe records." The records shown in Fig. 17.4 are called *logical records.* Each program refers to logical records, not the physical records that are stored in magnetic pulses on the discs or other storage media.

Data independence is one of the most important differences between the way data are organized in data bases and way they are organized in the file systems of computers that do not use data-base management software. The programmers or users can each have their own logical data structure, as shown in Fig. 17.4, and can be in blissful ignorance of how the data are really organized. When the data-base organization is changed, *the old programs still work.*

The total number of person-years that a corporation has invested in application programs grows steadily. The original programmers are long since gone, and it is too late to complain that their documentation is inadequate. The greater the number of non-data-base programs, the more horrifying the thought of having to modify them or their data, so there is increasing reluctance in the DP department to respond to the latest changes needed by end users.

A memo from a top DP executive expressed the maintenance problem as follows:

I believe that the present state of affairs in the operating areas with respect to data management makes it dangerous to continue on the present course.

    Many problems are apparent—such as the relatively high proportion of DP professionals devoted to maintenance activities, high cost and poor success in developing new systems for improving management information, and a variety of difficulties with inaccurate, inconsistent, and untimely reports, and the difficulty of supplying ad hoc information.

    It should be emphasized that these problems arise not so much for lack of available technology as they do for lack of understanding of what changes in management process and accountability need to accompany any move to sharing of common data—the primary problems are of a management rather than technical nature. Once the symptoms described earlier materialize, they tend to compound fairly rapidly.

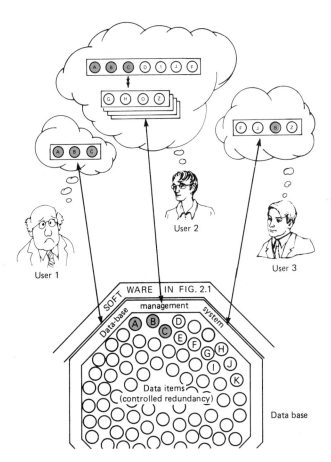

Figure 17.4 With data-base management systems, end users can live in blissful ignorance of how the data are really stored and structured.

PRINCIPLES OF A DATA-BASE ENVIRONMENT

Box 17.1 summarizes the problems that are typical in an established *file* environment. To help the user avoid these problems, Box 17.2 states principles of managing a data-base environment. It is important to recognize that these principles represent a change in management structure. *Data base is a change in management, not merely a change in software.*

In a well-managed data-base environment, data are recognized to be a corporate resource together with other resources, such as cash, people, plant, and equipment. It is sufficiently important to merit specialized and high-level management attention. Like other resources, it is necessary to:

1. Plan for it.
2. Establish a consistent approach to managing it.
3. Acquire it.
4. Maintain it.
5. Deploy it where needed.
6. Dispose of it when no longer needed.
7. Protect it.

BOX 17.1   Typical problems in established file installations.

- High proportion of DP professionals devoted to maintenance activities.
- High cost and slow speed in developing new systems.
- Inability to respond quickly to necessary changes.
- Inability to provide ad hoc management information.
- Inconsistent definition of similar data items across applications.
- Steadily worsening proliferation of separate files.
- Increasing proliferation of inconsistent values of redundant data.
- The greater the number of programs, the worse the problem of converting them when data change, so the greater the reluctance to respond to requests for such change by end users.
- Difficulty in maintaining inventory and control of data.
- Cost of redundant storage.
- Cost of repetitive data entry.
- Lack of overall management of the data resource.

BOX 17.2   Principles in managing the data-base environment.

- Data in a corporation should be managed directly and separately from the functions which use that data.

- Data descriptions should *not* be embedded uniquely in the programs which use that data. Instead, data should be designed by a separate data administrator.

- Data should be treated as a primary and vital resource in their own right, independently of current machines and systems.

- It is necessary to use standard tools and facilities throughout a corporation for managing its data.

- User departments should be given tools for extracting the information and reports they need directly from the data bases (with security and privacy control), and generating user-driven applications.

- The methods used by data processing management need to be changed when a data-base environment is employed.

- Many corporations have data management problems of strategic significance but do not know their extent. To deal with these problems, a high level of management needs to be involved in the data-base strategy.

8. Inventory it and know what effects will result when it changes.

9. Maintain records of its use.

All computer installations do 3, 4, and 6. Some installations do 7, although often poorly. Many installations do 5—badly, in that users often cannot obtain the data they need when they need them. Many installations, even multimillion-dollar ones, do not do 1, 2, and 8 in any formal sense.

In a well-designed and well-managed data-base environment, the data are relatively stable, although the ways of looking at the data and using them may change rapidly.

The reader should contrast in his mind the bowl of spaghetti described earlier, in which the number of pieces of spaghetti are steadily increasing, with the idea of a relatively stable data base from which users can exact new views of the data when they need them. The managers of the bowl of spaghetti have an application backlog of years. They are becoming increasingly frightened to change the data structures because of the chain reaction of problems that this causes. Therefore, for every new application a new file is created. By contrast, the data-base environment provides end-user management with high-level languages for querying the data, searching them, generating reports, creating their own temporary subfiles, and generating applications.

Many data-base installations have not achieved this degree of success. Indeed, data-base systems, like file systems, can plunge into trouble if they are not designed and managed appropriately.

SYSTEMS ANALYSIS The traditional methods of systems analysis focus on the flow of transactions and the functions to be carried out. Data are treated as an integral part of the individual systems that are designed. It is often designed as a *by-product* of the function analysis. The Deltak video course on structured analysis states: "Defining the *data flows* pretty much defines the *files*. All you have to do is add organizational information like Sequential-by-Date." Building applications on top of existing data bases is almost an inversion of this. An attempt is made to represent the inherent properties of the data in a stable data base which is independent of the data flows or functions that are programmed.

PROCESS-CENTERED VERSUS DATA-CENTERED APPROACH We can contrast a *process-centered* approach of systems analysis and a *data-centered* approach.

The *process-centered* approach is concerned primarily with processes and data flows. A *process* is often drawn as a circle and the *data flow* as an arrow. The files or data bases are treated as an important but secondary component.

The *data-centered* approach treats the data as a separate resource—a foundation stone on which applications are built. The processes are important but must employ data which are in the data base. Part of the systems analysis must determine what ought to be in the data base. This is sometimes called *data analysis*.

We could regard the whole of data processing as a succession of changes to data. A snapshot of a system or organization at any instant in time will reveal only a data structure. A process is, technically, a series of data changes, including changes to data in working storage and input/output data.

In the long run, designing a stable, well-documented, and largely nonredundant structure of data provides a simpler and cleaner form of data processing than embedding separately designed data into hundreds of processes. Attaching logic, such as integrity checks and decision tables, directly to the data structures so that this is shared by multiple processes can further simplify the overall processing.

ADVANTAGES AND   The data-centered approach has the following
DISADVANTAGES   *advantages:*

1. It avoids the problems with file proliferation, maintenance, and data redundancy and inconsistency described above.
2. Once appropriate data bases are in place, some types of applications can be created quickly with high-level data-base languages.
3. End users having direct access to the data bases can create their own reports and applications, often without the slow steps of formal systems analysis and often without waiting for action by the DP department.

The data-centered approach has the following *disadvantages:*

1. The data bases must be well designed. Although not inherently difficult, the technology of good data-base design is often not understood.
2. The data-centered approach implies the sharing of data. This needs different management from the management of separate files.
3. There are sometimes conversion problems in moving from the traditional process-centered approach to the data-centered approach. Some of these are human problems caused by users loosing control of data they previously "owned."
4. The data-centered approach is often more difficult to manage in its early phases, mainly because of pressures to take quick alternate solutions or to maintain the status quo. However, once set up, the data-centered approach is easier to manage than a process-centered approach with excessive file proliferation.

The data-centered approach, with data strictly separated from processing, is undoubtedly best in the long run if it is done well. However, it does not come into existence without firm management, at a suitably high level, knowing what they intend to achieve. Poor design, loose management, ill-defined objectives, or management easily pushed from its objective by corporate politics can wreck the data-centered approach. Too often, management has not understood the issues clearly.

FOUR TYPES   There are four types of environments of computer
OF DATA   data. It is important to distinguish clearly between
ENVIRONMENT   them. Box 17.3 summarizes the four types. Each
                 has a profound effect on management at all levels
in an enterprise, including top management. An efficient corporation ought to have a substantial foundation of Class III and Class IV data. These, however, are likely to be pervasive and successful only if there is top management support for them, as we shall see.

BOX 17.3 The four types of data environment.

CLASS I ENVIRONMENT: FILES

A data-base management system is not used. Separate files of data are used for most applications, designed by the analysts and programmers when the application is created.

EXAMPLES OF SOFTWARE: VSAM, BDAM, RMS.

CHARACTERISTICS:

Simple. Relatively easy to implement.

A large proliferation of files grow up with high redundancy, leading to high maintenance costs.

Seemingly trivial changes to applications trigger a chain reaction of other changes and hence change becomes slow, expensive, and is resisted.

CLASS II ENVIRONMENT: APPLICATION DATA BASES

A data-base management system is used but without the degree of sharing that exists in a Class III environment. Separate data bases are designed for separate applications.

EXAMPLES OF SOFTWARE: TOTAL, IMS, IDMS, IDS.

CHARACTERISTICS:

Easier to implement than a Class III environment.

A large proliferation of data bases grow up with high redundancy, like a file environment. High maintenance costs.

Sometimes more expensive than a Class I environment.

Does not achieve the major advantages of data-base operation.

CLASS III ENVIRONMENT: SUBJECT DATA BASES

Data bases are created which are largely independent of specific applications. Data are designed and stored independently of the function for which they are used. Data for business subjects such as customers, products, or personnel are associated and represented in shared data bases.

EXAMPLES OF SOFTWARE: IMS, IDMS, IDS, ADABAS.

CHARACTERISTICS:

Thorough data analysis and modeling needed, which takes time. Much lower maintenance costs.

BOX 17.3 *(Continued)*

Leads eventually (but not immediately) to faster application development and direct user interaction with the data bases.

Requires a change in traditional systems analysis methods, and in overall DP management.

If not managed well, it tends to disintegrate into a Class II (or sometimes a Class I) environment.

CLASS IV ENVIRONMENT: INFORMATION SYSTEMS

Data bases organized for searching and fast information retrieval rather than for high-volume production runs. Employs software designed around inverted files, inverted lists, or secondary key search methods. Good end-user query facilities. Most user-driven computing employs Class IV data bases.

EXAMPLES OF SOFTWARE: ADABAS, SYSTEM 2000, ICL CAFS, IBM STAIRS, THE RELATIONAL DATA BASES OF NOMAD, MAPPER, SQL, AND ORACLE.

CHARACTERISTICS:

Often easy to implement.

Should often coexist with a Class III environment.

Flexible. Low maintenance.

FILES

A Class I environment is that of *files*. A separate file is designed for each, or most, applications. Often a direct result of structured analysis, the data are embedded in the function. This has the problems discussed earlier and summarized in Box 17.1.

SUBJECT DATA BASES VERSUS APPLICATION DATA BASES

As we look back on years of data-base case histories, we can observe two types of approach; *application data bases* and *subject data bases*. It is quite clear which has given the best results *in the long term:* subject data bases.

Subject data bases relate to organizational *subjects* rather than to conventional computer *applications.* There should, for example, be a *product* data base rather than separate *inventory, order entry,* and *quality control* data bases relating to that product. Many applications may then use the same data base. The development of new applications relating to that data base becomes easier than if application-oriented data bases had been built.

Typical *subjects* for which data bases are built in a corporation include:

- PRODUCTS
- CUSTOMERS
- PARTS
- VENDORS
- ORDERS

- ACCOUNTS
- PERSONNEL
- DOCUMENTS
- ENGINEERING DESCRIPTIONS

Some applications use more than one subject data base. The programs make *calls* to multiple separate data bases. For example.

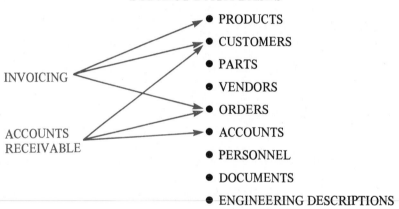

SUBJECT DATA BASES

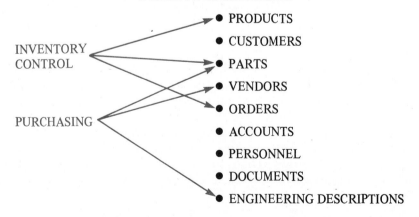

SUBJECT DATA BASES

By using *subject* data bases rather than *applications* data bases, the eventual number of data bases is far lower. A corporation builds up a very large number of applications but does not have a large number of operational *subjects*. If *files* are designed for specific applications, the number of files grows almost as rapidly as the number of applications, and results in the great proliferation of redundant data found in a typical tape and disc library today. Applications-oriented data bases can also proliferate rapidly. Using *subject* data bases, however, the number of applications grows much faster than the number of data bases.

CLASS II ENVIRONMENT

A Class II environment is one of application data bases rather than subject data bases. The systems analysts tend to create a separate data base for each new application as they do with file systems. Because data-base management systems are used, there is some degree of data independence, but proliferation of redundant data grows as with file systems and has most of the problems listed in Box 17.1.

It is sometimes said that a data-base management system is used like a file access method rather than as a true data-base system. This is the Class II environment.

CLASS III ENVIRONMENT

A Class III environment is one of *subject* data bases. When a collection of such data bases have been built, they represent the data resource we discussed—data independent from specific applications.

The types of data represented do not change very frequently, whereas the functions that use the data do. Therefore, it makes sense not to embed the data in the functions as in a Class I environment.

DISINTEGRATION

Many data-base installations have set out to create a Class III environment and have had problems. A new application comes along and for some reason a new data base is created for it rather than using the existing subject data bases.

It is easier and quicker to create application data bases than to carry out the overall design that is needed for subject data bases. However, as the years go by, installations that do this end up with almost as many separate data bases as they would have had *files* if they had not used data-base management. They do not then achieve the advantages of data base described in Chapter 16. The use of data-base management in such installations has not reduced the program maintenance cost as it should.

Too often the attempt to create a Class III environment disintegrates into Class II. This may be due to poor management or to poor subject database design.

Sometimes end users or analysts want their own data base, for reasons of pride, politics, or because it is easier. Management is not strong enough to enforce the principles of the Class III environment, or possibly does not understand them or their significance.

Sometimes the analyst needs a new view of data which cannot be derived from the existing data bases. Consequently, a new data base is created. This happens over and over again until there is a proliferation of data bases. The cause of this is usually inadequate design in the first place. Good design today can be ensured by using automated data-base design tools [3].

CLASS IV ENVIRONMENT

Much user-driven computing employs Class IV data bases: the relational data-base system of National CSS's NOMAD language, or IBM's QUERY-BY-EXAMPLE or Univac's MAPPER, or information retrieval systems such as Intell's System 2000.

The fields in a data base are arranged into groups called records or segments, and a single READ instruction results in one such record or segment being read into the computer's main memory. Many data base inquiries refer to *one* record—for example, "Display purchase order 29986"—or a small number of records—"Display the account of R.V. AGNEW" or "Display the details of the armaments on the ship INTREPID." Others, however, require the data base to be searched. Queries that cause searching can take much more machine time. If there are too many of them, they take too much machine time, slow down the main work of the system, and give unacceptable response times.

Some data-base languages for end users are powerful and easy to use, but they enable end users to take actions, often unwittingly, which cause expensive searching of data bases.

Some data-base software is specifically designed to permit the data bases to be searched efficiently. Spontaneous queries of a diversity of types can be handled quickly. The software employs data structures that are appropriate for this, such as inverted files, inverted lists, or multiple efficiently designed secondary indices [4]. In some cases special hardware is used to make the data searching fast, such as ICL's CAFS (Content Addressable Filing System).

Information retrieval systems are often separate from the production data-base systems that produce the daily paperwork and do the routine data processing. They are often easier to install and easier to manage. They use different software. The end-user language for interrogating the data base is often closely interrelated with the data structures. Some software can handle either a Class III or a Class IV environment, or both at the same time, but one or the other is handled without the highest efficiency.

An information retrieval system often contains some of the same data as a related production system. Why should they be separate? Primarily for reasons of efficiency. An information system needs its data to be organized differently from a routine high-volume production system. Often, it contains only a subset of the data. An information system could be highly inefficient if it contained and had to search the vast mass of data kept in a routine production system. On the other hand, the routine processes could be disrupted by many end users entering queries that trigger searching operations.

It is important in discussing data-base management to distinguish between Class III and IV environments. They have different problems, are managed differently, and both need to fit into the overall planning of a corporation's data resources.

EXTRACTOR PROGRAM

All or part of the data in the Class IV data bases may be spun off from the Class III data bases or other routine computing systems. For this purpose an *extractor* program is used. Figure 17.5 illustrates this. It transfers specified data to the Class IV data bases which serve the user-driven applications: the information retrieval systems, report processing systems, and decision support system. As the data are transferred they are rebuilt in the Class IV structures with inverted lists, secondary indices, or whatever is used.

The extractor program can work with several possible forms of timing:

- *Off-line, periodic.* For example, data are extracted at night and passed to the Class IV environment.

- *On-line, periodic.* For example, data are extracted every half-hour while the pre-scheduled system is on-line.

- *Trigger.* A preassigned condition triggers the extraction of certain data.

- *Ad hoc.* A human request may initiate the extraction of certain data.

- *Real-time.* Data of certain types are passed to the Class IV environment as soon as a change in them is made.

Inquiries can, of course, be made to the Class III data bases (or Class I or II data). These data bases may contain details of customers, transactions, or other entities which are not passed to the Class IV environment. The user may be able to make queries on either from the same terminal.

Sometimes the software permits *simple* queries to the Class III (I or II) data and *complex* queries to the Class IV data.

Sometimes data are extracted from public data banks and placed in the Class IV environment, where it may be searched, matched with internal data, graphed, or processed.

CLASS III DATA-BASE SYSTEM (or Class I or II)

PRESPECIFIED COMPUTING
(CONVENTIONAL DEVELOPMENT CYCLE)

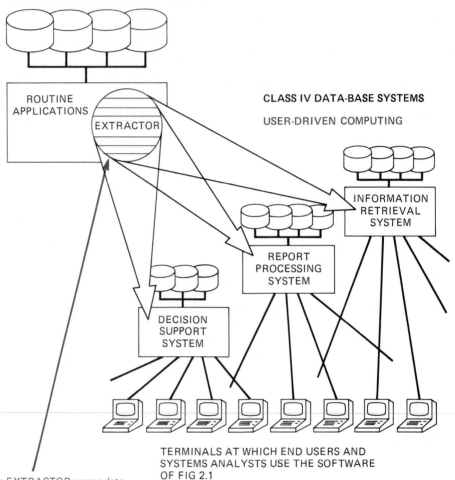

The EXTRACTOR passes data
to the Class IV data bases.
 It works in one of the
following ways:
  1. Periodic, off-line (e.g., at night)
  2. Periodic, on-line (e.g., every hour)
  3. Operated by a trigger condition
  4. Ad hoc, or on demand
  5. Real-time

Figure 17.5 Certain data are extracted from a Class III (or I or II)
system and transferred to Class IV systems.

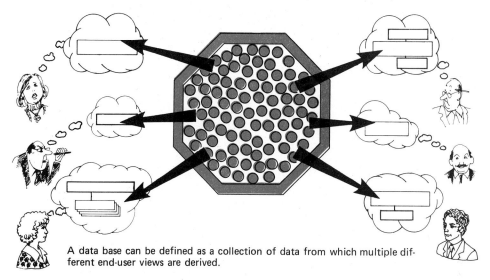

A data base can be defined as a collection of data from which multiple different end-user views are derived.

The task of designing the data is then to capture the end-user views and synthesize them into a data-base structure:

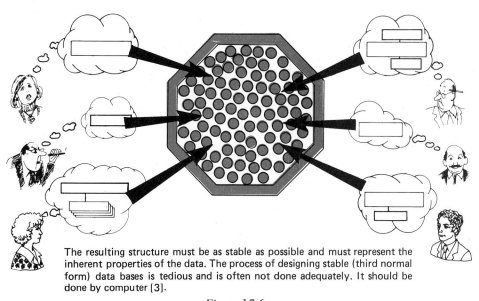

The resulting structure must be as stable as possible and must represent the inherent properties of the data. The process of designing stable (third normal form) data bases is tedious and is often not done adequately. It should be done by computer [3].

Figure 17.6.

REDUNDANCY   Data base has been sold in many organizations as a means of avoiding *redundant* data. The type of configuration shown in Fig. 17.5 introduces redundant data. Because of this, some DP staff argue against configurations such as that shown in Fig. 17.5.

There is no merit in avoiding redundancy for its own sake. Data base *should* be defined as using a data organization that avoids *harmful* redundancy. It would be harmful to have multiple copies of the same data being updated without coordination. The end-user data bases may use data without updating them. They may update and maintain data for a given set of user-driven applications. Summaries of this end-user data may be passed to a routine processing (Class I, II, or III) system. Data may pass in both directions between the user-driven system and the routine processing system.

DATA-BASE DESIGN   The process of designing a data base consists of capturing the user views of data which will be derived from it and synthesizing these into a suitable structure (Fig. 17.6). It is desirable that the resulting structure for a Class III environment be as stable as possible. A Class IV environment allows more flexibility.

The synthesis is done in such a way that redundant data items are eliminated where possible. The same data item does not generally appear twice in the final result. Also, redundant *associations* are eliminated where possible. A minimal number of links connect the fields in a chart of the data structure. A body of theory exists relating to stable (third and fourth normal form) data-base design [2], but too often it has been ignored, with the result that data bases are unsatisfactory.

The synthesis process should be a formal procedure following a formal set of rules. Because it is a formal procedure, it can be done by a computer [3]. This eliminates errors in the process, provides formal documentation that can serve as a basis for end-user discussion, permits any input view to be changed or new views to be added, and immediately reflects the effect of the change in the resulting data model.

A major role of the DP department is to design the data bases that a corporation needs. Increasingly, these will serve user-driven as well as prescheduled computing. The data administration process should involve the end users strongly in data-base design.

REFERENCES

1. Subject of a future Savant Institute report.

2. James Martin, *Managing the Data Base Environment,* Vol. I, Savant Technical Report 9, Savant Institute, Carnforth, Lancsashire, UK, 1980.

3. For example, DATA DESIGNER from Database Design, Inc., Ann Arbor, MI.

4. James Martin, *Computer Data Base Organization,* 2nd ed., Prentice-Hall, Inc., Englewood Cliffs, NJ, 1977.

18 PERFORMANCE CONSIDERATIONS

INTRODUCTION   The software and methods discussed in this book
                raise a number of machine performance questions.
There are two different types of concern. The first relates to efficiency questions. Do the generators produce less efficient code than that produced by conventional programs? Will response times be poor with the generators?

Second, if the end users are freed to generate their own applications, make data-base queries, sort their own files, and generally exercise the facilities of end-user software, who can control the effect they have on machine performance?

EFFICIENCY   Let us look first at the efficiency question. Some
                generators have been specifically designed to give
good machine efficiency; others have largely ignored the question. It is important to distinguish between these.

Many applications of data-base queries or report programs that are generated are run only *a few times a day*. In this case there is no need to worry about machine efficiency. With many applications the machine cycles used in running them for their lifetime are less than the machine cycles for assembling or compiling them [1]. This is true of both application generators and conventional languages.

In a survey of application programs conducted by IBM, it was found that 50% of the applications accounted for only 2% of the machine time. For 92.7% of the application programs, development and maintenance costs exceeded *lifetime* execution costs by a factor of 10 [2].

The type of generator that is likely to be machine efficient is one that selects precoded modules or modifies skeletal applications. These modules or skeletal applications may be precoded in assembler language with much tighter code than that which would result from a COBOL or PL/1 compilation. As we commented earlier, some application generators of this type can create object code which is better than the same application programmed in a conventional programming language.

The use of *precompiled* modules or skeletal applications can also greatly reduce the compile time in some cases. Several organizations have run performance evaluation studies on generators that use precompiled code, such as IBM's DMS and ADF. The following results were obtained by John Deere, Inc., comparing ADF with a COBOL version of the same application [3].

	Ratio $\dfrac{\text{ADF}}{\text{COBOL}}$		
	Nonconversational Programs	Conversational Programs That Did Not Update the Data Base	Conversational Programs That Did Update the Data Base
CPU time	2.4	1.8	0.8
Region time	0.7	1.1	0.5
Number of DL/1 data-base calls	1.0	1.2	1.3

These were not exact results because the machine was performing other activities, but they are thought to be typical. ADF tends to perform better when updating a data base in conversational mode, and slightly worse in some other situations. It was thought that performance degradation with the generator was nothing to worry about, even with high-volume applications. The applications did, however, use substantially more main memory.

A type of generator that would not have this property is one that generates COBOL code which must then be compiled. This is sometimes done with the idea that COBOL code can be modified or maintained if necessary.

Interpreted code is generally less efficient than compiled code. Some application generators, and some software for high-level languages such as APL, use interpreters only. These should, perhaps, not be used for heavy-duty applications.

For some applications high-level user-oriented programming languages such as NOMAD sometimes generate better object code than COBOL or PL/1. In one case a programmer was given a COBOL program to modify and expected to take 6 weeks. He had been quietly studying NOMAD and used this to completely rewrite the application *in one day*. Expecting the result to give poor performance, his management said: "What on earth did you do that for?'' It was benchmarked and in fact it performed better than the COBOL version.

In some cases the opposite effect can be found. Generator software whose designers have not paid careful attention to optimization can burn up an excessive amount of machine time. Some minicomputer installations have rapidly exceeded their machine capacity by using generators that make application creation easy, but not optimal.

Particularly dangerous is the use of files or data bases. An innocent-looking query or data reference may trigger the search of a whole file, a time-consuming, multiple-key operation, or expensive *joins* in a relational data base. Inefficient data-base operation can be tolerated for ad hoc requests which a user wants to perform once. They should not be tolerated for repetitive high-volume operations. With these the data-base administrator should check that the data-base design will work well for its intended use, just as in conventional high-volume application development.

COMMON CODE MODULES

A substantial advantage of generators using pre-compiled modules can occur when many generated applications run concurrently. In this case many modules of reentrant code may be shared by the applications. These remain in the main memory of the computer, so that there is substantially less paging than with conventional programs, for which every code module is different.

The improvement is sometimes dramatic. In one IBM installation PL/1 applications were replaced with the same applications written in DMS. Eight applications ran concurrently and shared modules of DMS. The average response time dropped as follows:

	With DMS Application Generator	With PL/1 Programming
Average response time (seconds)	0.6	3.4
Range of response times (i.e., difference between the shortest and longest response times measured)	0.8	7.1

The *drop* in response time is the opposite of the popular wisdom which says that the response time increases with application generators. It may increase if common modules of code are not used, or if data-base usage is such that it multiplies the number of access operations.

ACROBATS With most of the software in Fig. 2.1, there is much scope for tuning and performance improvement. This often requires a person highly skilled with the software and its file structures and access methods.

When a typical end user, or a systems analyst working with him, creates an application with the software of Fig. 2.1, the results may *appear* good, but the machine performance is far from optimal. Sometimes this does not matter. If the application will be used only occasionally by one person, who cares? If it will be run frequently, a rewrite is desirable to achieve optimal performance.

In one case a bill-of-materials application was written with NOMAD. It served as a useful prototype and many modifications were made to it, but to process the entire set of files required 20 hours. A NOMAD specialist worked on it for 5 days and reduced the running time to less than an hour.

Sometimes even more extreme performance improvement is achieved. Improvement can be achieved with application development facilities by restructuring the data, resequencing the files, reorganizing the accesses to the data, combining separate data bases, restructuring the processing, and maximizing the commonality of code.

The systems analyst who creates a prototype, or whose end user creates an application, may himself set about reorganizing the application to improve machine performance. On the other hand, he may pass it to a specialist with the software—the ADF or NOMAD "acrobat."

DANGERS OF END-USER LANGUAGES A powerful end-user language for data operations such as QUERY-BY-EXAMPLE or MAPPER allows users to take actions that could burn up machine time. They may be able to *sort* data or carry out large-scale relational *join* operations.

If they sort small files, no harm is done, but it is generally desirable to stop them from sorting large files. With MAPPER it is often said that if a user wants to sort more than 5000 screen lines, these data should be passed to an off-line sorting routine. The off-line program, which sorts more efficiently, notifies the user when the sort is completed. Users are instructed that they can do long sorts themselves if they block them into groups of 2000 lines and do not sort more than that with one command. Users are given other instructions about how to speed up sorts.

In the environment described in Chapter 11, where several hundred users can all create and manipulate files of reports using the same computer, they are all dependent to a certain extent on each other's good behavior. If some users employ an excess of system capacity, others will find that their response times are slower. Fortunately, not many of the worthwhile uses of the computer require that large files be sorted or matched on-line. The problem of finite computer capacity is explained to users and a community spirit encouraged. The magazine and notice board for users says: "Have some respect for the other guy." By and large there is no problem. If response times slow down, users are particularly careful to avoid initiating runs that worsen the system load.

It is necessary to monitor the use of such systems to expand the computing capacity as the load grows before it causes user frustration. Monitoring is also desirable to detect whether any users are hogging the system. Certain users have a habit of taking actions that initiate excessive file access operations. Sometimes they do this unwittingly and a system coordinator can stop them.

| TYPES OF DATA-BASE ACTIVITY | It is desirable to distinguish among different types of usage or different types of queries. Simple queries and updates can be handled by a Class II or III (or I) system, but complex queries require |

specially structured data.

Data-base queries can be classified into four types.

1. Primary-Key Activity

A record is accessed by means of its primary key. This can be done quickly and uses few machine cycles.

An example of a primary-key query would be "PRINT DETAILS OF THE SHIP *ACHILLES.*" SHIP-NAME is a primary key for accessing a naval data base. A single record is looked up, and its contents are printed.

2. Single-Secondary-Key Queries

This type of query may be represented on a data model diagram as a secondary-key path. If it is anticipated, a secondary index or other mechanism may be used. It requires far more machine cycles than does a primary-key query.

An example of a single-secondary-key query would be "PRINT DETAILS OF ALL SHIPS WITH A READINESS-RATING = *C1*." If the question was anticipated by the system designer, there may be a secondary-key index showing what ships have a given readiness rating.

3. Multiple-Secondary-Key Queries

This requires more than one secondary-key access. It can be substantially more complex and expensive in machine cycles than a single-secondary-key access.

An example of such a query might be "PRINT DETAILS OF ALL RUSSIAN SHIPS WITHIN 900 MILES OF THE STRAITS OF HORMUZ CARRYING TORPEDOES WITH A RANGE GREATER THAN 20 MILES."

A secondary index to the weapons data base may be used to find which weapons are torpedoes with a range greater than 20 miles. There may be a secondary-key index showing which ships are Russian. It may be necessary to examine their records to find whether they carry those weapons. This produces a list of ships. The area around the Straits of Hormuz is then examined to find which ships are within 900 miles of that location. These ships are compared with the previous list. This requires a considerable amount of machine activity, especially if there are many ships.

4. Unanticipated Search Queries

Secondary-key queries may take place relatively quickly if there is a suitable secondary index. If there is not, it may be necessary to search the records in question one record at a time. This is very expensive in machine time.

AUTOMATIC OPTIMIZATION

In Chapter 9 we used the term *automatic navigation* in a data base to refer to nonprocedural uses of the data base: for example, the use of the high-level relational data-base languages.

With automatic navigation it becomes the system's responsibility to select the access paths by which the data are retrieved. It is desirable that the system do this in an optimal fashion. How efficiently multirecord and multiple-key queries are processed varies greatly from one data-base management system to another.

There are three major aspects involved in achieving efficiency in automatic navigation. First, a set of special access paths or mechanisms may be created for data retrieval using keys other than the primary keys. These may be special indices, chains, or other mechanisms. If such an access mechanism does not exist when it is needed, the system will have to conduct a sequential search of the data, which is time consuming. A data-base administrator, or possibly a specially authorized end user, may instruct the system to create the special indices. Similarly, the data-base administrator may instruct the system to drop an index if it is not often used. The system may provide usage statistics to indicate what special indices are needed. The technical possibility exists of automatic creation and optimization of access paths based on system usage.

Some systems automatically optimize the handling of transactions to employ the special indices or access paths that exist. When changes are made, this may require the recompiling of previously compiled routines.

The second aspect involved in achieving efficiency in automatic navigation is that the system should determine in what sequence the various operations for combining records should be processed. There is much scope here for optimization to achieve good performance. This has been the subject of much research.

The third aspect involved in achieving efficiency relates to changes in hardware design. Many different hardware mechanisms are possible to speed up data-base researching, relational operations such as joins, and the processing of high-level data-base languages in general. Some hardware changes relate to the storage devices themselves, permitting parallel searching or faster relational operations. Other changes relate to the movement of data-base operations out of the mainframe and into a data-base processor that is attached to the mainframe channels—a *back-end processor.* Other changes relate to the modification of the mainframe instruction set and architecture. Hardware changes are more drastic than software operations, so at the time of writing, most automatic navigation is being done by software. Ultimately, however, data-base machines will be the best means to achieve efficient automatic navigation.

DEDICATED MACHINES

If a computer did nothing other than process one query at a time, a relatively inexpensive machine might be used. Even if it processed multiple similar queries at once, machine time need not be a serious problem.

Unfortunately, many systems are designed to do conventional high-volume data processing, with queries fitting in as required. A DP manager has to decide which activities have priority. Queries about Russian ships near the Straits of Hormuz may have very high priority, but ordinary commercial use of an end-user query language may not.

An end user with a language such as QUERY-BY-EXAMPLE can very quickly enter a query like the following:

EMPLOYEE	EMPLOYEE #	NAME	LOCATION	SALARY	YEAR-OF-HIRE
A	P.	P.		< 25000	> 1975

SKILLS	SKILL-TYPE	GRADE	EMPLOYEE #
	ACCOUNTANT	> 6	A

The user may have no concept of how much is involved in processing this query. The response time might be quite long. If this type of query is given a low priority, the response time might become degraded to a level that seems unacceptable to end users. If the necessary secondary indices do not exist and the EMPLOYEE or SKILLS records have to be searched, the time taken may be excessive.

EXPENSE   When a query initiates search of or joining data bases on a large system, it may be more expensive than the end user realizes. Often, there is no indication of the cost involved when a data-base facility is used. The user may not know the wide difference in cost between a primary-key query and one that triggers searching operations. It would be useful if computers would tell the user the cost before they process the query. Some end-user software does this. Viewdata systems, for example, often indicate the cost of accessing the next page. Information retrieval and query language systems sometimes indicate how many records would have to be retrieved to answer a query. Sometimes user management is surprised by the charges and unable to comprehend them.

CATEGORIES OF DATA SYSTEM   Figure 18.1 shows six categories of data system. In its early years data-base usage employed predominently primary-key access paths. The high-volume activity of most computers is category 1 in Fig. 18.1: production data proc-

	IS THE INFORMATION PRODUCED ON A SCHEDULED BASIS BY THE SYSTEM?	
	YES SCHEDULED	NO ON DEMAND
PRIMARY KEY	① PRODUCTION DATA PROCESSING	② SIMPLE QUERIES
ANTICIPATED SINGLE-SECONDARY-KEY AND MULTIPLE-SECONDARY-KEY	③ COMPLEX OFF-LINE QUERIES	④ COMPLEX ON-LINE QUERIES
UNANTICIPATED	⑤ SLOW-REACTING INFORMATION SYSTEM	⑥ GENERALIZED INFORMATION SYSTEM

Figure 18.1 Categories of data systems. Categories 4 and 6 may need to be in a different computer from category 1.

essing. Primary-key queries are used with the production systems with no problem (category 2).

Off-line secondary-key queries can be saved and processed in a scheduled batch fashion (category 3 in Fig. 18.1). This does not disrupt the production system.

Category 4 is much more disruptive of the production system. A data base designed to be efficient for high-volume production is usually not efficient for complex secondary-key queries, and vice versa. Category 6 is worse. The queries are not planned and may require that parts of the data base be searched.

It is often desirable that categories 4 and 6 be in a computer system separate from the category 1 high-volume production systems. End-user departments might have their own computer, either an information system or a production system. This may make sense both for performance and other reasons.

Category 5 in Fig. 18.1 is less useful. Non-predefined information requests might be satisfied by visual inspections of listings produced on a scheduled basis. Although this has been common with some computer systems, it is generally a rather unsatisfactory way of answering spontaneous requests for information.

SEPARATE
SYSTEMS
　　　　　　　Some data-base systems have severe scheduling and response-time problems. This is especially so when high-volume use is made of paths through the data base which are not primary-key paths. The languages for user-driven computing can trigger a substantial amount of such activity and their usage can grow rapidly. Given the falling cost of computers, it often makes sense to create user-driven systems that are *separate* from high-volume production systems.

Scheduling problems are generally caused by having conflicting types of activity combined on the same machine. Different forms of data-base activity, in particular, may conflict with the machine performance point of view. User-driven operations that trigger secondary key operations, sort, file matches, or relational joins can conflict with the high-volume production runs which need to be optimized. If the user-driven system is separate, the data can be selected and efficiently organized for that activity and the activity is then more efficient than if it used data organized for some other high-volume operations.

We have stressed the separation of Class IV data-base systems (which are usually user-driven systems) from Class II or III systems, as illustrated in Figs. 9.4 and 17.5. In some cases these are disjoint systems residing in the same computer. Often they are physically separate. An extractor program (Fig. 17.5) may be used in building the Class IV data base.

**SYSTEM
INTERFERENCE**
Sometimes the design arithmetic is correct in planning data-base runs, but the designer has no control over what other jobs may be run at the same time in the same computer center. If the computer center manager runs the wrong mix of jobs, the end users' response times may suffer badly. Sometimes he has to run large compilations or sorts alongside the on-line activity. He may be forced to do this because of job pressures or because another machine is down. Sometimes the degradation in response time is severe. In bad cases a 2-second response time has changed to 30 seconds or more. This is insufferably frustrating for the end users. The answer is often to separate the user-driven activities from the computer, which can play havoc with them.

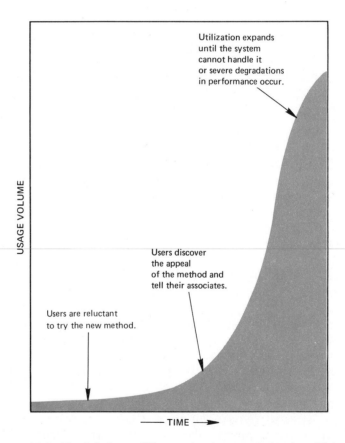

Figure within shows axes labeled USAGE VOLUME (vertical) and TIME (horizontal), with annotations:

- Utilization expands until the system cannot handle it or severe degradations in performance occur.
- Users discover the appeal of the method and tell their associates.
- Users are reluctant to try the new method.

Figure 18.2 Martin's Law: "If a service is created that is sufficiently useful, utilization expands until it knocks out the system!" Many end-user services have had a growth pattern similar to that shown here.

EXCESSIVE GROWTH IN UTILIZATION

One of the problems with user-driven systems is that when a service becomes perceived as being particularly valuable, the good news spreads and sometimes the utilization can expand too rapidly for the system to handle (Fig. 18.2). This has sometimes happened with powerful end-user data-base query languages.

Again, the answer is often to give the users their own system. They can do what they want with their own system and pay for it. The system may be designed to monitor usage and be expandable to larger sizes.

REFERENCES

1. R.C. Kendall, "Management Perspectives on Programs, Programming, and Productivity," *Proceedings* GUIDE 45, Atlanta, GA, 1977.

2. R.C. Kendall, *Management Perspectives on Programs, Programming, and Productivity*, IBM Corp., CHQ Div., White Plains, NY, 1978.

3. D.H. Holtz, "ADF Experience at John Deere," D303–SHARE 50, Denver, CO, March 1978.

19 INFORMATION CENTER MANAGEMENT

We have stressed the importance of user-driven application development. Today's software makes it practical for many end users to do their own application generation. Whether they do it themselves or with help from a DP specialist, it needs to be done within a *managed* framework. This chapter is concerned with that management.

THE NEED FOR MANAGEMENT   The reasons we need to manage user-driven computing are as follows:

- To ensure that data entered or maintained by the users are employed to their full potential rather than being in isolated personal electronic filing cabinets.
- To assist the users so they develop applications as efficiently as possible.
- To encourage the rapid spread of user-driven computing.
- To ensure that adequate accuracy controls on data are used.
- To avoid redundancy in application creation.
- To avoid integrity problems caused by multiple updating of data.
- To ensure that the systems built are auditable and secure, where necessary.

The Information Center concept, which we mentioned in Chapter 6, is intended to provide management of and support for user-driven computing.

The overriding objective of Information Center management is to greatly speed up the creation of applications which end users require. The queue for conventional development, with its long application backlog, is *bypassed*.

In most cases data bases are used: sometimes Class III, more often Class IV. Most Information Centers support the concept of end users developing their own applications. Some additionally use systems analysts working in conjunction with end users to develop applications, but without employing programmers, writing program specifications, or indulging in the time-consuming systems analysis techniques of flow charting, dataflow diagramming, or structured analysis.

The Information Center concept should support a natural division of labor between the end users and DP staff. Each group provides what it is best equipped for. The end users know what information, reports, and decision support they need in order to do their jobs well, and usually they need results quickly. The DP support group knows how these can be obtained. The two groups work together, balancing their resources for maximum productivity. To achieve this result the end users must be trained, encouraged, and motivated, and their competence developed to a point at which they can generate and manipulate the reports they need, perform calculations, answer "what if?" questions, perform simulations, and so on. In some cases end users have created many operations systems.

EXECUTIVE'S WORKBENCH   The terminal installed for an end user by the Information Center provides a variety of services. It has been described with the terms executive workbench, professional workbench, and administrative workbench.

Like a carpenter's workbench, the administrative workbench provides a set of well-organized tools. These assist the professional, manager, or their staff to manipulate data or carry out activities such as those shown in Fig. 8.1. Display terminals are used: sometimes with color and sometimes with graphics capability.

Information Centers differ greatly in the amount of data they make available to users. Some extract data from production systems and make these available for user manipulation and decision-support activities. Some merely support the user's own data input for his or her own applications. Others operate major general-purpose information retrieval systems to which new data can be added whenever requested.

Office Automation (Office-of-the-Future) facilities are spreading rapidly in some organizations, providing mailbox facilities, automated in-basket processing, and other services. These ought to be linked with the Information Center service. The office-of-the-future and Information Center concepts are becoming closely integrated in some organizations. Most office-of-the-future services should be regarded as additional tools for the administrative or professional workbench.

Figure 19.1 illustrates the administrative workbench concept.

A particularly important facility in an executive workbench is the capability for the executive to create and adjust his or her own control mechanisms.

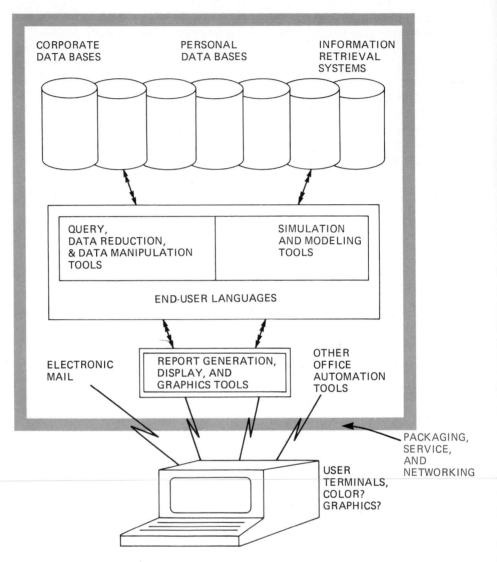

Figure 19.1   Executive/professional workbench.

VIRTUAL FILING CABINET   In some cases the data accessible by users is perceived as though it were in an electronic filing cabinet to which they have personal access.

They have several types of reports in their *virtual filing cabinet*. They can specify the type of data they want to see, what calculations should be done on it, and how it should be sorted and presented. They may ask to see data only when they exceed certain parameters. They can determine when "exceptions" should be brought to their notice.

In some cases the data in the users' virtual filing cabinets will be derived from the master data bases (or files), which are used for the main production processes. In some cases the users will create their own personal files. Often the users will enter and maintain data which is important to their area. This data, with appropriate security, audit, and accuracy checks, is moved across to the central master data bases.

The users can transmit data from their virtual filing cabinets to other users. They can generate reports that highlight important information, and have these printed if necessary.

The concept of users' virtual filing cabinets combined with computing and report generation capability is powerful. In IBM's Yorktown Heights research laboratory this approach led to an *increase of 1300% in computer utilization* by managers and professionals, *with no system development department* since all projects were handled by the users. A small, highly skilled support group helped the users and spread the usage of packaged tools.

In a much more spectacular example, end users on the Santa Fe Railroad created their own *operations* system to avoid paperwork and speed up railroad operations. This system grew until it processed more than $2\frac{1}{2}$ million transactions a day from more than two thousand terminals throughout the railroad. It had a major effect on the profitability of the railroad, allowing it to double the freight it carried without an increase in administrative staff. It permitted many changes in railroad operations and experiments in train and container usage, because the users could adapt the computer system quickly to reflect the changes.

Many DP executives and analysts are skeptical about this Santa Fe system until they see it in operation and investigate how it was created. It is a truly impressive computer system, with its development methods now being emulated elsewhere.

INFORMATION CENTER SUPPORT   DP executives in many organizations have tried to stop end users from developing their own applications. In other cases they have allowed it to happen, only too glad to get some of the end users off their backs. End-user development is a force which should be harnessed, encouraged, and supported to the fullest, but if it happens in an *uncontrolled* fashion it can store up trouble for the future because multiple versions of incompatible data come into existence, and multiple machines cannot be interlinked.

The Information Center concept encourages and supports end users developing their own applications. The Information Center is a group within the DP organization designed to serve the end users directly and speedily. The group is aware of what data bases exist and sometimes sets up other data bases. It makes this information available for end users to access and manipulate. Information Center consultants work with the end users. The consultants help users to create the decision support systems, personal computing facilities, information retrieval systems and organizational support systems. A major reason for establishing this mode of operation has been the extreme dissatisfaction expressed by end users about the way DP has been responding to their information needs.

The consultants encourage the users to employ the information facilities which already exist. They sit at terminals with the users to create the catalogued query procedures, report generation routines, or graphics generation routines. They train the users to employ these facilities.

Where more complex applications are needed, the information center consultants decide how they can be created, selecting, where possible, an application generator, language, or package which avoids the formal, slow, programming development cycle.

INFORMATION CENTER ORGANIZATION

Figure 19.2 shows a type of Information Center organization which works well in some corporations. Data processing development is split into two parts: conventional development and the Information Center. Both link to the data administration function, which has an important role in standardizing the data which must pass between the two areas.

The Information Center reports to the overall DP executive. Its staff consists of general consultants who work with the end users, and specialists who are expert on end-user products. These staff train and assist the end

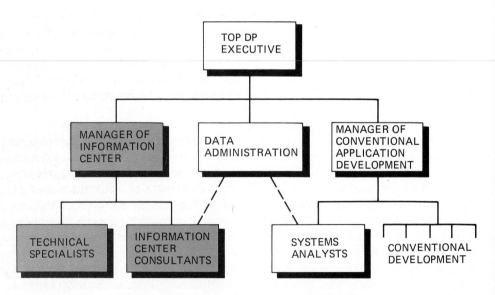

Figure 19.2 Information Center organization.

users, create applications for them, and, where practicable, encourage them to solve their own problems with the end-user languages.

An organization in the grip of traditional DP standards and methods can make a small beginning by initially having only a few staff members using the Information Center methods. The objective should be that as the Information Center methods are demonstrated to work well, they take over a rapidly increasing proportion of the DP development.

The Information Center must relate closely to the data administration function, which is a vital part of conventional DP development (if it is well managed). The Information Center consultants will use the data bases, request additional data bases, and participate in the logical design of data bases. The Information Center may design and operate its own data bases for decision support and information retrieval systems. The data in these will often be derived from conventional DP production-oriented data bases.

Sometimes an end-user application can be created partially but not completely with the application generators or nonprocedural languages. An important feature of these facilities is an *escape* mechanism or ability to call subroutines of conventional programming. For this purpose the Information Center may be able to call upon programmers from the conventional DP group. If, however, this can only be done with a long delay because of the conventional application backlog, the Information Center may acquire some programming skill of its own.

DIFFERENCES IN SCOPE

Information Centers in existence differ greatly in their scope.

Some are small operations within a DP department, sometimes without a full-time manager. Some support *only* development by end users. Some computer vendors' proposals for Information Centers state that a basic principle is that *only* end users should do the development, and the Information Center should merely give them the tools, systems, and training. However many of the most valuable Information Centers employ systems analysts or Information Center "consultants" who *do* create applications working hand in hand with the users, but do not write program specifications for separate programmers to code. These analysts employ nonprocedural application generators or report generators which can obtain results *fast* without conventional programming. They can complete the application faster than writing programming specifications, so the traditional development cycle disappears.

Some Information Centers do no work on routine production systems, but only on *ad hoc* systems—information systems and decision support systems. Others are organized so that *all* application development without programmers goes via the Information Center (which may be called a different name). Some of the nonprocedural languages which a nonprogramming systems analyst can employ are appropriate for creating certain production systems as well as information systems, and produce suitably efficient machine codes. IBM's DMS (Development Management System), for example, is used by nonprogramming analysts to create production systems.

Figure 19.3 splits application development into five categories. Some Information Centers do only category 1. Some do categories 1 and 2. Some do category 1 and some 1, 2, 4, and 5. In the author's view it is desirable to support all forms of application development without programmers.

Sometimes Information Centers have been set up with the blunt insistence that the staff should do *no* application development. Often in such cases the DP department itself has used the Information Center for its own development because this is quicker than conventional techniques. This leads to another type of organization in which the Information Center provides support staff assisting both the DP department and the end users. It is generally better that the Information Center is separate from conventional DP so that it can fully develop the counter-culture of application development by new methods.

The Information Center *should* develop applications itself so it becomes fully familiar with the problems, and thus can better support the user development, and also because the best form of development is often users and Information Center staff working jointly on creating applications. It should, where possible, insist that users document their own applications and learn how to modify (maintain) them.

The Information Center should avoid the trap of having a large number of (for example, APL) programs to maintain.

TECHNIQUES
ANALYST

When a demand for a new application comes up it is desirable to decide how it will be developed. Appropriate development software should be selected.

	DEVELOPMENT BY END USERS ALONE	DEVELOPMENT BY SYSTEMS ANALYSTS ALONE	DEVELOPMENT BY ANALYSTS AND PROGRAMMERS
INFORMATION RETRIEVAL AND DECISION SUPPORT SYSTEMS	1	2	3
ROUTINE PROCESSING SYSTEMS	4	5	6

Figure 19.3 Some Information Centers support development by end users only in category 1. Some support categories 1 and 2. Some encourage end-user development of routine processing systems as well as ad hoc systems—categories 1 and 4. Some support all application development without programmers—categories 1, 2, 4, and 5.

It should be developed by the *fastest* method possible and with a procedure that will minimize future maintenance costs. This means that languages like COBOL and PL/1 should be avoided where possible.

Specialists, sometimes called *techniques analysts* (TA), may make the decisions about how a new application demand should be handled. They will know the capabilities of the different software and will decide whether the application needs conventional programming and analysis, whether it can be created by a systems analyst with an application generator such as IBM's DMS, or whether it is appropriate for end users' development perhaps with a high-level data-base language.

The techniques analyst may act as a switch, to switch an application between conventional development and Information Center development.

A major objective of the technique selection should be to avoid programming in COBOL or PL/1 whenever it can be avoided. Not only is it expensive but it results in programs which are very costly to maintain and which cannot be changed quickly.

FUNCTIONS OF
IC STAFF

Selection of the techniques or software is one of many services that should be provided by the Information Center staff. They need to train, encourage, support, and assist the end users in obtaining the applications they need. Box 19.1 lists functions that should be carried out by the Information Center. It divides them into two groups—those performed by the analysts or consultants who work with the end users, and those performed by a technical support group or person. This follows the division shown in Fig. 19.2.

The size of the Information Center staff varies greatly depending upon the number of users supported and whether the consultants *develop* the applications along with the users or insist that users do their own development.

Some corporations have started an Information Center with a low-level commitment and allowed it to grow. In some small operations the staff carry out all of the support functions in Box 19.1; there is no division into technical and consultant staff as in Fig. 19.2. The staff play a role which is similar to that of an IBM Systems Engineer.

One large bank started this operation with a manager, assistant manager, two professional staffs, and a clerical coordinator. The manager was an enthusiast of the software used, had a technical background, and was chosen because he wanted to do the job. The assistant manager was an ex operations shift supervisor with no programming or systems background. It was argued that he was going to guide users who also had no technical background, so it would be an advantage for him to have gone through the learning process relatively recently.

This Information Center (which is called by a different name) is a low-key operation with a low budget compared to the bank's overall DP budget. In other cases a much more aggressive move has been made into this form of

**BOX 19.1   Functions that should be carried out by an
Information Center**

By the Consultants:

- Training the users to employ the tools and create applications
- User encouragement, education, and selling
- Generation of applications (without programmers) in conjunction with users
- Generation and modification of prototypes
- Specification of changes to prototypes that may be needed to make them into working systems
- Consulting on user problems
- Determining whether a proposed application is suitable for Information Center development, and selecting the software and methods
- Demonstrations of Information Center capabilities to users, including senior management
- General communication with senior management
- Communication with traditional DP development
- Linking to the data administrator(s) in defining and representing data
- Maintaining a catalog of available applications and data bases
- Coordination to prevent duplicate or redundant application development
- Creating Class IV data bases, or converting data for information retrieval.
- Operation of schemes for motivating users (as discussed in Chapter 14)

By the Technical Specialists:

- System set-up and support
- Dealing with technical and software problems
- Selection of languages and software and the versions of those which are used
- Assistance in choosing techniques or software for a given application (the job of the Techniques Analyst).
- Communication with vendors

BOX 19.1 (*Continued*)

- Monitoring systems usage and planning future resources
- Charge-back to users
- Tuning or reorganizing an application for better machine performance
- Auditing system usage and application quality

operation, with a tough executive heading it who believes that a high proportion of new application development can be done with techniques that bypass conventional DP programming and analysis.

SELLING   The more aggressive Information Centers regard
                           selling the new capabilities to end users to be of
primary importance so that advanced technology can make a more rapid penetration.

In the bank mentioned above there is a department that is responsible for the services the bank provides to its customers—a payroll service, a check reconciliation service, and so on. The bank put its Information Center in this department, arguing that people who were good at selling and supporting computer services outside the bank could also do it inside the bank. The manager of the department had experience in dealing with dissatisfied and disgruntled customers, and these talents were useful to the Information Center.

RIVALRY   Sometimes harmful political rivalry has grown up
                           between the management of the Information
Center and the management of conventional DP development. The manager of the Information Center naturally wants to satisfy as many user demands as possible and remove them from the slow conventional DP cycle. In some cases he assumes a missionary fervor about doing this. He sees conventional development as being cumbersome, expensive, and obsolete. He makes his views known about this and gains many disciples among previously frustrated end users. He advocates that rather than doing expensive maintenance on conventional programs, these should be scrapped and redeveloped with the Information Center methods, where possible.

The manager of conventional development may feel attacked and in danger of losing his empire. His rival running the Information Center appears like a hero and he does not. He may argue against the new methods. Great opposition is sometimes encountered to the setting up of, or expansion of,

Information Center operation. Box 3.2 listed some of the reasons given by the opposition. Most of these are invalid compared with the major gains in productivity that can be achieved.

The solution to the rivalry lies in good overall DP management by an executive whom both the Information Center manager and the manager of conventional DP report to. The manager of conventional DP should be encouraged to use new software techniques also, and challenged to demonstrate how productivity can be increased and maintenance costs cut with good data-base techniques and application generators like IBM's DMS or ADF, or Cullinane's OADS.

Often managers of conventional development perceive that all *routine* operations are their territory and that the Information Center should be used only for ad hoc development such as decision support systems. The argument against this is that some case histories show successful and spectacular development of routine, transaction-driven production systems by end users. We mentioned the Santa Fe Railroad, for example, where a vast system for routine operations was created entirely by end users. This system now processes more than 100,000 transactions per day, and is constantly adjusted by the end users to improve it and adapt it to changing needs. About a thousand end users have been trained to develop or modify the applications.

A better division of responsibilities is to say that the Information Center will encourage and support all types of user-driven development that make sense (and some do not); conventional development will support all development which involves the need for DP programmers using COBOL, PL/1, and new languages for DP programmers such as IBM's ADF and CINCOM's MANTIS.

Because they serve the same community, often with the same data bases, it is vital that Information Center management, conventional development management, and maintenance management work closely together and explore the most cost-effective trade-offs.

LANGUAGES   Information Centers differ widely in their choices
SUPPORTED   and ranges of languages.

Some support only one software package, such as IBM's VSPC (Virtual Storage Personal Computing) or Univac's MAPPER.

Given the *widely* varying capabilities of the software it is usually preferable when the center becomes well established to support more than one type of software.

What makes the Information Center possible is the software that it uses. What can make it excellent is a good choice of software.

An Information Center at the Equitable Insurance Company in New York employs the following software [1]:

- Languages to build systems: FOCUS   English-like languages used by
                                              RAMIS   managers and professionals

- Languages used for model   APL   (A Programming Language)
  building: ADRS   (An APL report generator)

- Statistical packages: SAS   These contain many formulas
                                          SPSS   for statistical analysis.

- Language for financial   FPS   (Financial Planning System)
  analysis:

- Language for querying,   QBE   (An easy-to-use query language)
  manipulating and selecting   ADI   (Giving APL programs access to
  data: data bases)

                                      FOCUS
                                      RAMIS

- Packages for preparing   SAS-graph
  graphs: FOCUS

Two types of color terminals are used with this Information Center. FOCUS and SAS-graph are used to display a variety of types of information in graphical form.

Some of the software needed is general purpose—query languages, report generators, application generators. Some is oriented to specify types of data such as financial planning data, project management, text processing, coordinate geometry, etc.

Box 19.2 lists software from IBM which is used in Information Centers.

It should be noted that much of the best software for Information Center use does not come from the major computer vendors. Excellent application packages, query languages, report generators, application generators, and graphics packages are marketed by independent software vendors. In the above list from Equitable, FOCUS, RAMIS, SAS, SAS-graph, and SPSS are from independent vendors. All run with the IBM hardware and operating system.

Some organizations have many end users creating valuable results with data-base languages such as software AG's NATURAL. More such software appears every month. Some of the earlier products are being constantly enhanced.

COMMUNICATION SKILLS

A particularly important skill of the Information Center staff is communicating with the end users.

Often the center is staffed by people trained as systems analysts. Their job changes fundamentally. They no longer write program specifications, draw data-flow diagrams, etc. They act more as consultants, listening to the end users' problems, solving them, determining the

BOX 19.2　Examples of IBM software used in Information
Centers. (Note: Many of the best packages and
end-user tools and languages are not from the
major computer vendors but from independent
software houses).

Financial

Financial Planning System

Financial Analysis and Credit Evaluation

PLANCODE/1 (PLANning, COntrol, and DEcision, Evaluation System—software for formulating, qualifying, evaluating,
and monitoring plans.)

Long-Term Debt Management System

Management Science

EPLAN—Econometric Planning Language
Forecasting and Time Series Analysis

APL Multivariate Time Series Analysis

APL Advanced Statistical Library

APL Statistical Library

Data Retrieval and Reporting

ADRS (A Department Reporting System II)

APL Data Interface

(IMS–APL Data Link, Interregion Access Method, Data Extraction,
Processing, & Restructuring System)

STAIRS (Information retrieval system)

QUERY-BY-EXAMPLE (QBE)

SQL—Structured Query Language, using a relational data base

Graphics Packages

Graphics Analysis Program

Graphic Attachment Support

Storage Tube & Plotter Simulation for 3277 Graphics Attachment

Plotter and Tablet Support

BOX 19.2 *(Continued)*

Graphs and Histograms
PANEL Line Art Technique
Graphical Data Display Manager

Text Processing

Document Composition Facility
APL Text Editor and Composer

Project Management

MINIPERT
Project Evaluation and Control (PECS)

Scientific/Engineering

COGO–APL Coordinate Geometry
Zeros and Integrals in APL
Continuous Systems Modeling
APL GPSS (General Purpose Systems Simulator)
APL Decision Table Processor and Code Generator
General Cross Assembler Generator

APL Programming Support

VS APL
APL Extended Editor and Full Screen Support
APL Computer-Aided Instruction
APL Handbook of Techniques
APL Workspace Structure Analysis
APL Data Language

Training

IIS (Interactive Instructional System)

users' needs for information, and encouraging, training, and selling ideas to the end users.

It is important to train the Information Center staff in the new languages and software, but this usually comes naturally to them. Sometimes the necessary communications skills come less naturally. A particularly valuable training for some Information Center staff has been courses on how to communicate well. The students in such courses should be followed by careful monitoring and guidance of their activities to help them acquire the style and techniques of a good consultant.

EARLY SUCCESS

It is generally desirable when an information center is established that it be seen to be successful *quickly*. If there are no early successes, it might be regarded as an oddball idea or DP plaything, rather than a facility that will revolutionize a major section of DP development.

The selection of the first users is particularly important. This should be a group keen enough to develop their own query and analysis services, and likely to cooperate well on what may be an experimental basis at first. They should have a definite business need for the new service so that there will be a strong payoff.

For this initial group the appropriate software products are selected, and data bases made available, possibly with separate Class IV data bases being extracted from established production data bases or files. A small number of users are trained and the Information Center staff work with them closely.

The initial experience with the service should be evaluated carefully both by users and DP. It may need substantial adjusting. When both parties perceive it to be working well, it can be extended to other types of users.

SPREADING THE SUCCESS

Eventually, when DP staff are confident of its success and capable of giving good support, the concept of Information Center operation will need to be sold throughout the organization.

A demonstration center should be set up and demonstrations given to all classes of users who will be employing the Information Center services. Demonstrations to senior management are particularly important. These should use *real* corporate data and be designed to show *interesting* results.

The objective of the demonstrations should be to show something of direct basic value to each area manager—something that affects how well his job is done. The demonstration content should be oriented to business results, not technical wizardry. The results-oriented data should be displayed as attractively as possible, for example, on color graphics terminals.

Various operating areas should be asked to contribute data for the demonstrations. Members of the EDP steering committee might each be asked to contribute a demonstration.

The author attended a demonstration in an insurance company before senior executives. Throughout almost the entire two-hour session the discussion was about business results and finances, not about computing technology. Data had been captured relating to the current concerns of the executives in question and had been converted to the relational structures which the software could manipulate. These top executives were fascinated to see how their business concerns could be explored: "What if the prime rate goes to 19%?," "What is the effect of holding down this budget to $600,000?," "Why did the Travellers Insurance Company do so well in this area?," etc.

Such demonstrations can constitute a powerful form of selling. They can help to improve communication between DP and top management, which is often not good enough.

THE IMPORTANCE OF DATA ADMINISTRATION

Perhaps the biggest danger of Information Center operation, or of the spread of minicomputers and software for user-driven computing, is that multiple uncoordinated data structures will be used. The answer to this is well controlled data administration. The data in the end users' files or Class IV data bases must be compatible, where necessary, with the data in the production data bases.

Data are often extracted from production system data bases and moved to separate Information Center data bases, as shown in Fig. 9.4. Sometimes they are moved back in the opposite direction, with suitable accuracy controls. These operations require common data administration and, ideally, the same data dictionary.

DATA COORDINATOR

If end users are given the capability to create their own files, using systems like Univac's MAPPER, for example, field formats and definitions should be derived from a common dictionary. Sometimes in such installations a *data coordinator* is used. This person, sometimes a specially trained end user, ensures consistency among the users' data. This data coordinator ought to report (at least for data administration purposes) to the official data administrator.

The data coordinator may have functions such as the following:

- ensure consistency among user's data
- make the data administrator's definitions of data available to the users

- guide and encourage the users in employing data
- train the users
- liaise with the data administrator
- move infrequently used reports or data off-line (if this is not done automatically)
- remove infrequently used "user views" of data
- establish techniques for informing users what data exists
- contribute to a newsletter about the systems and its available services

OTHER
REGULATION

It is clearly necessary to control the data that is created. A more controversial question is whether there should be any other regulation.

Most end users would say no. Users usually want to be left alone to use computers in the ways that seem best to them. A charge-back scheme is necessary so that they pay for the resources used. They can then make their own decisions about the financial viability of running their own applications.

Often the DP department has thought otherwise. In some cases DP authorization is needed before end users are allowed to develop their own applications. The reasons for this include the following:

1. The Information Center should check that it has adequate computer power and resources to support the application.

2. There may be strategic reasons why the application should not go ahead. For example, there may be a larger plan to develop systems which affect the application in question, or to develop data bases to which the system will link.

3. The project may require traditional DP involvement, for example, interface programming, network development, or large volume printing. This will have to be fitted into the DP workload.

4. A check should be made to ensure that the users know what they are committed to, that their application is practical, and that no DP rescue or maintenance will be needed.

5. A check should be made to see that the application has no adverse security implications.

6. A check should be made to see that the application is satisfactory from the auditor's viewpoint.

7. If a complete charge-back is not made, with the users baring the cost and financial responsibility, a check on the financial viability may be needed.

The problem with building up these types of controls is that they can destroy the end users' freedom to invent, which is one of the most important aspects of user-driven computing.

Excessive controls can put back the bureaucracy which exists in traditional data processing. They undermine the flexibility and speed of development which is a primary objective of Information Center operation.

A compromise may be that a description of all applications is maintained by the Information Center. This is provided to auditors and other interested parties. The user departments are made responsible for cost justification, and the Information Center avoids interfering with users' decisions as far as is possible.

AUDITORS

User-driven computing can be a problem for the auditors. It can increase the possibility that users can commit fraud. The auditors certainly need to know what is going on in this area.

One bank finds that the following arrangement for auditors works well. Every end-user-developed application is formally authorized. The chief auditor (who is a very powerful person in the bank) receives a copy of the authorization and a copy of any documentation which the end users produce. The end users are responsible for their own application documentation, and standards are established for this. If the auditor wants to investigate the user system further, that is a matter between the auditor and the users. The Information Center keeps out of it.

The chief auditor and his department became major users of the Information Center. This mode of operation pleased them because it enabled them to make investigations and write checking programs without the DP organization or programmers knowing in detail what the auditors were doing or looking for. Previously they went to each branch periodically and went through the books manually looking for irregularities. Now they write programs which go through each branch's computer files in the head office. The DP manager states that the auditors created these programs *far faster* than the DP department could have [2]. The auditors can modify the programs whenever they wish, maintaining secrecy over the modifications, and this improves the thoroughness with which they can search for irregularities.

In other organizations also the auditors ought to employ user software to improve the thoroughness of their inspections. Auditors should be one of first customers of the Information Center.

REFERENCES

1. Information from Mr. Jim Johnson, Operations Engineering Department, Equitable Insurance Co., New York.

2. Information from Mr. P.J. Entwistle, Chief Manager (Data Processing), Lloyds Bank Ltd., London.

20 INFORMATION CENTERS IN PRACTICE

While writing this book we surveyed the experience at a variety of Information centers. Many of them were not called "Information Center." Other names were used, and, as discussed in chapter 19, they differ considerably in their approach.

This chapter relays some practical experience and consists mainly of quotations from the executives involved.

FINANCIAL ADVANTAGES

To be worthwhile the Information Center must affect the bottom line of a corporation. We formed the view that flexible user-driven computing can have a greater effect on corporate profits than most traditional data processing.

An Information Center executive at a large insurance company wrote the following [1]:

INFORMATION CENTER EXECUTIVE:

The potential contribution to the assets of the corporation, from opportunities exploited by executives supported by their managers, could be in the hundreds of millions of dollars per year.

The Information Center concept has affected not only decision support and strategic planning, but also the day-to-day operations:

RAILROAD EXECUTIVE:

Since we put the techniques into place we haven't fired anybody because of them. But the freight we carry has more than doubled. That
increase has been handled without any increase in staff. We couldn't
possibly have handled the increase in business with our existing staff
without MAPPER.

USER EXECUTIVE:

For two years I was the Production Coordinator for the Oil Consortium
in Iran. The previous incumbent spent about 12 hours a day processing
detailed data to find out what was going on. The information system
had been designed so that information had to be available for all purposes before a single decision could be made. When a crisis arose the
coordinator was not in a position to contribute to the decision, so the
job had degenerated to that of a glorified accountant.

   By building an Information Center I was able to process selected
key indicators quickly, interpret them, and present an analysis of the
situation by the time of the daily operations meeting held at 7:00 A.M.
About 80% of the time nothing unusual was going on, and I was able to
use the Information Center data to debottleneck production capacity.
During the critical 20% of the time, I was in a position to work with
operational managers on an hour-by-hour basis to balance the flow
from the fields to the Abadan refinery and the Kharg Island export
terminal.

   The management system supported by Information Center concepts enabled Iran to export an additional million barrels a month at
no additional cost.

INSURANCE EXECUTIVE:

It enables us to make better decisions in cash management, and with
today's interest rates that means a large financial saving.

Financial savings also result from reduced costs of developing systems:

INFORMATION CENTER EXECUTIVE:

The *saving* in development costs of the Financial Information System

> and the Personel System alone will total six million dollars and cut development time in half.

Some users of the new techniques estimate that overall they can develop systems at about one-third of the costs.

More important, sometimes, they can obtain results very fast.

INFORMATION CENTER EXECUTIVE:

Users get reports on the day they ask for them, or at worst the day after. Before, it took two months. This completely changes the way they utilize information.

USER EXECUTIVE:

It enables us to spot potential troubles much more quickly. We get an overall view of supply and demand. We can spot short-term fluctuations in demand or supply problems quickly. This saves money and lets us serve customers better.

BUSINESSPEOPLE IN CONTROL

An objective of the Information Center ought to be to put businesspeople more in control of how computing is used.

INFORMATION CENTER MANAGER:

Our motto is "Put computing into the businessperson's hands." We are in business to support the business.

DP EXECUTIVE:

We tried to solve our age-old problem of turning programmers into bankers by instead turning bankers into programmers.

OPERATIONS EXECUTIVE:

An interesting by-product of the information system is that I have more feeling of control but my managers have more feeling of responsibility.

We have all the information on the projects we manage in the organization. Managers at the first level use information to do their job; they use it as a guide on how to manage. At the same time I can look at it any time I choose. I'm not handling them, asking them for special reports. I can generate those reports. If I look at it today and find everything is within the perimeters I'm comfortable with, I go about my business. They are operating as if they were independent entities; I rarely need to bug them at the operational level, and yet I have more control.

USER EXECUTIVE:

The Information Center has enabled senior management to participate in key decisions when they should, but keep out of them when things are going well. It provides *management distance* from the day-to-day operations.

USER MANAGER:

A lot of our people have started installing the terminals at home. When they have a problem they sometimes sit up late at night working on it.

I like to check on things at 7 in the morning (at home). If I take any actions or send messages these are available to people two seconds later. We can start the day in good shape.

One insurance executive compares the Information Center to a military war room [1]:

INFORMATION CENTER EXECUTIVE:

Information Center adapts the military command post and war room concepts to the needs of business executives. The Information Center is built around the dynamics of business decision making. To illustrate this point we can visualize a movie of a NASA mission control center. We may first be attracted to and impressed by the computers and technical support. However, when we watch "mission control," that is a complete mission—such as the recovery of the ill-fated Apollo 13, mobilization for a military alert, or an energy distribution crisis—rather than a still picture, attention shifts from technology to the total decision-making scene. Much frustration by executives and managers about management information systems can be traced to a misplaced and often distorted perception by systems people of information and processing needs in the real world of dynamic business decisions. Information *can* by systematically prepackaged so that it has the same strategic relevance and value that it must have in the "war room" context.

FLEXIBILITY AND RAPID CHANGE   Many executives stressed need for fast ad hoc computing as well as computing with traditional planning.

INTERVIEWER:

What do you think is going wrong with information systems in other organizations?

INFORMATION CENTER MANAGER:

I guess one thing is studying it too long.

INTERVIEWER:

So you're saying "Don't study it; get on with it."

INFORMATION CENTER MANAGER:

Yes. It's often delegated down to an analyst to go and study the users' needs: what they want and don't want. They do an elaborate study that gives minimal feedback, particularly if it's in the hands of someone who does not have a great deal of experience in understanding what managers may or may not want. So they're speculating about what the needs may or may not be, which is kind of what happened with the MIS direction in the early 1970s.

Instead of that we provide the users with tools and a service. We can convert and load up any information they ask for if it's in electronic form. The time taken to get the service in action is much less than the time some people take to do study which does not reveal the true users' needs. We add to the available data quickly as the users' needs change. The needs or perceived needs change all the time.

PILOT SYSTEMS — Often pilot systems are created and experimented with. Sometimes the users find them unsatisfactory and stop using them. This is not a disaster if the system is created quickly enough.

DP EXECUTIVE:

If we can put something up very quickly it doesn't really matter if we have to throw it away and redo it. This is better than excessive time spent in planning and specifying when we cannot be sure what the real needs are anyway.

The main argument for this seemingly sloppy approach is that with some applications the users do not know what they really want.

DP EXECUTIVE:

We all work in different ways. You could brainstorm for years trying to find out what is the right way.

The best approach is to get some people using the tools and see how they feel. You adapt to some of their feelings. Sometimes they so "No. That's no good," and that's useful feedback.

One of the reasons why this is practical now is that we've been able to get these tools into people's hands within days rather than going away for two years to develop a major system and then decide.

We put up a tool and test it on the users in a few weeks. It is better to do this than to conduct a detailed study, because the study would take longer.

Pilot systems reveal to end users what is possible. There is then likely to be many modifications made to the pilot to adapt it to the users' needs and ideas. Step-by-step adaption becomes a standard pattern when building user-driven systems with very high-level languages.

DP EXECUTIVE:

Once it began to gain hold our approach was to install pilots in every aspect of the bank. We have people in commercial banking using the system, people in trust and estates, people in international banking, and people travelling from country to country.

INTERVIEWER:

How about senior management?

DP EXECUTIVE:

We have several of the senior managers that are getting involved. Others are supportive in terms of having their staff do it, and are still not personally involved. And I guess my belief is that what is most important from a firm's perspective is that senior management is supportive, and that it's not necessary that they personally use the tools as long as they are getting the benefits from their organization using the tools.

TRANSITION PHASE   There is a transition phase in getting users to accept the new tools. It takes some time to overcome their apprehension, build familiarity, and advance to the stage where they are thinking creatively about how they might use the tools.

This is rather like learning photography. It takes some time to master the technicalities. Only when the photographer is familiar enough with the techniques to almost forget about them can he concentrate adequately on the creative aspects of picture-making.

INFORMATION CENTER EXECUTIVE:

People have got to get past the stage of becoming comfortable with the tool. Once it is a habit, like the telephone, something changes. They start to think up new ways to use it to enhance their work or how their area works. And that is infectious.

They've all got to go through the struggling transition phases, and then all of a sudden you've got everyone out there creatively thinking how to use the tools better. That's an extraordinary benefit in system development. It's light years away from what we accomplished with structured analysis.

To enable the users to forget about the mechanics and concentrate on creative uses of the systems, the user dialogue has to be very user-friendly— much more so than with many terminal systems of the past.

DP EXECUTIVE:

The old type of terminal operator used the terminal eight hours a day, was completely familiar with the system's quirks, and knew the account numbers.

Now we need to provide information to people who use the terminals just occasionally, are baffled by computer gobbledygook, and who want to go in on the first three letters of a name, or where you live, and do some searching around for information.

INTERVIEWER:

And STAIRS has that capability where IMS hasn't?

DP EXECUTIVE:

Correct. It does it very well. So it provides the capabilities we need to a much broader base of people.

GRAPHICS

Graphics give a particularly powerful way to communicate business information and understand the effects of "What if?" questions. Some Information Centers have emphasized the use of graphics. This has had a particular appeal to their user community.

INFORMATION CENTER EXECUTIVE:

The president of the corporation likes graphics and charts. He believes that financial management and other management participate better in meetings when information is presented graphically. It enables the whole management team to participate. In fifteen minutes you can get a picture of the entire situation.

Information presented graphically can enable you to spot problems quickly, and quickly understand the effects of "What if?" questions. Graphics can highlight problem areas.

Graphics software and terminals differ greatly in their quality. It pays to select the best in order to sell the Information Center capabilities to senior management and users.

DEGREE OF COMMITMENT

Because the Information Center represents a major change in culture, both for DP and its users, the spread of the new methods is likely to be slow in most organizations. To speed it up a major senior management drive is needed.

> *DP EXECUTIVE:*
>
> One problem is optimism. There was a point when we thought that once the tools were in place we would have the whole organization converted in two or three years.
>
> My current feeling is that once a firm decides to start it won't *fully* use these tools for seven to eight years.

In some cases the executive in charge of the new techniques is an aggressive senior "mover and shaker." More often the Information Center is given to a relatively junior person, and sometimes to a problem person whom the DP management want to side-slip to an area out of harm's way.

> *DP EXECUTIVE:*
>
> Our initial investment was very limited. At any time we could have abandoned the project at very little cost.
>
> . . . There were a number of nonconverts to the idea in the MIS division. I wanted to avoid a long and arid theoretical discussion as to whether and how we should go ahead.

In view of the success stories we feel that a thoroughly aggressive approach is needed, and should be backed by top management. It represents a major opportunity for an adventurous forceful executive to earn a name. Sometimes this has been a DP executive. Sometimes the drive has come from the end-user area.

TOP MANAGEMENT SUPPORT

Organizations which had achieved spectacular results, as opposed to relatively small operations, often stressed that top management supported the new type of development and helped to make it success.

> *USER EXECUTIVE:*
>
> The President of the railroad has access to one of our terminals. When the system was built he was Vice President of Operations. DP wasn't supporting us well enough and he knew it. So he decreed that we should have a go with this new software. DP opposed it, but he made it happen.
>
> There was a lot of pressure on the initial end-user team. We nearly killed ourselves getting the operations going. There were divorces, nervous breakdowns. . . . If we were doing it again today with that

experience we would have far more end users involved: spread the load. We didn't realize how big it would become.

USER EXECUTIVE:

We demonstrate it often to other firms. The computer manufacturer parades customers through here. And the reaction is always the same. The end users love it; the DP people go bananas. They think up all sorts of reasons why it won't work in *their* shop. Sometimes we've practically had fights break out here between DP and users.

INTERVIEWER:

What's the answer to that problem?

USER EXECUTIVE:

Demonstrate it to top management.

INTERVIEWER:

You have had much more success than most in penetrating the organization with these facilities. Why do you think you've been more successful?

DP EXECUTIVE:

I guess there would be two reasons. First, I had very good support from my executive vice-president and the corporate office. I had the responsibility to assemble an overall corporatewide picture without having to deal with many organizational levels.

Second, we chose not to package it as an Office-of-the-Future concept, or Information Center concept, or we're going to automate your office. We chose to break it down into products that had some meaning to different people and implement the products. The products were like pieces of a puzzle. We hoped that we understood the puzzle and how to fit the pieces together. The users just see the products.

INFORMATION CENTER STAFF SHOULD DEVELOP APPLICATIONS

As we indicated in the last chapter some Information Center proposals state that the Information Center staff should *not* develop applications. The managers of some of the most successful centers disagreed vehemently with this.

INFORMATION CENTER EXECUTIVE:

It is an absolute *must* (that Information Center staff develop applications). Most end users should not do it themselves. Most don't want to. They should work jointly with the systems engineer. Most are delighted when the systems engineer takes initiate, shows them results on the screen and then modifies the results to what they want. They have never seen this before and they often get excited about it. It's the first time I've really seen end users getting excited about DP's potential.

To work in this mode the Information Center staff need good communications skills.

INFORMATION CENTER MANAGER:

Our experience indicates that the Information Center needs a compassionate support staff, strong on communications skills, with experience to visualize the uses of the results in decision making. The support staff must be committed to assisting the professional and manager solve business problems, and feel a sense of responsibility for the outcome.

SPREADING THE TECHNIQUES

Once the techniques or pilot systems begin to succeed it is desirable to spread them as fast as possible. This needs aggressive sales within an organization.

DP EXECUTIVE:

About eighty percent of my information comes electronically and then there is another group of people that maybe one percent comes electronically. So one of our goals has been to get more people using the Center and then people using it more completely. And the next goal for the following year will be to increase the *penetration per person* and have more things electronically transmitted to each individual involved.

As the user-driven catches hold they can reach a stage of rapid growth. As this continues tools are needed to inform users what information and applications are available from their terminals.

INFORMATION CENTER MANAGER:

We are moving towards five thousand people in the firm using these tools. It's become a real problem to communicate change and upgrades and new functions to the users.

We think the only way is a computer-assisted tool for people to be able to educate themselves once they're over the hurdle of becoming comfortable with the basic systems.

DP EXECUTIVE:

The area of education is what, I think, we most underestimated. We expected that when people saw these capabilities they would immediately respond and be delighted. But what we found is that it takes a long time to get someone trained in the whole gamut of tools we made available.

It is different than when we automated something in the past. When we automated the payroll you had to use it. No choice. Here there is a definite choice. We teach people how to use these tools, and after they have learned, if they haven't personally decided to adapt and use the tool, they can stop. You need an ongoing reeducation or updating process so that they know what new functions might be useful to them.

INFORMATION CENTER MANAGER:

The staff act almost like a little marketing group, where people are assigned to different areas of the organization to spend all their time helping people use the tools that are available, and being on site so that you don't necessarily have to schedule a formal meeting, but just call them over and say, "Would you help me, I'm trying to find this kind of information." That's been very successful and it's been a very useful tool for us in terms of getting feedback on what people are thinking about, what they need, and what they would like.

STAFF WITHOUT
DP EXPERIENCE

Because of the change in methods from conventional DP, many managers and software vendors emphasized that bright people *who are new to DP* often achieve better results than experienced DP personal. This is true with both management and application creation.

END-USER EXECUTIVE WHO CREATED
A SPECTACULAR SYSTEM:

I think one of the reasons we succeeded so spectacularly is that nobody told us that it was not possible. No one in DP would have dared to do what we succeeded in doing.

INFORMATION CENTER EXECUTIVE:

We took young people coming straight off our training program and said "Your area is this. You will support the Trust department. Your goal is to get more people using the tools, and get those who *are* using them to use them *more.* You should locate yourself as much as possible in their area."

They had to help people use the tools, be available to answer users' questions, and get users over the transition of being willing to use a terminal and knowing how to access the information that was being made available to them.

These young people coming right out of college are doing an excellent job.

DATA ENTRY   Some Information Centers are used only for information retrieval or for manipulating data which already exists in on-line systems. The end-user languages, however, can also be used for entering data. This is done on a large scale in some systems. It has the advantage of moving the data entry process to the users who care about the accuracy of the data.

DP EXECUTIVE:

Many users enter their own data into their own virtual filing cabinets, and they are responsible for the accuracy of this data. Much of their data is used by other users or moved across to the production systems with various audit and accuracy checks.

We capitalize on capturing data at its source. There are usually so many steps in the process before a piece of data enters a computer.

It comes from a customer into a salesperson's hands, into some peoples' operations' hands, to some control clerks, and back into the computer. There are about six layers of prior potentials in there and even if that last person keys it perfectly, it's incorrect. So our migration is towards moving that entry back further and further until ultimately the customers can put in their own questions. And the next thing is, how to control it so that people can't mess up the files. You've got to have tight security controls and only update the master data base after thorough checking.

The degree of accuracy goes up exponentially as you eliminate steps in the process and deal with the person who is the most concerned that it is accurate.

AVAILABILITY   To be satisfied with Information Center systems users need high system availability. In some of the systems we surveyed this had not been taken seriously enough. The users find this very frustrating and harmful to their work.

LEASING EXECUTIVE:

If somebody phones us and asks us to quote a lease for twelve jet aircraft for Yugoslavia we can't tell them to call back in four hours when the machine will be up. They need immediate service.

The highest availability and suitably fast response time should be the rule. It is a mistake to put the Information Center operations on a back-up machine which can be preempted for other work.

On the Santa Fe railroad system availability was so important that the terminals, connected to large central computers, were backed up by microcomputers providing identical screen displays which operated when the main system crashed.

The users need to be completely shielded from design considerations relating to availability, networks, data-base access, or other technical matters.

INFORMATION CENTER EXECUTIVE:

The computer and the technology have got to go into the back room and disappear. People don't think about electronic generating plant or the telephone company central office as long as the service is there when you want it. The Information Center must become a service like that.

The users should have their own logical filing cabinets available when they need them, and have tools for manipulating the data in the files, viewing it in more useful ways, asking "What if" questions, investigating delays and problems, and so on. They should be able to move data from their logical filing cabinets to other people's.

HOW TO SUCCEED   Different Information Center managers had different interpretations of what "success" meant. In the author's view it means a substantial proportion of the application development being done by end users, or Information Center consultants working with end users, and the end users being pleased with the results.

INTERVIEWER:

Having created a successful Information Center operation yourself, what advice would you give to other organizations about how to succeed?

INFORMATION CENTER EXECUTIVE:

The concept needs to be extensively sold throughout the organization, and you cannot sell it on an intellectual basis. Users must try it, get their hands on the terminals, and roll it around.

We build pilots. We give demonstrations. We have given demonstrations to the president, to senior management, to DP personnel, and to all levels of end users. We have a demonstration center and have given so many demonstrations that we are the longest running show on Broadway!

INTERVIEWER:

I'm sure that's excellent advice. What else?

INFORMATION CENTER EXECUTIVE:

Pick the most important applications. Capture data for them, and show what can be done with them. Pick the best software packages, and particularly packages which give the best output—clear reports, really good graphics. Use these with the most important applications and demonstrate the results to those executives who will make things happen.

21 THE CHANGING ROLE OF THE SYSTEMS ANALYST

PRODUCTIVITY   The new facilities for DP development imply sub-
                stantial changes in the role of the systems analyst.
The changes should have one clear objective: *productivity*. Those methods
should be used which give the end user the best results in the shortest time,
or give the results with the lowest overall cost.

The analyst should understand that there are many ways to obtain
applications:

1. Conventional systems analysis and programming

2. Purchase of an application package

3. End users generating their own applications with the facilities in Fig. 2.1

4. End users working with systems analysts who generate the applications with one of
   the facilities in Fig. 2.1

5. End users working with systems analysts who create a *prototype* for the user which is
   then converted into efficient code

6. Method 3, 4, or 5, combined with programmer-created subroutines

The first method *gives much the lowest* productivity and therefore
should be avoided wherever possible. Methods 3 and 4 are appropriate for
user-driven computing that is frequently modified and adapted to meet the
changing needs and perceptions of the end users. Methods 1, 2, and 5 are
appropriate for relatively static computing, where a procedure such as printing invoices or processing insurance claims does not change much, or for
heavy-duty computing, where massive volumes of transactions are *routinely*
processed.

Heavy-duty computing requires techniques that are machine efficient.
Some application generators are designed for machine efficiency (e.g., IBM's
DMS); others are not. The distinction between these is important.

Most user-driven computing is not heavy duty, although there are exceptions. The Santa Fe railroad system for car and van control and way-billing, created by end users with Univac's MAPPER, processes 2½ million transactions per day.

The best case histories of user-driven computing are very impressive and it is clearly desirable to instigate this wherever possible. Very few end users have realized what can be done with today's software.

GUIDANCE FOR USER-DRIVEN SYSTEMS

Some vendors' literature on report generation and application generation software states that it avoids the need not only for programmers but also for systems analysts. Impressive systems such as those described in Chapter 11 were created without systems analysts. In fact, the systems analyst has a highly valuable role to play *even* when end users are creating their own applications. In most organizations user-driven computing is most likely to come into existence only if knowledgeable systems analysts are guiding it and giving a great deal of help to the end users. But for this to happen, both the systems analysts and their management must understand the new methods described in this book.

A large organization may create an *Information Center* style of DP management to work in parallel with conventional DP. Other organizations may train *all* systems analysts to employ the methods of application development without programmers and to judge where they should be used. There is much to be said for the latter. Often, the *Information Center* approach is applied on too limited a scale.

TOTAL CHANGE IN SYSTEMS ANALYSTS' JOB

Perhaps the most important point to make is that in most corporations there needs to be a total change in many systems analysts' jobs. The *most* effective use of the new software occurs with real-time creation of applications with the analyst and end-user interacting and employing a terminal to build and refine the application. This interaction results in either a prototype or a finished application. The *least* effective use of the new software occurs when the analyst is too influenced by the methods of the past—by COBOL-like thinking, a formalized development cycle, requirements specification documents, and structured analysis. These methods are valuable for certain applications that cannot be created by the new methods. Most commercial DP applications can use the higher-productivity methods, which avoid programming in COBOL or PL/1, *in part* if they cannot use them 100%.

ESCAPE FROM EARLIER DISCIPLINES

Specialists with many application generation facilities insist that a cause of problems or low productivity is systems personnel who approach these tools with an excessive familiarity with COBOL or conventional program development. A different way of thinking is needed. NOMAD specialists use the word "NOBOL" to mean NOMAD programs written with a COBOL-like way of thinking. The new languages and generators are much easier to use than COBOL or PL/1 and need to be approached without preconceived programming notions.

Similarly, the systems analyst should often avoid flowcharts and data flow diagrams, when generating applications. He needs to think from scratch regarding the most efficient way to operate. A technique called *event diagramming* is more appropriate to one-line data-base systems and leads to structured English specifications directly usable in fourth-generation languages [1].

Many aspects of the experienced analysts' knowledge are very valuable in the new environment. He understands security, error control, recovery, and auditing. He can learn quickly to achieve high performance with the facilities if he tries. But a frame of mind is needed that can free itself from the techniques of the past, even when those techniques are being sold as "converting systems analysis from an unruly art form to a scientific discipline." Experienced analysts find it difficult to throw off their hard-learned earlier methods. New graduates often produce better results with the new software than do experienced analysts. In fact, *end users* often produce better results.

Information Center managers have complained to the author that certain employees take much longer to create results than the majority of the Information Center staff. These are the ones that insist on using the techniques that were drilled into them on conventional systems analysis or structured analysis courses. They cannot give up their old types of diagrams even though they are not needed with the nonprocedural language.

Computer methodology is changing so fast that the best frame of mind for the systems analyst is to *search constantly for better methods* and challenge any approach that seems slow, unproductive, or does not quickly give the end user what is best for him. The systems analyst needs to be inventive, eager to try new things, and prepared to work to become skilled with tools such as DMS or NOMAD. He must shake off his COBOL-like thinking. He must understand the potentials of the new software and realize that it represents not just a change in software, but a revolution in methods and management.

There are several major aspects to the changing role of the systems analyst.

1. Avoid the Use of Programmers

The analyst should be instructed to avoid the use of programmers wherever possible. He should employ query languages, report generators, and application development facilities *himself* to create the results the end user wants. Only when these facilities cannot create the results or give bad machine performance on high-volume operations is he forced to write program specifications to be handed over to the programming team. He shows the reports, screens, and other output to the end users when he creates them and can adjust them quickly in response to users' suggestions.

2. Create Prototypes

When programming cannot be avoided, the systems analyst should create prototypes for the users. He should create reports, screen displays, and dialogues with the software of Fig. 2.1. The user can then see what is being planned, can try it out, and suggest modifications. This interaction should continue until the user is sure that the system is as valuable and easy to use as possible.

The prototype may be directly convertible into a working system by more efficient coding with the application generator that created it. A specialist on the software may be needed to accomplish this. If programs *have* to be written, the prototype replaces some or all of the program specifications. This saves time and tells the programmer more exactly what is needed.

3. Assistance with Data-Base Operation

Data-base operation is important in improving DP productivity. Logical data modeling is critical to its success [2]. In a well-managed data-base installation the design of the data is done centrally by a data administrator or data administration group. The systems analyst does not design the data base but in many cases is called upon to provide inputs to the design and to help check the resulting logical data model.

The systems analyst is often required to use an existing data base. He specifies inputs to the data base that trigger some action and specifies what the resulting action is. This changes the systems analysis methodology and, if done with the most efficient tools, removes much of the laborious work and documentation.

4. Encourage Users to Employ the Software Themselves

The users *themselves* should employ the data-base query languages and report generators whenever they are able to do so. The systems analyst should assist in this process. The users initially need much encouragement, training, and handholding. As they become more familiar with the new tools, they have many questions. They should be encouraged to invent how they put the tools to better use. The systems analyst aiding them encodes screen procedures in conjunction with the users and stores them.

An objective of using the new tools should be to respond quickly to users' needs, obtain rapid feedback concerning the results, devise improvements, and respond quickly to users' requests for changes.

5. Consultant Role

As facilities that are directly usable by end users spread, the systems analyst increasingly assumes the role of a consultant. In some cases a rich mixture of facilities are available at the users' terminals: information retrieval, electronic mail, calculator features, report generation, and so on. The typical user needs help to understand these and use them effectively. The systems analyst may conduct classes, conduct personal tutorials at the terminal, create a particular report, create subroutines or catalogued procedures for the user, and generally help to make the system use as effective as possible.

The analyst should determine how the end users' productivity can be improved and take action to accomplish this.

6. Salesman/Missionary Role

Much gentle persuasion is needed to make users employ the facilities described above as they become available. System analysts should act somewhat like salesmen to spread the use of valuable facilities. They need to appreciate the various subtle reasons why some users are hostile to the facilities. Like salesmen, the analysts may be given a quota for user acceptance and their compensation or bonuses related to their accomplishments. Some organizations have had great success using newly hired graduates to work in end-user areas to spread the use of terminals. They need both to make new users employ the systems and, where valuable, to increase use by existing users. They should identify and work with the *early adapters.*

7. Avoid Unproductive Study of Systems

When applications can be implemented rapidly, much of the need to study them disappears. If it takes a month to create a new application, this is less than the time that would have been taken to do a feasability study. Instead of spending a long time *studying,* it is better to *do* it and show the users the results. If it is scrapped, nothing has been lost because of the study time saved. Often it will need repeated modifying, which can be done fairly quickly, as succession administrative improvements are made.

In some corporations, especially in Europe, I have seen years spent on studying an application, after which nothing was done. With the new software, the right approach is often to do it, test it with users, and modify it as needed.

8. Create Practical Information Systems

With management information systems particularly, much time has been spent trying to identify the information needed by each manager. This has often met with little success because managers do not know their future needs. The change in hardware and software makes possible two other approaches.

First, with today's storage costs it is possible to put *all* valuable data on-line in some organizations and make it accessible with information retrieval software which enables users to ask for information when they want it. It was not practical to "give them everything" with batch processing or even with some of the early data-base systems, but it is practical with good information retrieval software, especially when this is combined with software for manipulating the data on a screen, extracting data, sorting them, matching data, and generating reports and graphics. The executive or his assistant can extract the data that interest him at a given moment and represent it appropriately.

Second, managers and professionals can keep their own files and use software for manipulating them. They may sometimes extract these from existing data bases or information retrieval systems.

Both of these approaches have produced information systems valuable to the end users. Ideally, they should be used together. Neither requires any application programming. They can be used in addition to attempts to determine specific information needs as with critical success factor analysis.

9. Cost Justification

The costs of user-driven computing should be passed on directly to the user departments where possible. Software such as MAPPER calculates the cost to each user of employing the system.

In one large bank the information retrieval system has grown to 90 disc drives. This is justified incrementally by the users. They are asked if they have information that ought to be added to the system. The principal cost of doing so is that of extra disc drives. The justification is three disc drives to the trust department, two to international business, and so on. To a large extent the end users make their own decisions about what they pay for.

The first implementation of such a system is the most difficult phase to cost justify. The initial expenditure will be recouped as usage grows. The risk of this first expenditure is like a business manager's risk in setting up a new facility. It should be judged similarly. Part of this judment should take into account the rapidly falling costs of technology. The big expense is often incurred by people *not using* the technology and employing lower-productivity methods. By the time they are persuaded to use it, the technology costs will have dropped, so the persuasion process should keep ahead of the falling cost curve.

SPECIALIZATION   The medium-sized installation discussed in Chapter 5 describes its systems analysts as being *responsible for all aspects of systems except programming and operating.* In common with analysts in many installations, they design the files, determine the data flows, and calculate what hardware is needed. They do a detailed requirements analysis and write detailed specifications for the programmers.

In today's environment, more specialization is needed. Various specializations are as follows:

- *Structured Analyst.* This person uses the techniques of structured analysis [3] to specify the requirements and data flows of conventional *prespecified* application development. He creates structured data flow diagrams and where possible employs data bases that already exist.

- *Information Center Representative.* This person works with end users to assist them in obtaining the information they require, and in generating user-driven applications or prototypes. He assists end users to employ query languages, report generators, information retrieval systems, and other office automation facilities. He is responsible for *user-driven* application development.

- *Data-Base Administrator.* This person collects the logical views of data that different applications need and synthesizes them to create logical data-base structures which are as stable and useful as possible. He maintains a data dictionary and logical model of the data [2]. Sometimes an end-user data coordinator is used with an end-user application development facility, as described in Chapter 11.

- *Data-Base Designer.* The data-base designer is a technical expert of the data-base systems that are used. (The data-base administrator may be nontechnical and concerned with the application aspects of the data.) The data-base designer is concerned with data-base hardware, software, and performance and sometimes with how the data are distributed [2].

- *Information Resources Planner.* This person carries out top-down planning of information resources. He uses formal and preferably computerized methodologies for the strategic planning of data bases and information systems [1, 4].

- *Techniques Analyst.* This person is an expert on the software discussed in this book and determines what software and techniques are appropriate for each application.

- *Software Specialist.* This person is a specialist in one software package for application generation. With it, he is able to create results quickly and achieve optimal machine performance (e.g., an ADF "acrobat").

- *Network Specialist.* Networks are becoming increasingly complex. Specialists are needed to ensure that the network can provide the services required [5].

● *Configuration Specialist.* The advent of distributed systems raises complex design issues. What should be distributed and how? Where should data reside? How is integrity maintained? A configuration specialist may deal with these questions [6].

● *Security Expert.* Maintaining security becomes more complex when end users have the power to create applications and update data. So many types of security breaches are possible that a trained security specialist should be involved in the design and operation of systems [7].

● *System Auditor.* This person ensures that the system is auditable where it needs to be and ensures that it is not being tampered with.

This list is too long for all of them to be separate people in a small installation. A small installation may have only one, or perhaps two, very high-level languages and only one expert on these (with a backup). The small installation may have one person doing all data-base and data administration functions (again with a backup person). The other tasks will be combined and simplified as appropriate.

INPUT TO INFORMATION SYSTEMS   Data processing to a large extent will consist of:

● Creating good data bases
● Extracting information when needed from these data bases
● Generating applications that use the data bases
● Creating and controlling input to the data bases

The last of these steps needs the attention of systems analysts.

There are often many steps in the process before a piece of data enters the computer. It comes from a customer into a salesperson's hands, into an operations department, to control clerks, and then to key entry. In some cases there are six layers, each with potential error, before it is in the computer. Even if the last person keys it perfectly, it is often incorrect.

It is desirable to perform the data entry as close as possible to its source of origin. It should be moved to the salesperson and even to the customer if possible. It should be moved to the originating end user. The dialogue facilities now existing enable end users of all types to enter data that are important to them. Some corporations are placing terminals in their customers' offices for sales inquiries or order entry.

Accuracy increases greatly as you remove the middlemen, and the person who enters the data into the computer is the person who is most concerned that it is right. Substantial systems reorganization may be needed to achieve this.

BOX 21.1 Factors that improve the productivity systems analysis

- Avoidance of the writing of requirements documents and specifications, where possible, this may be replaced partially or completely with prototyping using the software discussed in this book.

- Interactive screen, report, and dialogue design.

- Use of interactive computerized tools for accomplishing formal design and techniques.

- Avoidance of hand-drawn charts of excessive complexity and the replacement of these with computer-drawn charts.

- Skill with application generators, report generators, and dialogue generators so that these can be used efficiently and fast.

- End users doing as much of their own application creation as possible.

- End users obtaining their own information with data-base query languages and information retrieval systems.

- End users generating their own reports.

- Good training and skilled motivation of end users to do the above.

- An Information Center approach to support the end users in the above and to generate applications for them.

- Salesmanship by systems analysts to encourage the spread of end-user employment of the software and information systems. Concentration on early adapters in the end-user community.

- Automation of data-base design [2] and good management of the data-base environment.

- Data-base systems with formal descriptions of triggers that cause data-base actions and descriptions of those actions. Logic associated with the data base rather than with individual applications.

- Recognition of the distinction between Class 3 and Class 4 data bases. Simple, fast, implementation of Class 4 data bases.

- Use of self-documenting techniques and the creation of interactive documentation and HELP functions in end-user software.

- Motivation of systems analysts by creating better job satisfaction. This can result from working with users to finish a job, seeing it in actual use, and adjusting it to be as effective as possible. The analysts see the direct effects of their creativity. This helps to build their own effectiveness.

SUMMARY   The productivity of systems analysis can be greatly improved using the techniques described in this book. Box 21.1 summarizes factors that improve systems analysis productivity.

Today's falling cost of computers, storage, and networks necessitates software that enables systems analysts or end users to create their own applications and retrieve and manipulate the information they need. Much of this software now exists, and it presents a major challenge to end users, DP management, and systems analysts everywhere.

Systems analysts and DP management now have the opportunity to serve their end users much better and to have a major effect on corporate productivity.

The analysts' jobs can become much more satisfying. They can see the results of their work, obtain results much more quickly, observe the effects of their work on the users and make adjustments to improve those effects. They are more creative. This improvement in creativity and job satisfaction often causes analysts to work harder and improve their own psychological productivity.

A decade from now the DP profession will be greatly changed. Progressive DP organizations are making those changes now.

It is appropriate to end this book with a quote from an aggressive DP executive who is riding the crest of this massive new wave: "At least we are getting some real excitement back into DP."

REFERENCES

1. James Martin and Clive Finkelstein, *Information Engineering,* Savant Research, 2 New Street, Carnforth, Lancashire, England.

2. James Martin, *Managing the Data Base Environment,* Vol. I, Savant Technical Report 9, Savant Institute, Carnforth, Lancashire, UK, 1980.

3. Tom de Marco, *Structured Analysis and Systems Specifications,* Yourdon, Inc., New York, 1979.

4. James Martin, *Strategic Data Planning Methodologies,* Savant Technical Report 12, Savant Institute, Carnforth, Lancashire, UK, 1980.

5. James Martin, *Computer Networks and Distributed Processing,* Savant Technical Report 4, Savant Institute, Carnforth, Lancashire, UK, 1980.

6. James Martin, *Distributed Processing Software and Network Strategy,* Savant Technical Report 7, Savant Institute, Carnforth, Lancashire, UK, 1919.

7. James Martin, *Security, Accuracy and Privacy in Computer Systems,* Prentice-Hall, Inc., Englewood Cliffs, NJ, 1975.

INDEX

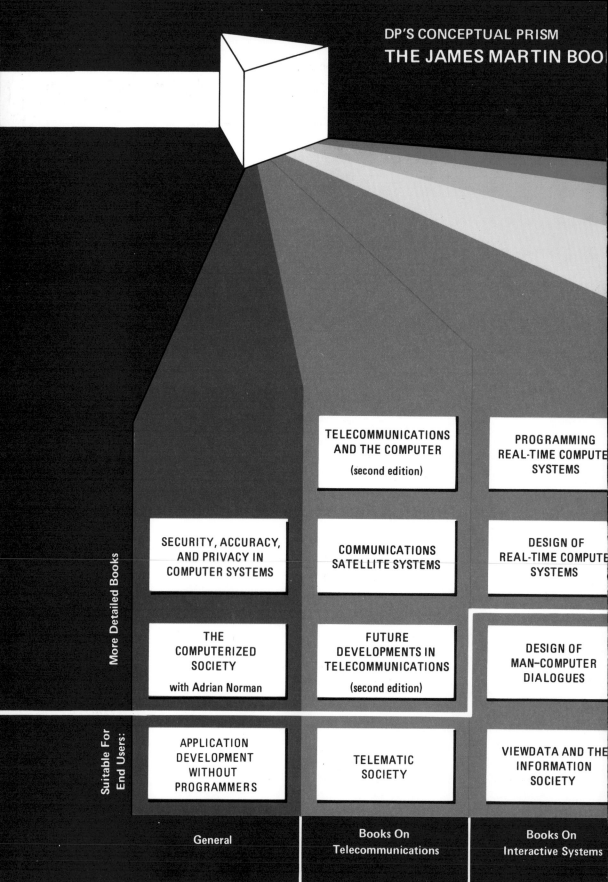

DP'S CONCEPTUAL PRISM
THE JAMES MARTIN BOO[K]

More Detailed Books

Suitable For End Users:

| TELECOMMUNICATIONS AND THE COMPUTER (second edition) | PROGRAMMING REAL-TIME COMPUTE[R] SYSTEMS |

| SECURITY, ACCURACY, AND PRIVACY IN COMPUTER SYSTEMS | COMMUNICATIONS SATELLITE SYSTEMS | DESIGN OF REAL-TIME COMPUTE[R] SYSTEMS |

| THE COMPUTERIZED SOCIETY with Adrian Norman | FUTURE DEVELOPMENTS IN TELECOMMUNICATIONS (second edition) | DESIGN OF MAN–COMPUTER DIALOGUES |

| APPLICATION DEVELOPMENT WITHOUT PROGRAMMERS | TELEMATIC SOCIETY | VIEWDATA AND THE INFORMATION SOCIETY |

General

Books On Telecommunications

Books On Interactive Systems